A personal
KIWI-YANKEE DICTIONARY

Lone & Ken
thinking of you

Love Dave

A personal
KIWI-YANKEE DICTIONARY

A personal
KIWI-YANKEE
DICTIONARY

Louis S. Leland Jr.

John McIndoe

To Ruth and Louis whose meeting is described under the heading 'A & P Show' and to Freda, Daniel and Cliff who provided the moral and practical support and harassment that made the 2nd edition possible.

© Louis S. Leland Jr

ISBN 0 86868 122 9

First edition published 1980, reprinted 11 times.

This revised and extended edition designed, printed and published 1990, by John McIndoe Ltd., 51 Crawford Street, Dunedin, New Zealand.

ACKNOWLEDGEMENTS

Once again I must thank Wm. S. Verplanck who suggested something like this book even before I came to New Zealand over 20 years ago. My wife, Dr Freda Walker, has proofread, critiqued, nagged, served as a walking Kiwi dictionary and taken on extra childcare time in order to enable this second edition to be prepared. Barry Dingwall and his crew and colleagues (Lady Di, Dianne I., Russell, Lindsay, John, Bradley, and William) have not only served as a court of last resort for meaning but set up my laptop computer so that I could write and revise wherever I found myself.

Apologies and thanks go to the reference department of the University of Otago Library, some of who's newer employees (a little bird told me) were of the opinion that their skills were being tested by this weird character in the Psychology Department who would phone several times a day with wildly disparate and unlikely requests for information ('On which Hawaiian Island was Captain Cook killed and what percentage of NZ high school graduates went on to University last year?'). One way or another they never failed me.

A special and unexpected thanks must go to Assoc. Professor Lawrence Jones of the University of Otago's English Department for easing my conscience as an academic for writing a popular book rather than the approved scholarly tome (I didn't even dare list the first edition as a publication in the University Calendar). Professor Jones actually used the first edition as a textbook in one of his courses and I only found out by accident. Mind you, he is an American and as such can be expected to do strange things on occasion.

Many thanks also to the following contributors in their personal, and in some cases, professional capacities: N. B. Body, V. G. Boyle, Bisten Buly, Kathy Campbell, Tim & Angie Davenport, Rex Forrester, Mike Gifford, Ruguste Jone, David Kerslake, Graeme Kitto, Tory Light, Nancy McMurray, Penny Otto, W. M. Peet, Charles C. Ransom, W. A. Rendall, Joan Schickert, Jennifer Selby, Ras Waters, W. S. Whitehead, Roger & Marsha Woodbury, and Ruth S. Woodside.

FOREWORD TO THE FIRST EDITION

Designed to amuse as well as enlighten, this is a very personal dictionary. It is written in the first person to emphasize that it is a picture of New Zealand, its people and its language, through my eyes. As such it emphasizes one man's interests and reflects his attitudes.

Your picture of Kiwis and their land will of necessity differ. That's what makes horse races.

> *Red sky at night, Shepherds' delight,*
> *Red sky in the morning, Shepherds take warning.'*

Not quite the way you learned it as a kid? That's New Zealand all over. 'Culture shock' in other countries comes from the radically different life-styles that you encounter. In New Zealand it is less obvious; it comes from things that look identical when you first see them, but are subtly or entirely different on closer inspection. Back in the days when I was attempting to learn French these were called faux amis (false friends), a list of these appears under F below.

This works both ways. My wife, a convent-schooled Kiwi bird (see below), went to California for a year of High School in her teens and on her first day in her first co-ed school, earned an entirely unfounded reputation by asking the boy sitting behind her if he had a rubber (see below). All she wanted was an eraser, but this experience colors her view of Americans to this day.

Not all Kiwis will recognize every entry in this collection, but most are in common use. Regional differences are indicated where known. To spare Kiwi readers culture shock note that all spellings other than those of words in bold type, italics and/or enclosed in parentheses, conform to Yankee, not Kiwi, usage.

Note that use of the terms marked with a single asterisk (*) will mark your low social class, and those marked with two asterisks (**) are not for use in polite, or at least mixed, company.

Louis S. Leland, Jr.
Dunedin, 1979.

FOREWORD TO THE SECOND EDITION

Everything written in the foreword to the first edition, above, remains true, however, the social fabric of New Zealand has altered over the past 10 years, as its people have been exposed to the harsh winds of economic change. Most government departments have revised their names, new terms for losing one's job (e.g., auroraed) and for the basis of the changes (e.g., rogernomics) have been coined.

In addition many readers of the first edition have written in with page after page of likely additions to the dictionary (see the partial list in the acknowledgements).

Having become a father in the intervening years since the first edition I have consequently learned many many words like 'feeder' for 'bib' and 'tig' for 'tag' (as in the children's game).

A substantial portion of the new words recorded here are things I have heard myself say and recognized as Kiwi-isms or that colleagues at Virginia Tech. (while I was there on sabbatical in 1985) pointed out to me as novel portions of my vocabulary, some of which they adopted, voluntarily or otherwise. Rumor reaches me that they still say 'sorry' rather than 'excuse me' when spilling coffee on each other or otherwise offending against good behavior.

Louis S. Leland, Jr.
Dunedin, 1990.

FOREWORD TO THE SECOND EDITION

Louis S. Leland, Jr.
June 16, 1990.

AA: Alcoholics Anonymous does operate here but in common parlance AA refers to the N.Z. equivalent of the U.S. triple A (or AAA). The AUTOMOBILE ASSOCIATION is even more visible here than in the U.S. since they have a contract to provide all the roadsigns outside cities; and naturally provide them in AA yellow with the AA logo discretely affixed to each. (see: *G.P.O.*)

A & P Show: The Agricultural and Pastoral Society Show. Local equivalent of a STATE FAIR. This is a major event in every region and nearly all businesses, government departments, etc., close down for 'Show Day'. This is often a Friday and the first and most important day of the (usually) three-day show. Remember that New Zealand depends on sales of agricultural products overseas for a large part of its living. Nearly everybody goes to the show (an urban couple I know well, met at the pig exhibit 50 years ago). Sideshows, skill tests, horse jumping, rodeo exhibitions, polo matches, etc. etc. Don't miss it (if it has been raining wear your gumboots). (see: *gumboots, primary products*)

A bit of all right then?: SO IT'S OK, IS IT?

a lamb is a sheep before you have carried it very far: Too true! Folk wisdom in New Zealand usually seems to go back to the farm. (see: *there must have been a stray bull in the paddock*)

a proper little madam: This young lady is TOO FULL OF HERSELF (thinks too highly of herself).

abattoir: A SLAUGHTERHOUSE for local consumption. Often owned and run by the larger cities, they do not have to meet the same health requirements as freezing works that slaughter for export. This seems to make no difference to the safety or taste of the food. (see: *freezer, freezing workers,* (the) *works,* (the) *season,* (the) *chain, gemel, primary products*)

academic year (University): The academic year consists of three teaching terms and an examination term and runs from February to December. Most students only sit in formal classes for 26 WEEKS, but academic staff work a full 11 months, doing lecture preparation, marking, thesis supervision and research during the times the students are not in class. Clinical courses run most of the year and clinical lecturers have clinical supervision duties on top of their other duties. (see: *Uni, Bursary, school, U.E., School Cert.*)

accelerator: When you wish to accelerate the speed of your automobile you naturally press your right foot upon the accelerator (GAS PEDAL). (see: *bonnet, boot, handbrake, windscreen, mudguard, petrol, gas*)

Access schemes: Any person over 15 years of age who is a N.Z. citizen or permanent resident and is unemployed or working less than 15 hours per week may apply to participate in one of these

TRAINING SCHEMES. They range from vocational (e.g., acting, horticulture, mechanics, electronics, woolhandling) through academic (English, Maths) and into 'living skills' (budgeting, cooking, legal rights, Maoritanga, job search). Trainees get the dole plus carfare and, if necessary, an accommodation allowance. (see: *dole*)

Acclimatization Society: A quasi governmental organization divided into regions and run by elected representatives of those holding hunting and fishing licenses. It is also financed by those licenses although the central government does get a rakeoff. They stock the rivers with trout (and enforce the rules about catching them), count waterfowl, set bag limits, and support some game reserves. (see: *quango, Plunket Society*)

act the goat: Someone who does a (see:) *down trou* is, in my opinion, PLAYING THE FOOL.

aerial topdressing: New Zealand's economic lifeline is her agricultural (particularly pastoral) produce. To deliver these products to North America, Europe and Japan at competitive prices, the inventive and industrious Kiwis have found ways to raise more and better food for less money. One key is the SPREADING of FERTILIZER FROM small single engine AIRCRAFT that take off from short grass strips (often comprising the total area of level land at the top of one ridge of an area of small ridges and valleys) and outperform most stunt fliers in their efforts to evenly cover the contracted area with powdered fertilizer. (see: *Kiwi, primary products, super, manure*)

aerogramme: A flimsy blue sheet of paper on which airmail letters can be written and which folds up to make its own envelope. It is considerably cheaper to mail than is an airmail envelope with letter enclosed. These are available in the U.S., where they are called AIR LETTERS.

affair: It can refer to what your boss and her male secretary have going but it is more likely to refer to a PARTY. 'It was a grand affair.'

age of consent: 16 YEARS (nuff said). Unless you want to marry her (or him) then you'll have to until s/he is 20 or get mum and dad to agree. (see: *carnie kid, mum, legal age for drinking, 21st*)

A.G.M.: Annual General Meeting. You will often hear people talking about the A.G.M. of a club or firm. This is the YEARLY BUSINESS MEETING of an organization. At this meeting, 'the committee' is elected. This group will run things with (usually) scant reference to the membership, for the other 364 days.

air conditioning: This is a tricky one, since it is a 'true friend' if you are talking about cold, and a 'false friend' if you are talking about heat. 'Turn up the air conditioning' can and does mean, turn up the heat, rather more often than it refers to turning up the cooling system. Kiwis have logically concluded that alterations in

10

both HEAT AND COLD amount to conditioning the air and that the one term should therefore refer to both. Very little of New Zealand has a climate in which air cooling is needed for any substantial proportion of the year which is why this dual purpose term more often refers to heating than cooling. (see: *central heating, false friends*)

air the washing: After drying wash on the line outside (local wisdom has it that clothes 'smell' and 'are' better after this treatment than they would be out of a drier. Some rude North American expatriates have suggested that this is making a virtue out of necessity), the clothing is put in a warm place, usually the cupboard where the hot water cylinder (tank) lives, until it is toasty warm (aired). (see: *hot water cylinder, rude, washhouse*)

All Blacks: Take the World Series winners, combine them with the Superbowl champs, add the prestige of a victorious Olympic team, and you have some faint idea of what this carefully chosen NATIONAL representative TEAM OF New Zealand's best RUGBY PLAYERS means to the nation. (Nearly) every boy wants to grow up to be one and most of the girls would just love to marry (or some reasonable facsimile thereof) one. If a Kiwi's (see: *Kiwi*) passions are, as commonly quoted, 'rugby, racing and beer', then the foremost of these is rugby and the All Blacks, its symbol.

The 1981 protest against the 'Springbok tour', a visit to N.Z. by the South African rugby team, pitted this love of rugby against Kiwis' equally strong sense of egalitarian fair play and led to rioting. A very rare event in N.Z.

A quick illustration of the All Blacks' importance. On my arrival in New Zealand, I saved $10.00 by purchasing a white electric razor rather than an otherwise identical black one which was colored in honor of the All Blacks and accompanied by a picture of the team. Note that these men are amateurs; there is very little professional sport in New Zealand. (see: *football* or *footie, Gleneagles Agreement, Springbok tour, tour, touring, All Whites, Kiwi*)

all flossied up: ALL TARTED UP. A nicer way of putting it.

All Whites: The NATIONAL SOCCER (test) TEAM. And, don't worry, there isn't any racism involved or even implied. (see: *All Blacks*)

all the guff: INFORMATION both useful and superfluous. (see: *bumf*)

a load of old cobblers: Information that isn't worth the paper it's printed on. 'That story you just told is a load of old cobblers!' 'That story you just told is BUNK!'

alpine stick or **frankfurters:** Available in the big city, these are tasty, OVERGROWN (extra long) HOT DOGS. Well worth sampling. (see: *bangers, saveloy, hot dogs*)

Alsatian: A GERMAN SHEPHERD DOG. This breed has an unfortunate local reputation for viciousness. I suspect this is based on its use as police dogs and reinforced by selective attention to any incidents involving German Shepherds. Dogs have a different social position in New Zealand than they do in North America. A dog is generally thought of as a working animal (used to herd sheep and cattle in a mainly pastoral country) and so not treated as a pet. Even urban Kiwis are often shocked at the idea that their pet dog might spend the night in the house. (see: *dogs, sausage dog, primary products*)

alterations: Changes, but not necessarily small ones. For example, you might alter your house by adding a second storey.

aluminium: Pronounced AL-YOU-MIN-E-UM.

amongst: 'AMONG other things.' (see: *whilst*)

anti-clockwise: COUNTER-CLOCKWISE; the direction in which the ancient Druid inhabitants of Britain used to dance after painting themselves blue with woad. Remember they were your cultural ancestors as well!

ANZAC biscuit: A COOKIE MADE OF rolled OATS and COCONUT. 'CARE' packages sent to first world war NEW ZEALAND troops always included some of these. (see: *ANZAC DAY, biscuit*)

ANZAC day: On APRIL 25, 1915 a World War I campaign, strongly supported and partially planned by the then (British) First Lord of the Admiralty (Winston Churchill) commenced. Combined Australian and New Zealand forces (ANZAC) hit one beach while French troops hit another. The French soon left but the ANZAC forces fought the Turks for eight and a half long months before 'withdrawing in good order'. A PUBLIC HOLIDAY is celebrated commemorating the heroism, loss of life (213,980 Commonwealth casualties) and waste of time and resources that the campaign entailed. Churchill resigned his government position and became infantry battalion commander in France where, it has been suggested, he felt that at least any tactical errors made would be his own. (see: *ANZAC biscuit*)

ANZUS: THE 'Security Treaty Between AUSTRALIA, NEW ZEALAND, AND THE UNITED STATES OF AMERICA', signed in 1951 committing each of these nations to '... act to meet the common danger in accordance with its constitutional processes ...' (the New Zealand Encyclopaedia says 'against the common threat' but this wording isn't actually in the treaty). As far as I can tell, the treaty does not obligate any country to take any action (other than informing the United Nations Security Council) in the event of an armed attack upon one of the other signatories.

Article II does say, in part, '... continuous and effective self help and mutual aid will maintain their individual and collective capacity to resist armed attack.' In the past this article was used by (see:) *National Party* governments to justify not only the joint military exercises of the three signatory powers but also the visits of Australian and U.S. warships to N.Z. ports.

The present (since 1984, see:) *Labour* Party *government*, like the last Labour government, has decided that the treaty obligations do not include the possibility of making New Zealand a nuclear target by playing host to nuclear armed or powered warships. This has understandably irritated the U.S. government, since of the three treaty partners it is the only one to have an admitted nuclear capacity. Furthermore the U.S. Navy has an announced, and usually adhered to, policy of never saying which of its ships is nuclear armed.

The combination of these two policies has, in effect, banned all visits by U.S. Naval vessels to N.Z. ports.

In retaliation, the U.S. has unilaterally suspended N.Z. from the ANZUS alliance, for failing to meet its obligations. In effect this has meant that the U.S. ceased sharing intelligence information with N.Z. and all planned and future trilateral exercises were canceled. One U.S. admiral has accused N.Z. of wanting protection without contributing. N.Z.'s contribution was never very great, but in the past it was as much as its two bigger partners could reasonably expect of a nation of 3.3 million people. The N.Z. Prime Minister at the time, David Lange, replied that N.Z. wished to remain part of ANZUS and was willing to make a greater contribution to regional defense than had been the case in the past. This contribution would, of course, consist of conventionally armed forces. Lange further stated that N.Z. did not want to be defended by nuclear weapons. Since he is a bright fellow, this seemingly stupid statement would appear to have been a repudiation of the military alliance with the U.S.

Despite the fact that the Labour government (under a new Prime Minister, Geoffrey Palmer) has come to cautiously admit that armed neutrality is much more expensive than the U.S. alliance, opinion polls indicate that the 'no nuclear ships' policy is supported by some 60% of the electorate. A large majority is, however, in favour of remaining in the ANZUS alliance. Those supporting both propositions want to have their cake and eat it too.

This issue has become a big deal because the U.S. has chosen to make it one, this time. At the time of the previous Labour government's implementation of a similar policy, the U.S. publicly ignored it although there were certainly private diplomatic efforts. The avoidance of the issue was an assumption that it would go away when the Labour government eventually fell; which it did after a single, three year term in office.

13

The U.S. State Department appears to have correctly estimated that the 1984 Labour government was going to be re-elected for a second, approximately three year period and decided to put on the pressure this time.

In any case the public U.S. pressure has been such that even those people who did not agree with the Labour government's policy, became angry at the U.S. which was perceived as the big bully picking on a much smaller nation which had democratically bowed to the will of its people.

Hang on Foggy Bottom, this too shall pass away! At least I hope so. In March of 1990 the major opposition party (the National Party) reversed themselves and said that if they got elected later in the year, as is highly probable, they would continue the 'No Nukes' policy.

The Australians have remained publicly neutral in this quarrel but have privately pressured N.Z. to change its mind. This, indeed, is what the current (1990) Australian Labour government did when, on first taking office in 1984, it discovered some of the realities of international politics and repudiated its campaign promise to ban nuclear warships. (see: *Lange, Palmer, Prime Minister, New Zealand Party, Social Credit Political League/Democratic Party, Labour Party, National Party*)

Are you being served?: Can you imagine a saleswoman or salesman saying this? They do! A phrase out of another era when the social line between salesclerk and customer was much greater than today, when there could easily be an argument as to who has the higher social position. CAN I HELP YOU? (see: *salesclerk, clerk*)

Are you Canadian?: A polite way of finding out where you're from originally. The assumption is that Canadians would be insulted at being mistaken for Americans but the reverse wouldn't be true. (The assumption is probably correct.)

Are you there?: Says the voice at the other end of the telephone just after you have picked it up but before you can open your mouth. A stream of replies runs through my head ('Of course I'm here, did you think the bloody thing answered itself?' 'Where should I be, after all we arranged to have you call (phone) at this time', etc.) before I politely say 'Yes I am' and repress the alternatives. HELLO. (see: *Is that you?, call, bloody*)

Armed Offenders Squad: A S.W.A.T. TEAM. As the police are normally unarmed (as are criminals) this is a very special group of armed police called out to deal with armed criminals who have shown a willingness to use their weapons. Those occasions on which the Armed Offenders Squad is called out are sufficiently

14

rare that such an event usually makes the national (television and radio) news.

as busy as a one legged man at an arse kicking competition:
AS BUSY AS A ONE ARMED PAPERHANGER.

as silly as a two bob watch: Any timepiece that sells for 20 cents could be expected to keep somewhat irregular time, if any at all. Usually used to describe people, e.g., 'Jack is as silly as a two bob watch', implies eccentricity approaching the HAREBRAINED. (see: *bob, ten bob each way*)

Associate Professor: A false friend (the term, not the individual). While this is an academic rank and the same term is used as an academic rank in the U.S. they are not equivalent. Associate Professor N.Z. = PROFESSOR (but not department head) U.S. Another N.Z. term for the same academic rank is Reader. (see: *Professor, Chair, Lecturer, Reader, false friends*)

aubergine: An aubergine by any other name would be an EGGPLANT. (see: *veges, capsicum, swedes, courgette*)

Auckland: Named for Lord Auckland, Viceroy of India in 1840, it comprises the area between Northland and Waikato in the North Island including New Zealand's biggest metropolitan area, Auckland (820,754 people in the 1986 census). Nevertheless if sheep had the vote it would be all over. The Auckland region had 887,448 people in 1986 and 965,000 sheep. It is, however, one of the few regions in the country where the people outnumber the cattle (504,000). Good on you big smoke! Oh yes, there are also 31,000 domestic (farmed) deer raised for the velvet off the stags horns and for venison. (see: *good on you, big smoke, North Island*)

auroraed: Not everyone will recognize this term but all the people in the media will! To be auroraed is to be R.I.F.E.D. (reduced in force or FIRED). The term comes from an exercise carried out in Radio New Zealand called Project Aurora. (see: *sent down the road, gave him the boot, Radio New Zealand, State Owned Enterprise, restructuring, Rogernomics, dole*)

Aussie: (A) Someone from that slightly declasse suburb of New Zealand called Australia, an AUSTRALIAN. (see: *Kiwi, Pom—Pommie*)

(B) AUSTRALIA (see above). Despite northern hemisphere rumor to the contrary, Australia and New Zealand are two very different(!) places. They are separated by a minimum of 1,200 miles of open water. Don't let anyone sell you shares in the Wellington-Sydney harbor bridge; at least if you purchase the connection between Brooklyn and Manhattan you can go look at 'your property'. Note that Kiwis tend to look down upon their Aussie neighbors as being rather coarse, a condition deriving naturally from their purported descent from prisoners involuntarily exported from Britain

15

to Botany Bay. On the other hand, Aussies tend to look down on New Zealand as a junior partner without the resources and get-up-and-go of Australia and Australians. (see: *Trans Tasman, Oz, CER, Ocker, Pom*)

an **award:** Not what you get for achievement (see: *Honours*). An award, or more properly an Industrial Award, is the CONTRACT BETWEEN UNION AND EMPLOYEES. Awards specify pay, fringe benefits, types of work etc. (see: (the) *British disease, C.T.U., industrial unrest, industrial action*)

away with the fairies: DAYDREAMING. I just said hello to Myrna and she didn't even hear me, she's away with the fairies.

B

bach: A WEEKEND COTTAGE on lake, mountainside or coast. This term applies only to the 'North Island'. (see: *crib* — watch that, your thoughts are showing!, *North Island*)

*backside: the politest term (it isn't very polite) for that portion of your anatomy on which you rest while in a SEATed position. (see: *fanny, bum*)

backwards: Some aspect of each of the following is exactly opposite of what you would assume to be: (see:)

bathwater	*salt and pepper shakers*
date	*Saturday paper*
dress circle	*switches*
driving	*toasted sandwiches*
electric blanket	*walking*
entree	*zippers*
4 × 2	

bad lot: A description of the other guy, or more likely, his son or daughter. 'S/he's a bad lot', is just a bit stronger than saying, 's/he's NO GOOD'. This term usually applies to individuals rather than groups, and people rather than objects.

bags: 'I bags that red one'. I CLAIM that red one. Children's slang, probably originates from the hunter's practice of putting the game he shot into his game bag.

balaclava: A SKI MASK that covers all of the face and head except for the eyes. Just the thing for skiing down a glacier in winter (you don't need the balaclava in summer), or robbing a bank. Skiing down glaciers is an everyday occurrence in the South Island; bank robbery is unusual enough to make the national news, no matter where it happens.

(a) **ball:** (A) Another name for a FORMAL DANCE. Most social organizations, and many that are primarily professional or business ones,
hold an annual ball. (see: *graduation ball, ball frock, spray, bash*)
   **(B) Fornicate.

ball frock: It's the 7th form ball (senior Prom) and she's dressed in
her best BALL GOWN. Any formal dance is likely to be called a ball
(and is likely to be one). Being under the influence is a much better
excuse for violence or exhibitionistic behavior than it would be in
North America. I have seen (at a black tie, formal dress, University
graduation ball), a man peel off completely in the middle of the
dance floor and climb a trellis to an overhanging balcony. (see:
graduation ball, spray, down trou, school, ball)

ball of muscle: usually referring to children:
   (A) a BALL OF FIRE (complimentary)
   (B) a hyperactive child (derogatory)
   Which of the two meanings is employed, depends more on the
circumstances than the child.

Banda: Remember the duplicating machine that used to get the
purple ink all over your fingers? A *Banda* is a DITTO machine. A
very few of these dinosaurs still lurk in the back of some N.Z. offices.
(see: *cyclostyle, drawing pins, Cellotape*)

bangers: New Zealand SAUSAGES. For those used to Oscar Mayer,
they are best avoided. An inexpensive meal. This is a slang word,
say 'sausages' in the butchery. (see: *saveloys, alpine sticks, hot
dogs, butchery*)

barbe: No relation to the famous doll. This is a term that has crept
over from Australia, meaning BARBEQUE. A barbe is the device on
which you cook and is also the name of the function to which you
have invited your friends at your home on Sunday afternoon. (see:
service)

barrack: You ROOT for your favorite team, Kiwis barrack for theirs.
Don't use the word root. (see: **root*)

barracks week: a WEEK OF voluntary R.O.T.C. for high schoolers.

barrister: Those masters of courtroom oratory and procedure who
do the actual arguing in front of the bench (judge). The case itself
has been largely prepared and investigated by the other half of the
legal profession called solicitors (I kid you not) who then engage
and brief a barrister. Although in the U.S. LAWYERs do both of
these things you will find that any large firm splits into those who
do conveyancing, etc. and never (well hardly ever) go into court,
and those who deal with cases that do require the adjudication of
a court. In New Zealand most attorneys are qualified to do both
(they are Barristers and Solicitors) but as in the U.S. they tend to
specialize. (see: *solicitor, brief*)

bash: An informal PARTY. As 'she (that) was a good bash at your place last night. I've never been so pissed in my life'. (see: *she, ball, pissed*)

basin: The marvel of technology in which you wash your hands. This has nothing to do with toilets, it is rarely even in the same room. (see: *bathroom, lav, toilet bowl*)

*bastard: (A) It means what you think it does, but it can also be a term of ENDEARMENT and ADMIRATION. You are a right bastard, aren't you? (see: *hard shot, false friends*)

(B) A common variety of coarse metal FILE. (see: *long nosed pliers, false friends*)

Bastion Point: Shades of the occupation of Alcatraz by American Indians. Bastion Point is a park in Auckland that was occupied (on April 4th, 1982) by members of the Ngati Whaatua Maori group in much the same way and for much the same reasons. Most of this land has now been returned to the tribe. (see: *Waitangi Day, Waitangi Tribunal, Treaty of Waitangi, Maori, Iwi*)

bathroom: Literally means a ROOM CONTAINING a BATHTUB, a SINK, and nothing else. I have been embarrassed in the past to ask the way to the bathroom, and on arrival to find that the convenience I was looking for wasn't there. (see: *toilet, toilet paper, basin, lav, loo, bog, grot, dunny*)

baths: The public baths are not places to get clean but SWIMMING POOLS, also called swimming baths. Before you say 'how quaint', remember what you call the clothing in which you swim. Now who's being illogical?

bathwater: There is a rumor that when you pull the plug the water runs out of your bath clockwise in the northern hemisphere and counter-clockwise down under. Well, if your bath is a symmetrical tank, preferably of some stable substance like concrete, and it is firmly anchored, and the water in it has been there for a month or so (to get rid of random eddies introduced by pouring it in) and you devise a way to pull the plug straight down out of the bottom, then this is true. Otherwise, you pays your money and you gets either result in either hemisphere with about equal probability. (see: *backwards*)

Bay of Plenty: The name was bestowed by a pleased Captain Cook who had just come from a much less hospitable area. Sandwiched between the Coromandel peninsula to the northwest, East Cape to the east and encompassing the Rotorua district to the south this is a must area to visit. The largest cities are Tauranga whose metropolitan area comprises 59,435 people and Rotorua (52,001, 1986 census). The whole area has 187,462 people (1986), 1,406,000 sheep, 444,000 cattle and 47,000 domesticated (farmed) deer. Beautiful country with thermal areas that make old faithful look as if it was misplaced. (see: *North Island*)

Bazzer: An alternative pronunciation for the name BARRY. New Zealand is well populated with Bazzers and Trevs (Barrys and Trevors).

B.C.N.Z.: (bee-c-n-zed) BROADCASTING CORPORATION OF NEW ZEALAND. It used to be a government owned but quasi-independent body that operated both of NZ's channels (now there are 3 and one is privately owned) and about $^3/4$ of its radio stations. It has (like so many others) just changed its name, fissioned into two parts and become corporations, albeit state owned ones. (see: *Radio N.Z. Ltd., Television New Zealand, State Owned Enterprise, national programme, concert programme, wireless, TV3, zed*)

B.D.S.: Bachelor of Dental Surgery, your DENTIST who spends one year in ordinary university studies and five years in dental studies. Dentists, like physicians in New Zealand, do not have doctorates, and unlike physicians, do not even have the courtesy use of the title (see: *choppers, murder house, gum digger, M.B. Ch.B.*)

beaut: BEAUTIFUL in the sense of 'that was a beautiful dive into the swimming bath', or she's a beaut horse or sheila, etc. (see: *sheila, baths*). Note that unfamiliar words in New Zealand are likely to be contractions of familiar ones, as beaut for beautiful, or speedo for speedometer, or park for parking place (see: *park*). Another distinct possibility is that they are familiar words pronounced in unfamiliar ways as re-valley for reveille, or tomahto for tomato. (see: *veges, strawbs, ciggies, tomato/potato*)

be away — be away laughing: To SUCCEED EASILY. 'That driving test is in the hand, you'll be away laughing'. That driving test is easy, you'll pass with no sweat. (see: *in the hand, *piss in, *piss in the hand, not a problem*)

bedclothes: What you wear to bed, like pajamas or nightgown, right? Wrong. Bedclothes are what the bed is dressed in, sheets and blankets.

(the) Beehive: New Zealand has lots of conventional ones, and you must try manuka honey, but The Beehive isn't likely to produce anything so sweet. It is the PARLIAMENTARY OFFICE BUILDING in Wellington, named for its shape. (see: *Parliament, Fowl House*)

(I've) been inside: I've been IN PRISON. (see: *guest of Her Majesty, gaol, wooden aspro*)

beer: If, as is commonly quoted, a Kiwi's passions are 'rugby, racing and beer' then beer is the most available and hence most commonly indulged passion. It is usually served in jugs, (pitchers that hold one liter these days, they used to hold 2 imperial pints or 1.2 U.S. quarts), sold in half g's (half imperial gallon bottles) and delivered to hotels (bars) in tank trucks. Shortly after my arrival in New Zealand, I commented to a friend on, what appeared to me to be, the vast amount of beer drunk by most of my acquaintances. (By the way, they couldn't believe the amount of water I drank and were dumbfounded by the amount of ice I wanted in it.) He replied that it just wasn't true. Take himself for example; he only drank 3 jugs (3.6 U.S. quarts) when he went to the hotel and he rarely went to the hotel more than twice a week.

One other point. Kiwis don't like a foamy head on their beer and bartenders are skilled at pouring your beer without this head. Inquiry reveals that this is because they think that the head is cheating (waste) and if you pay for 8 oz. of beer you should get 8 oz. A concern more with substance than with froth. (see: *Kiwi, pissed, half g, draught beer, jug, boozer, hotel, booze barn, sink a few, brew, six o'clock swill, skinfull, litre, ice blocks*)

beetroot: Red BEETS (just the thing for borsch) usually served in slices and found on every plate, in every salad and in every filled roll. Ugh! (see: *filled roll, marrow, swedes, silverbeet*)

beggared: (A) Probably derived from (see:) *buggered*, this is a politer way to indicate that you are TIRED OUT. 'I've been fencing with Sam all day and that bastard works so hard I'm beggared'. I've been stringing fences and putting in fenceposts with Sam all day, and that character works so hard that I'm exhausted. (see: *bastard, stuffed, stonkered, puffed, clapped out, bugger, buggering around*)

　　　　(B) DAMNED. 'I'll be beggared if I'll spend another day working with that sod.' (see: *sod*)

Belgium (sausage): LUNCHEON MEAT, sort of a low grade liverwurst. This is a South Island term only. It is interesting to note that this stuff was called German sausage prior to World War I. (see: *Friesian, Chinese gooseberries, false friends*)

belly-buster: is not an excess of candy and ice cream although the term conjures up interesting visions. It is the inexperienced swimmer's least favorite dive—a BELLY FLOP. (see: *honey pot/bomb, duck dive*)

(kitchen) bench: A piece of kitchen furniture that is not designed for taking the weight off your feet. This is the kitchen COUNTER. (see: *false friends*)

Benmore breakfast: Patients in mental hospitals who are scheduled for ELECTROCONVULSIVE THERAPY have to refrain from eating for approximately 12 hours. Therefore ECT tends to be scheduled for first thing in the morning. One major source of electricity is the hydropower station at the Benmore dam, hence South Island patients call such therapy sessions a 'Benmore breakfast'.

berk: a berk is a STUPID JERK. 'That berk then tried to change lanes right in front of me'. (see: *clot, thick, no hoper, jerk, clueless*)

Berkeley: pronounced (Barkley) The name of a famous Irish Bishop (George Berkeley, 1685–1753) who maintained that for each of us the world exists only as we perceive it through our senses. In the world inhabited by a color-blind man, there is no color.

An alternative view is that of Benjamin Whorf (an American engineer) who proposed that we think the thoughts and make the perceptual discriminations for which we have words. Therefore, a Kiwi sees the world differently from an American, because he analyses it through somewhat different language (as you will have noticed throughout this volume). A Frenchman or Russian would perceive a very different world indeed, according to this logic.

All this boils down to the observation that if you come from Berkeley, California, in New Zealand you come from 'Barkley', California. (see: *caramel*)

berko, or **to go berko:** GO BERSERK, committing violence upon persons and/or property. Kiwis go berko about as frequently and within the same class strictures as North Americans. The only difference is that if the person who goes berko is under the influence of alcohol, people are likely to be much more understanding than in the U.S. or Canada. (see: *down trou*)

best of British luck, or **Best of British:** Usually means, I WISH YOU GOOD LUCK BUT I DON'T THINK YOU HAVE A SNOWBALL'S CHANCE. For instance, when you ignore form at the races and bet on Lame Dog ('Ran well back in all previous races, never a chance') because he is paying $200 – 1, your mate, who bet on the favorite, is likely to wish you 'Best of British'. (see: *mate*)

*Bible basher: A very religious, often AGGRESSIVELY RELIGIOUS PERSON. This term is often applied to the door-to-door advocates of religion, usually Fundamentalists or Mormon missionaries; however, anyone more religious than the speaker can earn this appellation.

bickies: BISCUITS meaning crackers or cookies. (see: *biscuit, water biscuit, big bickies*)

bicultural: In the U.S. (these days) this usually refers to the promotion of both Hispanic and North American-English speaking culture. In New Zealand it is the Maori and Pakeha-English speaking cultures. This is the flavor of the month in N.Z. at the moment, much to the annoyance of members of other non indigenous and less numerous minorities who, while not begrudging the Maori their recognition, would prefer a multicultural policy that included themselves. (see: *Maori, Pakeha, false friends*)

biddy-bids: Very small SEEDS/fruits equipped WITH hundreds/thousands of tiny HOOKS that fasten them to anything that walks by like pant legs, dogs, sheep, etc. Cleaning these off your clothes is a pain.

big bickies: LOTS OF MONEY. 'Sam just got promoted, he's in the big bickies now'.

big smoke: 'Off to the big smoke are you?' Off to the BIG CITY are you? This phrase long predates concern about pollution and in fact is a term of approbation and admiration.

bike: Usually a MOTORCYCLE not a bicycle. (see: *pushbike, motorbike, town bike, bikie*)

bikies: There are a number of MOTOR-CYCLE GANGS in New Zealand whose young MEMBERS model themselves largely on the 'Hells Angels'. (see: *bike, motorbike*)

billberry: Billberry ice cream, billberry cheesecake, sorry no go, English billberry (BLUEBERRY) jam is the best you can do in New Zealand, although I am pleased to say that a now thriving blueberry growing industry was established about 14 years ago and fresh blueberries are now obtainable during January and February. The term used to refer to these fresh billberrys is the one you are used to; blueberries. (see: *strawbs*)

billet: Shades of WW II; a billet is a PLACE TO STAY. The term is most often used when childrens' sports teams go to another town to play and are billeted with families in the host town providing both financial savings and chaperonage. In addition it provides a look at how others live but I suspect that this last point is an unplanned bonus. (see: *hostel*)

billion: If you could find an New Zealand billionaire he/she would be much richer than his/her U.S. counterpart, since a billion is equal to a TRILLION in the U.S. That is to say:

1 billion U.S. = 1,000,000,000

1 billion N.Z. = 1,000,000,000,000 (see: *thousand million*)

bird: There are two major types of birds. There is the feathered kind that you are familiar with, and the (to my mind) much more attractive featherless kind. I suppose that gentlemen hippopotami feel the same way about lady hippos. A bird is a GIRL. (see: *sheila, bit of crumpet, bit of fluff*)

Biro: A brand name that has become a noun. *Biros* are BALLPOINT PENS. You very likely won't be understood if you refer to a ballpoint, the word is *biro*. (see: *Snowtex, Clayton's, Witches-Britches, hoover, lux, Lilo, Fairydown, Twink*)

biscuit: These come in two varieties, dry biscuits which are CRACKERS and sweet biscuits which are COOKIES. What you think of as a biscuit is a scone. (see: *scone, bickies, water biscuit, Queen cake*)

(a) **bit:** Teenage slang for MAKING OUT. (see: *slap and tickle, bit of fluff, bit of crumpet, bit on the side*)

bit of all right: 'She's a bit of all right'. VERY ATTRACTIVE.

(a) **bit of a step:** 'It's a bit of a step down to my place, about 25 miles!' 'It's a bit of a step to change from school-teaching to farming.' 'It's a LONGISH WAY from …'

*bit of crumpet:** (A) a SEXY LASS. (see: *bit of fluff, crumpet, bird*)
(B) COITUS (see: *shag, have it off, get one away, root, on with, stuff,* (a) *naughty*)

bit of fluff: A patronizing description of a young lady. The term tends to reflect more on the intentions and attitudes of the speaker than the attributes of the subject. A FEATHER-BRAINED GIRL.

It has been suggested that the fluff in question is made up of the lady's natural feathery covering usually hidden by the bottom of her bikini.

bit on the side: LOVER, other than one's usual cohabitant. (see: *bit of fluff, bit of crumpet, fancy boy, toy boy*)

(Getting a) **bit on the side:** Getting it on with someone who is not your primary sleeping partner. (see: *getting it on, have it off, defacto*)

bitumen: (Pronounced bitch'a min) meaning ASPHALT (pronounced ash'falt), what roads are made of.

black Budget: The government's annual financial plan, including taxes and expenditure is announced annually in the Budget. A black Budget is full of bad news, with increased taxes and decreased funds going into social services. (see: *Budget, mini Budget*)

blimin': As in 'some blimin' thing'. Actually it's the local version of 'blooming' and means 'DARNED'. (see: *bloody, flaming, ruddy*)

block: In the U.S. you buy a (building) LOT. In New Zealand where open spaces are even more taken for granted than in Texas, you buy a block of land. (see: *land agent, lot*)

bloke: A MAN. 'He's a good bloke.'

bloody: Often used in referring to the British (bloody Pommies), Inland Revenue (tax collectors), etc. For most people, it occupies approximately the same place in the New Zealand lexicon as 'DAMN' does in ours. (Damn Yankees anyone?) However, for some it is an extremely strong and highly objectionable word. I have heard it suggested that this comes from a double entendre 'By our Lady' stated as an insult to the Catholic Mary Queen of Scots, implying that she and the Virgin had little in common. It also suggested that she was physiologically female and had not yet reached menopause. (see: *blimin, whinge, flaming, Kiwi, Pom — Pommie*)

23

bloody minded: From the point of view of the individual to whom you are applying this appellation he is probably sticking to the letter of the law. From your point of view he is being DIFFICULT, OBSTRUCTIONISTIC, RIGID, and OBNOXIOUS. (see: *bloody*)

blow it: (A) A relatively polite way of saying 'to hell with it', or 'I GIVE UP'.

(B) 'I'm afraid I will blow it.' 'I'm afraid I will FAIL.' (see: *done your chips, dipped out*)

blows: The STROKES OF the SHEARS which are used to remove the wool from sheep without (with skill) otherwise harming the animal beyond those nicks that you might inflict on yourself, while shaving. (see: *shearing gang, Golden Shears, sheep, wide comb*)

bludger: a bludger is a SPONGER — someone who is always borrowing and rarely repaying. To bludge is to borrow. It's socially acceptable to say 'may I bludge a cigarette (or a cup of sugar)' but calling someone a bludger can be a fighting insult. (see: *cadge*)

blue: a GOOF or mistake. 'I made a blue in trying to get on with her on the first date'. (see: *boob, on with*)

Blue Duck: A strange New Zealand bird (feathered). Unlike most other ducks in the world, this one lives in swift flowing mountain streams. It looks as if it has a moustache, since the beak has two flaps at the end that are used to strain caddis fly larvae out of the streams for dinner. The Maori name is WHIO because that's what its call sounds like. (see: *bird*)

bob: Now it means a DIME. It used to mean 12 pence but decimalisation changed everything to 10's. Yes, New Zealand used to have (pre-10 July, 1967) the same incomprehensible monetary system as the Mother country. (see: *quid, not the full quid, as silly as a two-bob watch, ten bob each way, decimalisation, metrication, pound, shilling, sixpence, penny, florin*)

Bobby: Often used for the COP on the beat. Part of New Zealand's British heritage.

bod: a PERSON. Derived from body as 'I need a few bods for this job'. It is perfectly ordinary parlance and not in the least derogatory. (see: *odd bod*)

(a) ***bog:** a SOJOURN on the TOILET.

(the) ***bog:** TOILET (Not a term used by the most refined.) Also refers to an area of swampy ground, but you knew that already. (see: *toilet, toilet paper, lav, loo, grot, dunny*)

***bog in:** BEGIN to engage enthusiastically in an ACTIVITY, usually eating. (see: *Kiwi grace, bog*)

boiled lollies (boiled sweets): Sound unappetizing? They're little pieces of clear HARD CANDY for sucking on, just like you can get at home and just as tasty. (see: *lollies, lolly scramble*)

bollicking: When you rush into the house to give your wife a big smacker (kiss) and she screams at you for tracking mud across her nice clean carpet, the CHEWING-OUT you are getting is a bollicking. Whether it's a rocket from your boss or a dressing-down by your nearest and dearest, a bollicking is no fun. (see: *smacker, give them arseholes*)

**bong: A term borrowed from Australia where it is used to refer to aborigines; in New Zealand, it is a derogatory reference to Maoris and occasionally Pacific Islanders. This is a fighting word; use it only if your neck is red and you enjoy a punch up. (see: *coconut, Maori, punch-up, wog*)

bonkers: NUTS. Someone who is bonkers has a screw loose. (see: *drive you crackers*)

bonnet: that's the HOOD of your car and you had better remember that, because hood won't be understood. (see: *boot, windscreen, accelerator, handbrake, mudguard*)

Bonus bonds: The New Zealand treasury operates a lottery through Post Bank and N.Z. Post outlets. The tickets are in $5, $10, $20, $50, $500 & $5000 amounts. These bonds draw no interest but each $1 is a lottery entry and there is a major draw on the second Tuesday of each month and a minor draw every Saturday. The prizes, like all gambling winnings by non professionals, are not subject to income tax. A reputable local organization has calculated that the overall return on these is about 2%, but we can all dream. (see: *Lotto, N.Z. Post Ltd., Postbank*)

boob: (A) A GOOF or boo-boo, e.g., 'I made a boob.'

      (B) It can also mean what you think it does.

      (C) In addition it is criminal slang for jail or PRISON.

    (see: (in the) *nick, boobhead, gaol, tats*)

boobhead: Criminal slang for PRISON INMATE. (see: *boob, gaol, tats*)

booeye: So far OUT IN THE COUNTRY, mountains, or woods that carrier pigeons lose their way trying to find the nearest town. I'm told this comes from 'up the Puhoi River', near Auckland, which was the back of beyond when the term was coined. (see: *wops or wop-wops*)

(to) book: To MAKE A RESERVATION at a place of entertainment where one 'books a seat' or at an eating establishment where one 'books a table'.

boomer: 'She's a boomer.' REALLY GOOD. (see: *mighty*)

boot: Can be used for the things you hike in, and there is an expression 'to put the boot in' which means metaphorically to kick someone, as 'then he really put the boot in and sent him down the road' (fired him); or gave him the boot. However, the commonest use of

boot refers to what you would call the TRUNK of your car. (see: *bonnet, windscreen, accelerator, handbrake, mudguard, gave him the boot, sent down the road*)

booze barn: Any large open room devoted to the 'purveyance of spirituous liquors'. One of these, that I used to frequent in a provincial center measures approximately 50 ft by 300 ft of open room with a bar that spans $^3/_4$ of the 300 ft wall. There has been some argument that the neighborhood pub should return and replace such barns. To a limited extent, this has been happening, in that new pub construction tends to be smaller and cozier. (see: *hotel, boozer, tavern, beer, six o'clock swill*)

boozer: the place where you drink. 'Meet you down at the boozer (BAR)'. Except for a few new-fangled 'taverns' the boozer is always, by legal requirement, part of a place that (at least nominally) offers bed and board as well, and is consequently called a hotel. (see: *hotel, beer, licensed hotel, plonk*)

borer: Wooden antiques and houses must be carefully inspected for the presence of myriad tiny holes looking like randomly scattered periods produced by a mad typist. These are made by a local insect with the dendrophagic habits of a TERMITE. If there are many of these holes, it is said that the object is held together by all the borer holding hands. In the earlier stages, this condition is curable by fumigation or if holes are few, using a syringe to shoot kerosene into each hole.

borstal: If you are a borstal graduate you have spent time in REFORM SCHOOL.

Boston buns: This term refers to a sweet bun, filled with jam or cream and iced with coconut. (see: *bread roll, iced buns, raspberry buns*)

(the) **bot:** A TUMMY BUG or intestinal flu.

bottle store: Attached to every (licensed) hotel is not only a bar but a separate shop which sells your home supplies of booze. In other words, a LIQUOR STORE, PACKAGE STORE or SPIRIT SHOP. (see: *hotel, private hotel*)

bottles on lawns: All around N.Z. and Australia you will find plastic pop bottles, partially filled with water, sitting on people's lawns. Folklore has it that, since a dingo won't foul his own water hole, dogs won't defecate on lawns that have these bottles. Research (mine) has shown that there is a small, but statistically significant, increase in the probability that fertilizer will be deposited on your lawn if you put a bottle there. (see: *Alsatian*)

bottling: Home CANNING as in fruit. Since all home preserving is now done in bottles rather than cans this makes more sense than the

North American version which harks back to an earlier era. (see: *clothesgrips* or *clothespegs, cement block, hairgrips* or *hair clips*)

bottom drawer: The place where young ladies (and perhaps some of their male counterparts) store away those things which will enable them to set up housekeeping when grown and married. If you can't afford a HOPE CHEST you always have a bottom drawer. (see: *glory box*)

bowler: (A) The PITCHER IN a CRICKET game. (see: *bowling, cricket*)

(B) Someone who plays bowls (there are U.S. style Bowling Alleys in New Zealand but that isn't bowling, that's 'ten pin') (see: *bowling, ten pin*)

(C) A bun shaped HAT. Not often seen these days.

bowling: (A) indoor and outdoor, and neither of these is ten pin bowling. This refers to the game of bowls which is a cross between shuffleboard (without sticks and with six-inch diameter balls substituted for the pucks) and horseshoe pitching. This is usually done on lawns like putting greens, only flatter, by white clad (customary, it used to be obligatory but pastels are occasionally sneaking in now) middle aged (optional) sportsmen and women (separately, of course).

(B) pitching the ball in a cricket game. (see: *bowler, ten pin, cricket*)

bowls: (see: *bowling*)

bowsers: No, this is nothing to do with beer. A bowser is a GAS (petrol) PUMP. 'Pull up to the bowsers and I'll fill her up'. (see: *petrol, gas, Motunui synthetic petrol plant*)

boxer shorts: Sorry, if you wear this variety of underwear you will have to go to Oz (Australia) to get them or have them sent from home. No one here wears them and most sales clerks wouldn't even know what you were talking about if you asked for them. (see: *Oz, sales clerks, skivvy*)

box of birds: 'How are you today?' 'I'm a box of birds today'. I'm on top of the world, RIGHT AS RAIN. (see: *box of fluffy ducks*)

box of fluffy ducks: I'm a box of fluffy ducks? I'm just as WELL/HAPPY/ SUCCESSFUL AS CAN BE. (see: *box of birds*)

box on: CARRY ON or FORGE AHEAD.

Boxing Day: A pugilists' bacchanalia. Well no, but I couldn't resist. Traditionally, on the DAY AFTER CHRISTMAS, wealthy Englishmen and their ladies used to have their servants box up the leftovers from Christmas dinner and distribute this largesse (sometimes along with a few presents) to the local poor. The custom has died but the name hasn't. (see: *Christmas*)

boys on the hill: Not usually the boys in the band. This phrase refers to the MEMBERS OF PARLIAMENT, New Zealand's unicameral legislature. (see: *Parliament*)

BP: (A) SON or daughter OF YUPPIE. An acronym for 'beautiful person'. Right clothes, right car, right accent, no financial worries and sitting next to you in university. A law or commerce major. (see: *ski bunny, varsity bunny*)

(B) *British Petroleum* a petrol company. (see: *petrol*)

braces: Remember those elasticized straps over your shoulders that held up your pants in the dim distant? Well, if you want a pair of SUSPENDERS, just ask for braces. (see: *suspenders*)

brandy snaps: A latticework cigar-shaped CONFECTION made of golden syrup, flour, ginger, brandy essence, etc. stuffed with cream and calories. (see: *golden syrup*)

brass me off: MAKE ME ANGRY.

brassed off: ANGRY.

bread: The supermarket and (see:) *dairy* does not carry quite as wide a variety as you are used to, however, a development of the last few years is hot bread shops in major and provincial centers. These make a wide variety of delicious fresh breads seven days a week.

The other thing about bread, is that in this land of abundant food, where restaurant servings are usually generous, it is very hard to get more than one piece of bread (or one roll). Unlike North America, where they seem to hope you will settle for smaller servings if you fill up with bread, in New Zealand restaurants appear afraid that you will spoil your appetite with the stuff. The major exceptions to this rule are Chinese Restaurants which are traditionally generous with half slices of standard white bread. Do note that the slices tend to be cut half the thickness that you are used to. If you want bread sliced to North American thickness you must purchase a 'toaster loaf' as toast in N.Z. is cut to North American dimensions. (see: *sandwich, toaster loaf, toasted sandwiches, doorstops*)

bread rolls or **hamburger rolls:** These come in two basic shapes — hamburger buns and HOT DOG BUNS. The terms, hamburger roll or bread roll, are used for both shapes. The term bread roll usually refers to hot dog buns. No one has ever heard of a hot dog bun; there is a thing on a stick that goes by the name hot dog and 'American Hot Dogs' which bear a visual resemblance to the real thing are becoming more common street stand fare. (see: *bangers, saveloys, alpine sticks, hot dogs, sandwich, hamburger*)

break up: The day SCHOOL ENDS for the academic year or any firm closes down for the Christmas holidays. Sometimes an end of year function, which may precede the actual end of school or work by a few days, is called a break up. (see: *Christmas*)

break wind: To release internally generated gases through one's anal orifice. A genteel expression. (see: *gas*)

(a) **brew:** a GLASS OF BEER. (see: *beer*)

brief: What a solicitor does for and to a barrister. Gives him or her the facts, a summary of the relevant law and any other tips he/she can think of. (see: *solicitor, barrister*)

(the) **British disease:** STRIKES. (see: *award, industrial unrest, demarkation dispute, industrial action, C.T.U.*)

brolly: That's what you hold over your head to keep the rain off (an UMBRELLA).

brown derby: A CONE, usually of plain (vanilla) ICE CREAM, with the ice cream part DIPPED IN hot CHOCOLATE which quickly hardens around it. Very tasty. This term is used only in the South Island. It is called a chocolate dip in the North Island. (see: *derby, North Island, South Island, chocolate dip*)

(to) **brown eye:** TO MOON. A Maori (and Pakeha, for that matter) sign of disrespect. The exposure of one's anal orifice, while bending over, to someone to whom you wish to express your disapprobation. It does render the exposer somewhat vulnerable to immediate forms of retaliation. (see: *down trou, drop your tweeds, take the mickey*)

bubble: A fishing FLOAT. Most often made of clear plastic with a plug on one side so that you can weight it with water. (see: *trace wire, false friends*)

bubble and squeak: If someone offers you a 'bubble and squeak' it isn't the latest breakfast cereal, it's VEGETABLE HASH. Chop up yesterday's left-over veges and fry them up with a bit of butter. Not as bad as it sounds and just the thing for impecunious student meals. (see: *veges*)

bubbly: Any SPARKLING WINE but most particularly champagne. 'The ladies always like a drop of the bubbly.' (see: *champers*)

buck in: Some years ago, the then Mayor of Greymouth was on TV praising his townsfolk for the way they bucked in (PITCHed IN) to help the city and each other during a flood. I've heard it privately since, but not through the media. (see: *muck in*)

bucket of bolts: a JALOPY.

(The) **Budget:** Once a year (more often in bad and changing times) the Minister of Finance presents the government's proposed financial management package to Parliament for approval, his/her caucus presumably having already approved it. This includes all tax changes as well as expenditure items such as health, education, welfare, defense etc. All the country listens carefully to find out what is happening to the price of cigarettes, alcohol, imported cars, etc. In addition we find out about what will probably happen to personal income taxes in six to twelve months. Changes in rates and allowable deductions are announced, at least in broad terms and often in detail, in this document. (see: *Minister of Finance, Parliament, caucus, Inland Revenue, mini Budget, black Budget*)

**bugger: A term of derision. When used as a noun, it refers to someone you don't like. When used as a verb, it refers to the male act of SODOMY with a member of one's own sex and species. (see: *buggering around, buggered, beggared, sod*)

*buggered: EXHAUSTED, worn out, beat. Deriving from the putative state of someone who has been sodomized, it has lost all but the faintest hint of this origin. There are other ways to declare your imminent collapse. (see: *beggared, stonkered, stuffed, puffed, clapped out, bugger, buggering around*)

*buggering around: 'He's been buggering around with that job for weeks.' WASTING TIME. (see: *bugger*)

*bugger off: GO AWAY.

*bugger up: To CREATE a SNAFU or to otherwise render less functional than before.

*bum: is what you sit on. Les Femmes in New Zealand appear to have an unusually high proportion of generous ones and sturdy legs to match. Pioneer heritage? (see: *backside, fanny*)

bumf: These days it tends to mean INFORMATION IN PRINTED FORM. However, this term has an inglorious past. It derives from 'bum fodder' a.k.a. toilet paper, which was (and is) what many consider the reams of paperwork generated by bureaucrats is best suited for.

bummer: A BAD TRIP, drug or just everyday activity, as, 'yesterday was a bummer'.

bun: As in 'use your bun' (HEAD). (see: *scone*)

bun in the oven: PREGNANT. (see: *up the spout, up the duff, sprog*)

bunch of fives: Hold out your hand flat, palm up. Now curl the index finger into the palm, now the middle finger, now the ring finger, now the little finger. Put your thumb across the backs of the middle sections of the index and middle fingers. Now shake the FIST under someone's nose and ask, in a belligerent tone of voice if he'd like a 'bunch of fives'. (see: *knuckle sandwich*)

bungy jumping: An ankle harness attached to a rubber rope is fitted to the intrepid tourist's lower extremities and then she or he leaps off a bridge up to 250 feet high. Great therapy for compressed spines and a fine example of 'flooding' therapy for those with fear of heights.

Bursary: 7th formers (or bright 6th formers; in any case 17 – 18 year olds) take this exam to earn some financial support (above tuition, for University). The top 4% of Bursary passers who do some extra exams (scholarship) get a little more. These amounts are not large but they are the icing on the cake. Each N.Z. student under 21 who is accepted by a University gets some financial help from the government. It ranges from $11 per week for a student who is under 18 and living at home, to $260 per week for a student with dependent spouse or child.

On top of this a Bursary exam pass of higher than 250 out of 500 gives them an extra $100 per year. 300 – 500 gives them $200 per year, and a Schols pass gives them $300 per year. These latter amounts are net, not additive.

As of 1990 they have to pay $1250 tuition per year plus living expenses, textbooks, exam and student union fees, etc. (see: *U.E., school, School Cert., 6th Form Certificate*)

bush: In New Zealand there may or may not be any bushes in a patch of bush. Any UNDEVELOPED LAND covered with vegetation is bush.(see: *bushwhacker, go bush*)

bush carpenter: Those of us who are more concerned with function than looks. You know, the nail may be in crooked, but it holds.

bush shirt: Characteristic outdoor work and leisure dress for male New Zealanders consisting of a very thick and heavy WOOL or wool-blend, colorful, checkerboard patterned SHIRT that pulls over the head but has a conventional shirt collar with three or four buttons below it. (see: *bushwhacker*)

bushwhacker: not an evil man in a black stetson who shoots people in the back from ambush, but simply a MAN WHO WORKS in the backwoods or BUSH. (see: *bush shirt, hard case, land agent, false friends*)

butchery: This is not your local slaughterhouse (see: *works, abattoir*) but rather an institution you may be old enough to remember. The neighborhood BUTCHER'S SHOP. 'And not too much fat on that, Mr. John'. (see: *T bone, fillet, topside, silverside, lamb's fry*)

buttercup: Sorry, wrong again! This isn't the familiar yellow flower; it is a variety of PUMPKIN. (see: *butternut, marrow, runnerbeans, veges, false friends*)

butternut: This has nothing to do with butter or nuts. Butternut is a kind of PUMPKIN. (see: *buttercup, marrow, runner beans, veges*)

by crikey: BY GOLLY (gosh). (see: *by ginger*)

by ginger: BY GOSH (golly). (see: *by crikey*)

B.Y.O.B.: on a party invitation, means BRING YOUR OWN BOTTLE.

C

cabbage tree: No, even in N.Z. cabbages don't grow on trees. This is a small tufted tree (Cordyline australis) that resembles a palm but is, instead, a relative of the N.Z. flax bush. (see: *false friends*)

cadge: (cad-je) TO BORROW. 'May I cadge a cup of sugar?' 'Sam is a perennial cadger. I wouldn't lend him anything if I were you.' (see: *bludger*)

*(your) **cake hole:** is your MOUTH. Neither friendly nor commonly used; avoid this one. 'Shut your cake hole.'

Califont: You may rent a flat that has a SMALL GAS WATERHEATER over the tub or shower. You switch this on and it roars into life, startling the hell out of you and providing the frightening sight and sound of a violent conflagration that quickly heats the water. (see: *flat, hot water cylinder, gas*)

callipers: (A) The usual measuring instruments.

      (B) LEG BRACES so unfortunately common in the days before Salk and Sabin. (see: *false friends*)

call: I once received an official message from an organ of the N.Z. Government asking me to '... call if convenient, otherwise telephone'. To call means to COME IN PERSON, it does not mean 'to telephone'. (see: *Telecom N.Z., ring, ring off*)

camp as a row of pink tents: OVERTLY HOMOSEXUAL.

can I heat up your tea/coffee: MAY I REFILL YOUR CUP? Since the action of pouring in an amount of fresh hot liquid accomplishes both the refill and heating functions, neither statement is any more logical than the other. No matter how strange it sounds to our ears. It is just a matter of the priority one gives to the two functions. (see: *false friends*)

can I loan: MAY I BORROW.

can off: 'Then he went round the corner and canned off his bike which went on to win the race without him.' Then he went round the corner and fell (violently) off his motorcycle which ... FALL (VIOLENTLY) OFF (see: *come a greaser, come a gutser, can out*)

can out: To OVERTURN one's yacht, canoe or other WATERBORNE CRAFT, spilling oneself into the water, under circumstances that imply that this was not your intention. (see: *yachtie, can off*)

Candy floss: That light, airy, sweet, carnival fare COTTON CANDY. It seems a much more elegant name. (see: *toffee apple*)

cane: A verb referring to the practice of applying a leather strap vigorously to some portion of the anatomy of an errant schoolboy (it used to be illegal to cane girls, over 10 years old, clearly a case where it was only just that equality for the ladies should have been energetically pursued). The current state of affairs, where it is theoretically possible to cane girls, has come about much more from the repeal of regulations rather than any active desire to achieve an equality of discomfort. None the less, caning girls would still be an event so rare as to be nonexistent. Most any adult male Kiwi will be happy to recall his caning(s) (PADDLINGS) during his schooldays. Private schools seem to distribute these more freely than public ones and a sociologist (American) claims that there is a bonding process between Masters and boys brought about by caning process. Every boy appears to feel that to be caned once is a necessary proof of manhood. Some boys, however, appear to collect canings, keeping a tally of beatings on their belts. Everyone wants to be special in some way! (see: *get the strap*)

canoe: The usual meaning of canoe in New Zealand is an eskimo KAYAK, just the thing for shooting the rapids. What you think of as a canoe, is a Canadian canoe or an 'Indian canoe' to most Kiwis, and they've probably never seen one. (see: *Kiwi*)

Canterbury: This area is comprised of the middle $^2/_3$ of the east coast of the South Canterbury Plains which is some of the best farming land in N.Z. However, in the late 1980's a severe and protracted drought in north Canterbury has put many farmers out of business. Canterbury also includes N.Z.'s most English city, Christchurch (metropolitan area population 299,400, 1987), with stone buildings and a very English cathedral. Take a trip up to 'The Sign of the Takahe' in the Port Hills above Christchurch for a Devonshire tea. The building is fascinating, the view spectacular, and the tea fattening. Here (Canterbury) too is Mt Cook, N.Z.'s highest mountain, set in a national park of wilderness, glaciers, and mountains (a must). Canterbury's (1986 census) statistics are as follows: 348,700 people, 5,192,000 sheep, 233,000 cattle and 22,000 domesticated (farmed) deer. (see: *South Island, tea*)

capping: In May of each year, the seven University level institutions hold their GRADUATIONS after a week of traditional hi-jinks. These include parades, skirted (not kilted) male bag-pipe players entering every bar in town to give off-key concerts and multiple large scale practical jokes. The police tend to look tolerantly at such activities during the week. Why, you may ask, is graduation in May when the academic year runs from March through November? Well, when all final exam papers had to go by ship to Great Britain to be graded, the results just didn't come back till the following May. The exams no longer go to the Mother Country, but the major time of graduation hasn't changed. However, an increasing number of people are choosing to formally graduate at a new ceremony, held in December of the year in which they complete the requirements for their degrees. (see: *capping concert, capping mag, procession*)

capping concert: At graduation time each year, the students of all of New Zealand's Universities used to put on a stage show. Sometimes they are risque, sometimes downright crude, but always funny. Now the only one left is at the University of Otago. One warning, if you sit in the front rows you may find yourself an involuntary participant in the activities on stage. (see: *capping, capping mag*)

capping mag: or capping magazine: is the GRADUATION week STUDENT PUBLICATION. It serves one official purpose, to provide a list of all the graduates, and a host of unofficial ones. It is the students' chance to satirize their elders and their society, morals, politics, education, all fair game. Capping magazines range from witty to obscene. Many cities have restricted the sale of these magazines in time or place but none have dared to ban them outright.

capsicum: Bite into a crisp, tasty capsicum. It sounds like you are asking for a mouthful of broken teeth but it's only a GREEN PEPPER. (see: *veges, aubergine, courgette, swedes*)

Captain James Cook: The commanding officer of the first British ship (the Endeavour) to reach these shores. He arrived for the first time on the 6th of October 1769. Abel Janzoon Tasman had paid a fleeting visit 127 years earlier but had been discouraged by the Maori who had themselves arrived some 600 years before him. Initial Maori efforts to discourage Cook as Tasman had been discouraged failed. Cook was later to reach an untimely end at the hands of the polynesian inhabitants of Hawaii (the big island) on Feb 14, 1779. (see: *Captain Cookers, pig island*)

Captain Cookers: Feral pigs, purportedly descended from swine released by the good captain. (see: *Captain James Cook, pig island*)

caramel: Pronounced KARMEL as in Carmel, California. Still good candy. (see: *Berkeley*)

caravan: In far off days of yore, these crossed the deserts, strings of camels swaying, chewing and spitting in the breeze. Today, I'm afraid it is a remote and prosaic, but comfortable, descendant of that romantic, but smelly and uncomfortable, parade. In short, a HOUSE TRAILER. Note that most of these are small and mobile, partly as a result of a law which forbids their use as a permanent residence. Hence motorcamps have strictly temporary accommodation. (see: *motorcamps*)

carbonettes: (North Island): Hard packed BRIQUETS of COKE. They burn long and hot. The biggest bit of culture shock I've experienced in New Zealand was moving from the North Island, where these are sold in every neighborhood store (dairy) and gas (petrol) station, to the South Island and trying to buy some. No one knew what I was talking about. (see: *dairy, petrol, gas, mainland*)

cardigan or **cardie:** A SWEATER that is cut like a jacket in that it buttons up the front. These grow more common as you go south into the colder weather. Sweater sets that include cardigans are popular with some of the ladies. (see: *twin set and pearls, jumper*)

careering: 'And then the lorry, whose brakes had failed, came careering down the hill.' And then the truck, whose brakes had failed, came CAREENING down the hill.

cark out: To GO TO SLEEP, often as a result of alcohol intake or exhaustion, or to DIE.

carless days: On the 30th July 1979, New Zealand introduced a drastic fuel conservation measure (in addition to banning petrol sales on weekends). This was the banning of operation of all privately and petrol powered motor vehicles weighing 4,400 lbs or less (except for motorcycles) for one day per week. That day to be chosen by the owner of the vehicle in question. There were several exceptions, public transport (taxis, buses, ambulances) rental cars and those (about 20% of vehicles) who have a good reason to drive on their carless day.

  The introduction of this measure created some unexpected difficulties, e.g., the most popular days turned out to be Wednesday and Thursday, while the government had expected (and printed stickers for) the weekend.

  As far as effects went, research (mine) has shown that it certainly alleviated the parking problem on Wednesday and Thursday. As far as saving petrol went, the absolute savings, over the previous year, brought about by both savings measures combined was appx. 2.8%. The notional savings, assuming that demand would have grown if steps hadn't been taken, was 8.5%. You pays your money and takes your choice. Carless days were suspended when the international oil crisis passed but I'm sure that there is a contingency plan, gathering dust in a filing cabinet in Wellington, to reintroduce them if the crisis recurs. (see: *petrol*)

carnie kid: JAIL BAIT (from carnal knowledge). (see: *age of consent*)

carpark: A PLACE in which automobiles can find temporary surcease from their labors in the salubrious open air. A PARKING LOT. (see: (a) *park*)

carriers: These are your local MOVING COMPANY. Makes sense doesn't it? (see: *hair grips, clothesgrips*)

cassia: If you have an American cookbook, and it calls for CINNAMON, use what is called cassia in New Zealand. Otherwise you will wonder why it doesn't taste quite right (with thanks to Mrs. Bear). (see: *cinnamon, icing sugar*)

casual meals: If you go to a hotel restaurant for a meal or telephone for a booking (reservation), you will be asked if you are '... in the house or casual'. Unless you are a registered guest, your answer should be 'casual'. (see: *hotel*, (to) *book*)

cat: The New Zealand branch of the felis domesticus family makes (most of) its North American cousins look like kittens. An average adult cat weighs upwards of a stone (14 pounds). (see: *stone, pussy, moggy, dirt box, sandpit, pet*)

cattle stop: In a pastoral country with 67,478,000 sheep, 8,279,000 cattle, 149,000 domesticated (farmed) deer and 3,307,084 people (all 1986 figures), opening and closing gates can get to be a terrible nuisance. The cattle stop is a horizontal arrangement of railway rails with 4-inch gaps between them set into the road at a break in the fence. The cattle and sheep jam their hooves between the rails and find it easier to stay on their own side. (see: *Taranaki Gate*)

caucus: When I first came to N.Z. I assumed that the laws of the country were made in Parliament. However, after listening to Parliament on the radio for a few years it became clear that the debates were totally irrelevant and that those Bills sponsored by the government (majority party) always passed, everyone else's were always defeated and no one ever seemed to cross party lines on any vote (it does happen but very, very, very rarely). So who makes the decisions? My next hypothesis was that it was really a dictatorship with the Prime Minister calling all the shots. In 1979 this was a theory with considerable popular backing (see: *Muldoon*). In 1989 it seemed rather less likely although there were (unlike 1985) those who gave it serious consideration (see: *Lange*). In 1990 with yet another new Prime Minister (see: *Palmer, Geoffrey*) dictatorship is once again on the wane, however, wait until he finds his feet. This is assuming that Labour will be re-elected in late 1990 which doesn't seem to be the most likely outcome in March 1990.

However, independent of who is P.M. it turns out that there is meaningful debate on the government sponsored Bills but this debate takes place in private. Each party holds caucus meetings consisting of all the representatives of that party in Parliament. Debate is presumably free and fierce in these caucus meetings and this is the place WHERE DECISIONS ARE actually MADE! Once a decision is made, party discipline is very strong and all members of the party caucus are expected to support the group decision independent of their own judgement. Presumably if someone consistently didn't, s/he would lose his/her voice in caucus and his/her seat at the next election. The loss of the seat without party support is not a foregone conclusion but it always works that way.

As I write there is a quarrel between the Labour Government and the Labour Party and the Government caucus is seeking to expel the one parliamentarian who is trying to support the party line and consequently defying caucus decisions. Watch this space for further developments. [Further developments: The parliamentarian in question has left the Labour Party and started a new party, the 'New Labour Party'] (see: *Prime Minister, Parliament, conscience vote, boys on the hill, National Party, Labour Party, New Labour Party, shadow cabinet ministers, M.P., P.M.*)

caught short: An immediate NEED TO SEE A MAN ABOUT A DOG. An explanation to any shopkeeper that you've been 'caught short' will usually result in an immediate offer of his toilet facilities, or directions to nearby public ones. Strangely enough, it is only men who seem to use this phrase. Either the ladies are better planners, have better control, or just know something we don't. (see: *relieving oneself, pointing Percy at the porcelain*)

Cellotape: SCOTCH TAPE (see: *sticky tape, cyclostyle, drawing pins*)

cement block: a CINDERBLOCK. I think the Kiwis have the right of this one. (see: *hair grips, clothesgrips* or or *clothespegs, bottling*)

central heating: Not bloody likely mate (except for a few effete sorts, probably North American or Pommie immigrants. 'Do you know why you Yanks get so many colds? It's because you keep your houses so hot the contrast gives you colds.' It is customary, even in the coldest parts of the country to turn the heat off completely at night, and most people consider 65° F a warm house. (see: *air conditioning, Pom — Pommie*)

century: Think it refers to 100 years, do you? Well, possible, but more likely when someone uses this word in New Zealand they're referring to 100 runs made by their favorite player in a cricket match. 'Ian made a century yesterday!' (see: *cricket, test, sticky wicket, wicket keeper*, etc. etc., *false friends*)

C.E.R.: On the Australian side of the Tasman this has a dreadful ring, 'COMPULSORY EARLY RETIREMENT'. Which is a pension from the Government (if you are over 65), and possibly from the firm, but no gold watch. In times of economic difficulty the number in each lifeboat is reduced (one way or another). On the New Zealand side of the Tasman it has quite another meaning, it refers to the 'CLOSER ECONOMIC RELATIONSHIP' with, guess who? Australia, of course. This attempt at a South Pacific EEC has been tried before but this is the most serious and successful attempt to date. No doubt there will be an expansion of the scheme or something new directed to the same ends in the 1990's. (see: *Aussie*, (the) *Tasman, white goods*)

(the) **chain:** In the freezing works where meat animals are butchered for New Zealand's most lucrative export trade, there is a kind of

disassembly line where each person chops out the same portion of
each carcass as it reaches him on an endless belt. Extremely boring,
but by local standards, extremely well paid work and considered
the choice job to have in the works. (see: *works, freezing works,
abattoir, gemel*)

Chair: (A) What you sit in.

(B) The ACADEMIC APPOINTMENT held by a University Professor,
e.g., the Chair of Physics at the University of Otago. A Chair and a
department headship used to be almost always synonymous. These
days 2 or 3 professors in a large department is not uncommon. (see:
Professor, false friends)

chalkboard: A BLACKBOARD which, these days, is just as likely to be
green.

champers: Weddings, (see:) *wedding breakfast* s, celebrations of all
kinds call for CHAMPAGNE. (see: *bubbly*)

charge hand: The Japanese would call him the honcho, you would
tend to say FOREMAN. This latter term (foreman) is also used in New
Zealand. (see: *leading hand*)

Charlie Browns: Lace up BROWN SHOES with crepe soles FOR KIDS.
Remember Buster Brown shoes?

*charlies: A teenage slang term for the physical characteristics
which identify the female homo sapien as a mammal.

chat up: is to engage in conversation. Usually this refers to a discussion with a member of the opposite sex whom one has met for the
first time. 'I saw you chatting up that beaut sheila at the hotel last
night.' I saw you TALKING IN AN ANIMATED AND ENGAGING WAY to that
beautiful girl in the bar last night. (see: *beaut, sheila, hotel*)

cheek: The guy who invites himself to dinner and then complains
about the quality of the food has this in excess. GALL or HUTZPA.
(see: *false friends*)

cheeks: A term most commonly used to refer to one's BUTTOCKS,
although it is also used for the fleshy parts of the face. (see: *false
friends*)

cheeky: Someone who exhibits a lot of cheek (not necessarily cheeks)
is cheeky. (see: *cheek, cheeks, down trou*)

cheerios: These round little 'O''s bursting with ... Sorry, wrong
again. *Kellogg's* has floated to these distant shores but wisely
they have avoided confusion by not introducing this item. In New
Zealand cheerios are COCKTAIL FRANKFURTERS. The rude and lewd
also call these 'little boys'. (see: *bangers, saveloys, alpine sticks,
rude, hot dogs*)

cherry bye: a cheerful GOODBYE. (see: *hurray*)

cheesed off: When my tax bill arrives, I am usually very cheesed off
(a cross between ANGRY and ANNOYED). (see: *Inland Revenue*)

*cheesehead: A DUTCHPERSON.

chemist shop: The place where you purchase your chemicals such as acetylsalicylic acid, vitamin B_1, shampoo, etc. In other words, a DRUG STORE. These establishments come much closer to being genuine drug stores than their North American counterparts, since they sell little beyond drugs, cosmetics and toilet articles. (see: *shop, bottle shop, Op shop, bottle shop, tuck shop*)

chilly bin: A literal description of the inside of the ideal picnic hamper which is a STYROFOAM COOLER (made of foamed polystyrene). You put in frozen *Slikka pads* and you've got a well-insulated portable refrigerator. If you tour New Zealand by car (or bicycle) one of these will save you money and let you lunch in the most beautiful spots. (see: *Slikka pads, coolibah*)

chin wag: a CHAT or a good old fashioned gossip.

Chinese burn: INDIAN ROPE BURN. You know, when you grab someone else's wrist with two hands and twist them rapidly in opposite directions, simultaneously and painfully pulling their skin in the two opposite directions. Childhood has it's downside.

Chinese gooseberries: You may know this as KIWI FRUIT, since the New Zealand merchants changed the name in order to facilitate sales to the United States during the days when the U.S. didn't officially recognize Red China's existence. (see: *Kiwi fruit, goosegogs, tamarilloes*)

chip: A North Island term for a SMALL BOX of berries, the equivalent of (see:) *punnet*, also a North Island term. The South Island term (Christchurch south), is (see:) *pottle*.

chippies: (A) Those crunchy thin slices of fried potato (POTATO CHIPS). One of my first language laughs in New Zealand was a sign in the Palmerston North Opera House which said:

NO CHIPPIES
ALLOWED

I hadn't realized that soliciting was such a serious problem although every city has its (legal) solicitors. (see: *solicitor, false friends, Opera House*)

(B) The men who produce chips and sawdust as a regular part of their work (CARPENTERS).

chippolatas: Frankfurter shaped spicy sausages, not recommended. (see: *bangers, saveloys, alpine sticks, hot dogs, cheerios*)

chips: These are FRENCH FRIES. Don't let the fact that some take-away bars advertise french fried potatoes fool you. If you were to ask for them you'd most likely get a blank look. You must ask for chips. (see: *fish and chips, take-aways*)

chocka: Fibber McGee's closet could have been accurately described as chocka. For younger readers, it will have to be Scrooge McDuck's money bin. Chocka means FULL TO BURSTING.

chockies: CHOCOLATE COOKIES.

chocolate dip: An ice cream cone, vast and inexpensive by American standards, and dipped in a vat of chocolate which hardens into a delicious brown shell over the ice cream part. This is a North Island term only. In the South Island they are called brown derbys. (see: *brown derby, North Island, South Island*)

chocolate wheel: At school fairs and other charity gatherings, the chocolate wheel is a traditional fundraiser. This is a WHEEL OF FORTUNE with a box of chocolates for the person who has purchased the ticket marked with the winning number. Occasionally other prizes are offered (e.g., chickens) but chocolates are the staple.

chook: Another name for one of the most prestigious meats in New Zealand. If a Kiwi invites you to dinner, odds are about 4 to 1 that he (she really) will serve CHICKEN. This is because it isn't long since chicken was the very most expensive meat in New Zealand and in many households was served only for Christmas and honored guests. Even the advent of Colonel Sanders hasn't eliminated this heritage. (see: *veges, strawbs, chook*)

choppers: (A) 'Sink your choppers into that chook and you'll think you died and went to heaven'. TEETH decay faster in New Zealand than they do in Britain according to a recent investigating commission (soil deficiencies?). Dental bills, however, are laughably low in New Zealand by North America standards. Would you believe an average of $143 for a (single root) root canal job or an average $44 for an ordinary amalgam or glass filling (1989 Otago-Southland prices)? (see: *B.D.S., chook*)

    *(B) Slang term for Malaysians, used on some University campuses. (see: *bunga, wog, coconut*)

Christmas: That lovely time of year when all the shops shut up (and many of them remain closed through January as well), the sun shines and the beach beckons. Most people do eat a traditional (cold weather) English Christmas dinner, and exchange gifts, but otherwise there is no resemblance. This is the start of the summer holidays when the cities empty and the resorts fill. Bloody marvelous, unless you want to get some work done. If your work involves anyone else, just forget it! (see: *January, school holidays, Father Christmas, cracker, Boxing Day, seasons*)

Christmas cracker: (see: *cracker*)

Christmas drinks: It is a time-honored tradition that you have your friends over before Christmas and ply them with liquor and little goodies. In fact, this is the (see:) *bottle store*'s best time of year and a common enquiry is 'have you bought your Christmas booze yet?' (see: *New Zealand Christmas tree, Christmas*)

chuffed: A combination of cheered up and puffed up. When I see my name in print (over an article) I am PROUD AND HAPPY (chuffed).

chunder: A term which is used freely by people who engage in occasional massive over-indulgence in alcoholic beverages; REGURGITATE. (see: *Technicolour yawn, *spew, *puke, chunder, drive the porcelain bus*)

ciggies: CIGARETTES (see: *veges*)

cinnamon: A somewhat milder taste than you would expect. Do not use this in American recipes when they call for cinnamon. Use cassia instead. (see: *cassia, icing sugar, false friends*)

city: A collection of human habitations is by law entitled to call itself a CITY when it has achieved the overwhelming population attributed to a name of such dignity, i.e., 20,000 INHABITANTS. There used to be one loophole clause — if such a collection of habitations contained an Anglican Cathedral, it was a 'city' independent of size. I believe this provision was wiped in 1987.

clapped out: 'After lugging my baggage from one airline counter to another for two hours, I was totally clapped out (EXHAUSTED).' This also applies to mechanical devices. 'That old car is totally clapped out.' (see: *stuffed, buggered, beggared, stonkered*)

Clayton's: ERSATZ (non-alcoholic) whiskey. 'What you drink when you are not having a drink.' Any sort of ersatz has come to be called a '*Clayton's*', e.g., 'My *VW* is a *Clayton's Porsche*'. (see: *Snowtex, Biro*)

clean your shoes: a chorus dinned unceasingly into my ears. It doesn't mean to scrape the dirt off or even to saddle-soap them. To clean one's shoes, is to POLISH THEM. (see: *clean your teeth*)

clean your teeth: a command often honored in the breach by youngsters of any western nation. Such cleaning is done with a toothbrush. BRUSH YOUR TEETH. (see: *clean your shoes*)

clerk: means clerk, pronounced clark. He/She could be a Town Clerk, a most important post, the office manager for a city. Alternatively, this could refer to a salesclerk, or a bookkeeper. (see: *salesclerk*)

clobber: Your clobber is what you wear. Some wear flash clobber and others wear more conservative CLOTHING. Depending on the context, this can also refer to violence, either direct as: 'then I clobbered him with a crank handle', or indirect as: 'then the judge clobbered me with a stiff fine'. Alternatively, the term is often used as we would use 'stuff', as 'how will I ever move all this clobber into that little room?' (see: *flash, stuff*)

(The great New Zealand) *clobbering machine:* It is said that N.Z. suffers from the TALL POPPY SYNDROME. Those who dare to stand out

41

from the herd attract an inordinate degree of opprobrium, just as tall poppies tend to be the ones that get their heads cut off. It is my impression that in 1990 this is rather less true than it was in 1980.

clot: A clot is an individual whom you might uncharitably describe as a dumb CLOD. (see: *thick, clueless, no hoper, berk, jerk*)

clothesgrips or **clothespegs:** CLOTHESPINS. You must admit that they make more sense than we do. (see: *hair grips* or *hair clips, knitting pins, cement block, bottling*)

clueless: Someone who is clueless DOESN'T HAVE A CLUE. Since there appears to be a certain amount of correlation between intelligence and having a few clues, this has become a synonym for STUPID. (see: *thick, clot, no hoper, berk, jerk*)

cobber: My cobber is my FRIEND. (see: *mate*)

**cock in a sock: A tradesman's or engineers term for two things that are supposed to fit together with very little clearance but which, in practice, make a very sloppy fit indeed. (see: *rattling good fit, there's an old boot for every old sock, tradesman*)

cocky: (A) a cocky is a New Zealand FARMER. These come in several varieties: cow cockies (ranchers) tend to be the only ones who rate a modifier to the cocky, but there are also men who you could describe as sheep cockies, dairying cockies, horticultural cockies and mixed cockies. A Kiwi would, however, leave off the descriptive words for all but the cow cockies. (see: *sheep, primary products, high country station, station, dogs, fencing*)

(B) A COCKATOO. This is a (Australian) parrot sized, white feathered, yellow crested bird with a disconcerting habit of addressing you in English. Such immortal phrases as 'Cocky wants a peanut' and 'Cocky wants a cup of tea', come to mind. I've often been tempted to honor that last bird's request and see what happens.

*coconut: In addition to referring to the usual hairy milk filled nut, this appellation is used as a derisive name for Pacific Islanders living in New Zealand. The term is most often used by Maoris who resent the Islanders' attempts to move into the jobs and neighborhoods that are their customary preserve. (see: *Maori, bong, wog, choppers*)

college: This is not a term that (with 1½ exceptions) refers to University level institutions, nor does it (as in some British and North American institutions) refer to the component parts of a University. These parts are called Faculties or Divisions, e.g., the Faculties of Medicine and Law. Most colleges are HIGH SCHOOLS and this is a general term for a high school. The institutions that train teachers are also officially called Colleges of Education, however, they have so recently changed to this name that to make yourself understood you must use the old name: Teachers' College. These do not give a Bachelor's degree, but rather award a 'Certificate'. The only remaining 'college' that awards the Bachelor's degree is Lincoln (the exception noted above) Agricultural College. In 1990 there are moves afoot (mostly at Lincoln) to turn it into a University. Massey University is still known as Massey College to some of the old-timers who remember it as an Agricultural College. (see: *Uni, varsity, College of Education, school, grammar school, P.P.T.A., false friends*)

College of Education: If you are old enough to remember NORMAL SCHOOLS in the U.S. that's what this is (careful, Normal Schools are something different here). It takes New Zealand's equivalents of high school graduates and puts them through a three year course designed to train them as teachers. At the end of this period, the successful student will be awarded a (teaching) 'Certificate' of their College of Education, this is not the legal or moral equivalent of a B.A. or B.Sc. Teachers consider this 'Certificate' a 'Diploma of Teaching'. Colleges of Education are now starting to offer their brighter students the opportunity to gain a Bachelor's degree in conjunction with the Education Departments of nearby universities. University graduates who wish to go into teaching must spend a year at a College of Education getting the practical training they've missed. They are then awarded a (teaching) Certificate on top of their Bachelor's degree. No one will, however, know what you are talking about if you use the name 'College of Education'; you must use the old (up to January 1, 1990) name: Teachers' College. (see: *Uni, varsity, college, Normal School, School Cert., U.E., Teacher's College*)

collywobbles: A NERVOUS UPSET STOMACH. 'Before exams, I always get the collywobbles'.

colonial goose: If fowl is New Zealand's most expensive meat, mutton (which you might think is lamb overseas) is the cheapest. Hence a ROLL OF MUTTON filled WITH A BREADCRUMB STUFFING is substituted. (see: *chook*)

come a greaser — come a gutser: (A) HAVE BAD LUCK (of any kind) (B) To FALL OFF as from a bike, skis, etc. (see: *can off, bike*)

come again: Kindly REPEAT your statement. It is not improbable that your North American accent and idioms will elicit this request from Kiwis on occasion, although you will find that thanks to TV they are acquainted with most American word usage even if they wouldn't say it that way themselves. (see: *Kiwi*)

come off it: PULL THE OTHER ONE or, you don't really mean what you are saying. (see: *take the mickey*)

come round: (A) You don't have to fatten yourself up or even stuff a pillow in your shirt in order to come round. Just COME OVER and see the speaker. (see: *go round*)

(B) 'He's come round to my way to thinking.' 'He's showing some sense at last' (CHANGED HIS MIND).

comparisons-differences: There is a tendency to rank order things when comparisons or differences are requested. If you are asked what the differences between North America and New Zealand are, people are usually looking for a conclusion at the end; stating that one or the other is better. Similarly if you ask someone about the differences between, say, the North Island and the South Island, the end of the description will always include a comparative value judgement. Labeling isn't enough, ordering is required.

Concert Chamber: A SMALLish (seats 100 – 300) HALL used for functions of appropriate size, often but not always musical. (see: *theatre, Town Hall, Opera House, flicks*)

concert programme: The (commercial free) YC radio network that has news (including the B.B.C. news), symphonic music and readings from intellectual novels. This, like the national programme and one of the local commercial radio networks, is a subsidiary of Radio N.Z. Ltd. (see: *Radio N.Z. Ltd., Television New Zealand, State Owned Enterprise, national programme, wireless, television license, TV3, zed*)

concrete yacht: Ever considered building yourself a seagoing yacht? Haven't enough money? Then do as the Kiwis do, pour one. That's right, the art of making concrete yachts originated in New Zealand and is still widely practiced. I'm told that the results float well, are nearly maintenance free and are one whale of a lot cheaper than the other construction methods for large yachts. So there! (see: (Hamilton) *jet boat*)

conscience vote: A PARLIAMENTARY vote in which the M.P.'s are FREE to make up their own minds and VOTE the way their consciences dictate rather than being required to follow the party line as established by a prior caucus meeting. These votes are unusual but are employed by political party caucuses to avoid taking a stand on very contentious issues like abortion and occasionally on other issues where there doesn't seem to be any benefit in having a party line. (see: *caucus, Parliament, M.P.*)

constable: An official representative of Her Majesty's law; a POLICE-MAN.

convert a car: In this genteel society 'down under', one does not do anything so crass as to STEAL A CAR, one merely converts it to one's own use.

cookie: 'What's that you say? Ah! You mean a CUPCAKE. Sorry mate! Fancy food like that is rare, have a piece of pav instead.' As the influence of Cookie Bear and United States television spreads, more and more people are coming to understand that cookie really means biscuit (cookie to you). (see: *biscuit, pavlova, Cookie Bear, Queen cake*)

Cookie Bear: New Zealand's version of the 'Jolly Green Giant', only this one wears a bear suit and sells *Hudson's* cookies (Ho!Ho!Ho!). Actually, I'm very fond of Cookie Bear; not to mention his cookies. Don't let his name fool you, this is an isolated instance of borrowing American usage. (see: *cookie, chips, biscuit*)

coolibah: An Australian term perverted to unnecessary commercial use in N.Z. The same meaning as (see:) CHILLY BIN.

(the) copper: 'Mum is out back in the washhouse heating up the copper. There are a lot of nappies with a new baby, you know.' A large (usually approx. 20 inches in diameter by 15 inches deep) round WASHTUB formerly (and in a very few households, presently) used to boil up washing water, soap, and clothing which were then agitated with a 'hand operated' wooden paddle. Heating was usually provided by burning wood or coal on a grate under the copper. Most homes 40 or more years old have a washhouse behind them with built in copper, grate and firepot. Today, coppers are often found, highly polished and varnished, in living rooms, holding firewood or plants. (see: *mum, washhouse, nappies*)

cordial: a concentrated bottle of liquid flavour essence. A tablespoonful with cold water makes a sweet-flavored drink, popular with children's sweet teeth. Some cordials (particularly lemon) are considered therapeutic for colds, other act as a painless way of increasing vitamin (especially vitamin C) intake. (see: *lemonade*)

corker: 'She's a corker.' Meaning that the subject under discussion (not necessarily female but definitely not male), is VERY GOOD indeed. (see: *cracker, she*)

corn: Not necessarily those yellow bits on the cob. This is a term referring to GRAIN of any kind. (see: *maize, false friends*)

corned silverside or **corned brisket:** (lower quality): CORNED BEEF; not like your local delicatessen. For one thing it is much cheaper and for another, it comes in roast-like chunks rather than paper-thin slices, but the taste is easily the equal of the beef you corn yourself. You will enjoy this very much provided you have been away from the corner deli for no less than four months. (see: *delicatessen*)

cornflour: when your North American cookbook says CORNSTARCH, use cornflour. This isn't masa. (see: *cassia, cinnamon, icing sugar*)

cot: a cot is an infant's CRIB. (see: *crib*)

cotton: This is what you use to sew up that tear in your frock or trousers. A needle and cotton instead of a needle and THREAD. The word is also used for garments made of the boll weevil's favorite munch. (see: *frock*)

cotton wool: I had the most difficult time understanding what this was, because it has absolutely nothing to do with wool. Finally, someone showed me a package of COTTON BALLS. They do look a bit like a pile of woolly sheep (if you have a good imagination).

courts: There is the court of St James which is Her Majesty's official British location. But, I was thinking of the New Zealand judicial system. The bottom rung is the District Court. One step up is the High Court and if you don't like their decisions you can appeal them to, what else, the Appeals Court. If you don't like their decision you can appeal to the court of St James or, more specifically the Judicial Committee of the Privy Council. (see: *Privy Council*)

country service: Ten years and more ago in order to be eligible for promotion beyond basic levels of pay, public school teachers under 30 years of age had to spend three years teaching at schools considered rural. If they were over 30 this requirement disappeared. Some of these schools were, and are, a reasonable driving distance from cities, or even located in good sized towns; others were, and are, the one teacher primary school of little red schoolhouse fame and two years of this teaching was considered equal to the three otherwise required. Some people decided they liked the life and never came back from country service. After all, country teachers can find themselves the community's intellectual leader plus being the family with the tennis court, swimming pool and possibly library, since a house is provided (for what used to be nominal rentals and are, in 1990, what the teachers consider exorbitant rentals) in these isolated jobs and it has access to all the school's facilities. With the removal of the country service requirement, and the rental increase, many of these remote schools are having trouble attracting teaching staff.

courgette: A gorgeous little ZUCCHINI. (see: *veges, capsicum, swedes, aubergine*)

cove: (A) 'He's a right rum cove, that bartender', translates as he's a very peculiar PERSON, that bartender.

    (B) An INLET. (see: *false friends*)

cow pat: Not a bovine caress. (see: *manure*)

cracker: (A) SOMETHING really GOOD. 'She's a cracker', is high praise for any non-male person, object, animal, or event. (see: *corker, she, false friends*)

(B) A Christmas cracker is a 3" long cylinder covered with crepe paper that is twisted at both ends. It is traditional at Christmas dinners to share one of these with a friend. You each take a hold of one of the twisted ends and pull. The result is a bang (from a gunpowder charge approximately equal to that in a cap pistol) and a prize reminiscent of those found in cereal cartons.

crate: Teenage slang for the most prominent feature(s) of a buxom wench. (also: old car, wooden box, etc.) (see: *charlies, lusty wench, town bike, scrubber*)

cream: comes in only one version in New Zealand. The N.Z. version is the equivalent of double cream or WHIPPING CREAM in the U.S. If you want something lighter you'll have to ask for (see:) *top of the milk*. A warning, Kiwis normally drink their coffee with milk in it rather than cream. If you want cream you must ask for it. If you like your tea black you must ask for that. (see: *tea*)

creche: (A) A DAY CARE FACILITY for pre-school children. (see: *kindy, playcentre*)

(B) A NATIVITY SCENE.

crib: House of ... No, sorry. This term refers to a WEEKEND COTTAGE in South Island parlance. (see: *bach, cot*)

cricket: (A) A ballgame from which baseball could be very loosely said to be descended. The ball is rock hard, the pitcher is called the bowler, a short game takes all day and a proper one five days and usually winds up in a tie. Top cricket players are national heroes but the stands appear to be largely deserted most of the time.

(B) FAIR! If it is cricket it is fair; if it isn't cricket it is an unfair thing to do. (see: *bowling, bowler, not on, test, century, sticky wicket, wicket keeper*)

crikey Dick or **cripes:** GOOD LORD! Possibly a reference to Dick Seddon, a prominent Liberal Party (later to become half of the National Party) Prime Minister (1893–1906) of New Zealand (a.k.a. King Dick). (see: *Labour Party, Prime Minister*)

crim: A crim is a CRIMINAL, this term is used by police, social workers, prison officers, criminals, etc. (see: *guest of Her Majesty, gaol, wooden aspro, been inside*)

crook or **gone crook:** If you are talking about an inanimate object, it is NOT WORKING well; an organic one is SICK or ANGRY. 'Jim was feeling crook (sick) when he drove home last night and it didn't help that his engine went crook (broke down) half-way there. He sure went crook at (got angry with, berated) his wife when he got home, for not taking the bucket of bolts into the garage as she had promised.' (see: *bucket of bolts*)

crooked as a dog's hind leg: Some of the back, metal roads in the mountains of Central Otago (e.g., Crown Range Road) could be safely described this way. It is seldom used as a reflection on someone's honesty. ZIGZAG. (see: *metal, Otago*)

crossed cheques: If you write a CHECK on a New Zealand bank and you wish it to be FOR DEPOSIT ONLY, then you should draw two parallel lines slanting slightly off the vertical across the check and enter the words 'Not Negotiable' between the lines. (see: *direct credit*)

Many people leave out the words and just cross the check. They (as I was), might be surprised to find that the lines by themselves have no legal force.

If someone gives you such a check you cannot legally cash it or endorse it to someone else, you can only deposit it in an account. These crossed lines override the words 'or bearer' which appear after the 'Pay' blank on all N.Z. checks. Most Americans in N.Z. tend to cross out the 'or bearer' thus making it on the face like a U.S. check. As far as I know the legal validity of this practice has not been tested. (see: *'Words'*)

(the) Crown: This is not a physical chunk of gold and jewels, instead it is the GOVERNMENT acting, as it does (a fine legal fiction), on behalf of the sovereign. (see: (the) *Queen, Governor-General, Treaty of Waitangi*)

crumpet: sold commercially, this version of an ENGLISH MUFFIN (the batter is somewhat more liquid) resembles a thick silver dollar pancake on one side and a Swiss cheese on the other. They are just the right size to fit into your toaster. These can be found in the shops during the colder (April – November) months only. (see: **bit of crumpet*)

crutch — crutching: The crutch is the GROIN and the crutching is the removal of fecal matter adhering to this area of sheep. (see: *dag, short and curlies, minge*)

C.T.U.: New Zealand's version of the A.F.L.-C.I.O. (American Federation of Labor-Congress of Industrial Organizations) or the British T.U.C. (Trades Union Congress). The Kiwi version is called the COUNCIL OF TRADE UNIONS and has as its members the multiplicity of unions that represent and control the New Zealand work force. The laws which once made the unions monolithic and so powerful that they really only had to deal with government (employers being caught in the middle) have been eroded over the past ten years, to the extent that the balance of power now appears to be with the employers rather than the unions. The government has now retired to the sidelines with a sigh of relief. (see: *P.S.A., industrial unrest, industrial action, union bashing, demarkation dispute, freezing workers, wharfies*)

cuda: a cute cuddly name for a BARRACUDA! (see: *white pointer*)

48

cup: as 'a cup of flour' in a recipe book is a standard 8 oz. cup but in the recipe you got from the lady next door, is usually a teacup. (see: *tablespoon*)

cuppa: A CUP OF TEA or coffee. 'Have a cuppa' is a friendly neighborly greeting repeated thousands of times a day throughout New Zealand.

curley cues: Ugly to look at and sometimes painful to use, these are OLD-FASHIONED HAIR CURLERS.

curling: A game brought over to Central Otago from Scotland. It's a bit like shuffleboard on ice, except that you use 40 lb ellipsoids of stone equipped with a gooseneck shaped steel handle and a man with a long-handled broom moves nimbly in front of the moving curling stone clearing the path and effectively guiding the onrushing boulder. This was an Olympic sport as late as 1932 (I don't know about more recent Winter Olympics). (see: *hockey*)

cushy job: What most of us think the other guy has, an EASY (cushioned) JOB. (see: *These crossreferences have been removed as in the current economic climate there don't appear to be any jobs that fit the category.*)

cyclostyle: 'Bazzer, please cyclostyle these two notices, *Cellotape* them together and use drawing pins to put them up all over the factory.'

'Barry, please MIMEOGRAPH these notices, Scotch Tape them together and use thumb tacks to ...' The photocopy machine has largely superseded these devices. (see: *Bazzer, Banda, Cellotape, drawing pins*)

D

D's: Criminal and police slang for DETECTIVES.

dag: literally, this refers to a clot of FECAL MATTER sticking to the tail end of a sheep. It has however, become part of the language as in 'What a dag!' — an admiring statement directed at someone who has done something slightly risque. Some joker threw a pie in the Prime Minister's face, what a dag! (see: *Fred Dagg, joker, rattle your dags, crutch — crutching*).

dairy: a NEIGHBORHOOD mom and pop STORE. It will typically sell dairy products, canned goods, fresh vegetables, ice cream cones, magazines, newspapers and paperbacks. This store is usually open seven days a week and often 14 hours a day. Many young couples get their first stake to start a business by running one of these for a couple of years. (see: *milk treatment station, milk shed, milk bar, milk bar cowboy*)

Dallies: New Zealanders whose forebears came from Dalmatia in what is now Yugoslavia. The Dallies are concentrated in the North of the North Island and tend to be farmers and winemakers.

Dame: A Dame is female, however, socially the resemblance stops there. Except insofar as "Rosie O'Grady and the Colonel's lady are sisters under the skin". A Dame (capital D) is the FEMALE equivalent of a KNIGHT (as in round table). (see: *Honours, Kiri Te Kanawa*)

Darby and Joan: The ARCHETYPAL, happily married ELDERLY COUPLE. They've been together so long that they not only think alike, they look alike. Fibber McGee and Molly without the closet. They were the subjects of a ballad written by Henry Woodfall in 18th century England. The ballad is long forgotten by the general public but the phrase Darby and Joan is instantly recognized and understood by any Kiwi.

date: 1/2/95 in the United States implies the 2nd of January 1995. In New Zealand, it implies 1st February 1995. That is, the month precedes the day in the United States and follows it in New Zealand. (see: *false friends, backwards*)

dear: EXPENSIVE. Fillet mignon at $7.39N.Z. per lb is very dear, or wouldn't you agree? (see: *fillet*)

death duties: These are not the loyalties one owes the dear departed. These are the INHERITANCE TAXES you owe the government. Any inheritance over $450,000 attracts the unwelcome attention of the Department of Inland Revenue (see: *Inland Revenue*)

decimalisation: On the 10th of July 1967, New Zealand went from a pounds (£), shillings (s) pence (d) system to dollars ($) and cents (¢) system (in 1989 inflation and the N.Z. Treasury did away with the 1¢ and 2¢ coins as being uneconomic to make). Everyone has adjusted very well by now, but you will hear the older terms still used, especially for very expensive purchases and in phrases such as 'as silly as a two bob watch'. (see: *bob, as silly as a two bob watch, ten bob each way, shilling, pound, florin, sixpence, penny, penny-farthing, metrication*)

defacto: A LIVE-IN LOVER without benefit of clergy or court. Originally this appellation was confined to those whose liaisons had lasted long enough to legalize the status, even though the formalities had not been observed. Now, it has come to refer to either half of any heterosexual couple who are living together in other than a platonic relationship. (see: *bit on the side*)

dekko: Probably picked up, like a lot of other things, on the Indian sub-continent by troops of the British 'Raj'; it was originally a Hindu word. 'Let's take a dekko at that new car.' Let's take a look at that new car. (see: *shufti, squiz*)

delicatessen: With about four exceptions nationwide, it ain't kosher, there is no chopped liver, pastrami, lox or smoked whitefish and the quality of much of what is there leaves much to be desired. By local standards, it is dear. (see: *dear*)

Democratic Party: The Social Credit Political League decided to shed its 'funny money' image, especially since it had a couple of parliamentary representatives. Hence it adopted this new name. Unfortunately many of the party faithful liked the old name and philosophy. So after a few years the party split and the Social Credit Political League was reborn. It left behind a party that has less general public support (appx. 1%) than does the new offshoot with the old name (appx. 3% as of Feb. 1990). This Democratic Party and the U.S. one appear to me to have only a coincidental name in common. (see: *false friends*)

demarkation dispute: I bet you thought that industrial unrest was a dispute between employers and employees. Well, at least $\frac{2}{3}$ of the time it is. However, the remaining third is a quarrel between unions about who should do particular kinds of work and the employer is often caught in the middle in these disputes (and occasionally precipitates them). (see: *industrial unrest, industrial action, award, C.T.U.*)

derby: One of those funny looking ENGLISH BUN HATs. No one ever wears one of these but everyone knows what they are. (see: *brown derby*)

destructor: A small closed stove usually located in the kitchens of older homes and used to dispose of any burnable waste. (see: *wetback destructor*)

dial: 'If you don't behave, I'll wipe your dial (bash your FACE) for you.' (see: *knuckle sandwich,* to get your *face re-arranged*)

DIC Ltd.: This is the name of a chain of department stores in N.Z. (now a subsidiary of Arthur Barnett Ltd.). Most Kiwis who have lived with one of these in their towns all their lives don't realize that the DIC is an acronym for the DRAPER & GENERAL IMPORTING COMPANY LTD. (see: *Kiwis, Ltd.*)

diddle: 'He diddled her out of her life savings.' He SWINDLED ...

(oh) diddums: (A) affectionate babytalk when talking to a baby.

(B) a heavily SARCASTIC expression of sympathy when addressed to an adult. 'Oh diddums, did you really lose all your money at the races yesterday? If you had taken me to the beach instead, as you promised(!) it wouldn't have happened, would it?'

differences: (see: *comparisons-differences*)

dim sims: Chinese MEATBALLS rolled in BATTER and sold in the ubiquitous fish and chip shops. (see: *fish and chips, pie-cart*)

ding: Bells do this but as a noun a ding is the DENT your offspring put in the family car.

dinkie: A beautician's metal clip used for holding back HAIR. It is similar in shape to an alligator CLIP.

dinner: a word infrequently heard. You will, however, be understood if you use it. A very SPECIAL afternoon or evening MEAL, e.g., Christmas Dinner. (see: *tea, supper*)

dipped out: 'Trev (Trevor) dipped out on his driving test'. FAILED. (see: *blow it, done your chips, Bazzer*)

direct credit: AUTOMATIC PAYMENTS made into a bank account without going to the payee first in the form of cash, check, or other negotiable instrument. (see: *crossed cheques*)

dirt box: Very few people in N.Z. use one of these since Kiwis put their cats out at night and don't, as a rule, let their dogs inside at all. However, there are a few apartment dwellers who do employ a LITTER BOX. (see: *cat, moggy, dogs, false friends*)

dissertation: The equivalent of a TERM PAPER. A Ph.D. research report is a Ph.D. thesis, not a dissertation. (see: *false friends, thesis*)

dissolution of marriage: The latest legal term for DIVORCE.

divy: A dividend, but not the kind you get from stocks. This divy is obtained by investing in the chances of a horse doing well in a race. It is GAMBLING WINNINGS FROM BETTING usually on horses. (see: (have a) *flutter, T.A.B., trots, gallops, punt, punter, punting*)

do a foreigner: To do a personal job on company time, or with company resources, e.g., the baker who takes time out from his work to bake his girlfriend a cake.

do a Hollywood: For those folk who come from the Los Angeles area, it won't surprise you that this term means TO EXAGGERATE. It usually refers to the histrionic exaggeration of an injury on the playing field. (see: *do your bun, throw a wobbly*)

do a party: THROW A PARTY.

do the ton: DRIVE a self propelled petrol powered vehicle in excess of 100 MILES PER HOUR.

Do you think it would pass in a crowd?: IS THIS thing I have (made, built, cooked or possibly bought) ANY GOOD? (see: *just like a bought one*)

do your bun/do your scone/do your nana: is to BLOW YOUR FUSE. This is a temper tantrum but is less general and more directional than to throw a wobbly. One does one's bun at someone. These terms are more often used for adults, while children are more likely to throw a wobbly. Considering the meaning I can't figure out why these are all food words. (see: *throw a wobbly, nana, do a Hollywood*)

docket: is an INVOICE.

dog ranger: Sounds exotic, doesn't it, a cross between Lassie and a Texas Ranger. Unfortunately, this employee of the Society for the Prevention of Cruelty to Animals is the local DOG CATCHER. This can be a somewhat more important job in a pastoral economy than in an industrial one, as loose dogs can harry and kill sheep, and there are sheep everywhere. (see: *dogs, huntaway, strong-eyed bitch, sheep*)

dogs: To most North Americans a dog is a friendly tail-wagging pet. To most Kiwis, a dog is a WORKING ANIMAL, an integral part of a farm's equipment and has no more place in your house than does a horse or a tractor and equally should be locked away in a pen when not working. Immigrants from Britain don't feel this way. Usually, the first thing they do, unless it is to go right home, is to buy a large dog as a pet. Something they couldn't have coped with in London. The attitudes of some urban Kiwis have likewise begun to change, but very slowly. This change is not necessarily desirable, as loose dogs in rural or semi-rural areas (most of New Zealand) can be an economic menace. (see: *dog ranger, Pom — Pommie, huntaway, srong-eyed bitch, get in behind, Alsatian, sausage dog, pet*)

**dogs balls: Something OBTRUSIVE.

dog's breakfast: A MESS, e.g., my office.

(the) dog that bit you: HAIR OF THE DOG.

dog trials: New Zealand's superbly trained sheep-herding DOGS and their trainers get to strut their stuff at these rural COMPETITIONS. A common task is for the dog to go to a hill three or four hundred yards way, go to the far side of the hill (where his trainer can't see him), collect a small flock of three or four sheep, bring them back to a pen near the trainer, and put them in the pen. The trainer is allowed to whistle, gesture and close the pen gate. This is something you must see to appreciate. Highly recommended! The national championships are also televised. (see: *dogs, huntaway, strong-eyed bitch*)

dole: Officially this is known as the Unemployment Benefit. Unofficially everyone calls it the dole. Seventeen years ago, I wrote:

In a country that prides itself on being a highly socialistic welfare state, it shouldn't be difficult to get on RELIEF, but this country also rarely has over 1% unemployment, so to get on the dole you need a really good reason as to why you are incapable of working, since work is usually freely available. A solo parent of very young children would qualify.'

Ten years ago I wrote: 'Alas, those days are gone, unemployment plus special work (even by the government's very conservative method of calculation) runs around 6% (1979) and government-sponsored make-work schemes abound. Young people for the last 4 years have had to scratch for jobs upon High School or University graduation and can no longer assume they have their choice. This is a hard adjustment to make when it happens all of the sudden to you. Older folk hark back to the 30's and say, "it isn't as bad as that, yet!"'

Today (February 1990) I'm forced to write that nearly 13% of the workforce is unemployed or on one subsidized work scheme or another (appx. 180,000 in total) as the economy 'restructures'. (see: *solo parent, family benefit, Access schemes, restructuring, State Owned Enterprise, dole bludgers*)

dole bludgers: This is what people were called who chose to draw unemployment when jobs were going begging for workers. There are some berks who still use the term but they have no justice on their side. Most unemployed want to work, there just aren't any jobs. (see: *dole, Labour government, Access schemes, restructuring*)

domain: a domain is a locally administered PARK usually in the COUN-TRY. (see: *park, reserve*)

domes: The SNAPS that you commonly find on garments in North America and don't find in some expected places in New Zealand. Would you believe pajama flies? (see: *pyjamas, cotton, haberdashery*)

done in: BEAT, tired.

done your chips: 'You've done your chips.' You've FAILED. What a useful expression this would be in Las Vegas, Monte Carlo or Tasmania. (see: *blow it, dipped out*)

don't come the raw prawn with me: DON'T TRY TO FEED ME THAT LINE. (see: *have me on, prawn*)

doorstops: This is what my Kiwi friends call the perfectly ordinary AMERICAN SANDWICHES that I cobble together. These are by no means Dagwoods, but compared to a New Zealand sandwich (e.g., one slice of bread, half normal thickness, buttered and rolled around two thin slices of cucumber or one stick of asparagus), they are enormous. (see: *sandwich*)

double: When placing a long-distance telephone call in New Zealand or any other circumstance in which you are giving a telephone number, and that number has two recurring digits, e.g., 778846, you must say, double seven, double eight, four six, rather than seven, seven, eight, eight, four six. Otherwise you are in danger of being misunderstood and told that you have left out two numbers (the second 7 and the second 8).

down the road: (A) IN THE FUTURE (down the track). 'That job is down the road.'

(B) On the other hand, to be sent down the road is to be FIRED. (see: *sent down the road, get the boot*)

down trou: The ceremonial SELF-REMOVAL OF A MALE'S LOWER GARMENTS, often while standing on a table in a crowded bar so as to afford a view to the widest possible public. This is usually enhanced by choosing Saturday night for the display. An activity sanctioned by tradition and alcohol, its practitioners are usually in their late teens or early twenties and in a bar largely patronized by their peers. (see: *berko, drop your tweeds, brown eye,* (to) *take the mickey, public bar*)

dragging the chain: Someone who is dragging the chain is NOT PULLING HIS/HER WEIGHT. Perhaps this one comes from Australian chain gangs where everyone had to help carry their share of the chain's weight on the march as well as working when the destination was reached.

drapers-drapery: Well, you can get drapes there but that's an understatement; a draper is a DRY GOODS STORE. Clothes, sheets, towels, material, buttons and bows etc. (see: *manchester, mercers, DIC Ltd.*)

draught beer: DRAFT BEER drawn from a tap rather than a bottle or can (see: *pissed, half g, jug, boozer, hotel, booze barn, sink a few, brew, six o'clock swill, skinfull*)

draughts: Have you ever seen two old men sitting in the park playing draughts? Well, if you have, you patronize different parks than I do, but that's the way the story goes. Draughts are CHECKERS. (see: *noughts and crosses*)

drawing pins: THUMBTACKS. (see: *cyclostyle, Cellotape*)

drench: To drench a sheep or cow no longer means to dump them in a vat of something. Instead, farmers with tanks on their backs connected by a hose to a waterpistol-like device in their hands, grab each animal, shove the pistol down its throat and shoot in a dose of medicine or just squirts the medicine/parasite killer on its back. (see: *sheep, false friends*)

Dress Circle: Remember sitting in the cheap BALCONY seats in your local movie theater as a kid? A little popcorn for the people below and/or a little slap and tickle with your date? Well, in New Zealand these same seats are the expensive seats with plush seat coverings and (given a less expensive alternative) not frequented by children or adolescents (except on first dates). When they are available it is the downstairs seats that serve the same social and economic groups in New Zealand that sit in the balcony in the United States. Many more recently built movie theatres have simply dispensed with the downstairs seats and many old ones have closed them off. (see: (the) *Gods, flicks, slap and tickle, backwards*)

dressed pie: A (approx. 4 inch diameter) MEAT PIE that has a crust DECORATED WITH PEAS, beetroot and mashed potatoes (see: *meat pie, mince pie, pea, pie and pud, pie cart*)

dressing gown: BATHROBE.

dribble a ball: (A) Believe it or not this is a 'look Ma, no hands!' To move a soccer ball from A to B by running forward kicking it with alternate feet, never letting it out of your immediate control. (see: *football* or *footie, false friends*)

(B) Bouncing a basketball alternately off the floor and your hand. But you already knew that.

drive the porcelain bus: To REGURGITATE usually as a result of overindulgence in spirituous liquors. (see: *Technicolor yawn, chunder, *spew, *puke, *pointing Percy at the porcelain*)

drive you crackers: 'That amplified music will drive you crackers.' That amplified music will DRIVE YOU CRAZY. (see: *bonkers*)

driving: If you are right-handed and you ride your horse ON THE LEFT-hand-side of the road, then your sword arm is in the best position to engage oncoming traffic. Australia, New Zealand, Great Britain, Japan, Cyprus, Jersey, Kenya, Malaysia, Malta, Mauritius, Mozambique, Surinam, Tanzania, Thailand, Uganda, Rhodesia, South Africa (etc.?) have taken precautions against the day that the horse and sword return. You will find that your reflexes cope quite well until you have to make a right turn. Then the training of many years will probably put you in the wrong lane. Expect to be a bloody menace for 3–5 days while you retrain yourself. One more problem; you will continuously find yourself arriving at the left hand door of the car you plan to drive. This would be fine but the steering wheel is on the other side. (see: *walking, quite, bloody, backwards*)

drongo: A DRIP. This refers to people, not plumbing. (see: *berk, jerk, hoon*)

drop kick: a FIELD GOAL ATTEMPT

drop your tweeds: And just how long is it since tweed was standard trouser material? (see: *down trou, brown eye*)

drying green: There are bowling greens, golf greens and then there is the PLACE WHERE YOU HAVE ERECTED YOUR CLOTHESLINE. (see: *bowling*)

duchesse: The hereditary New Zealand title for a LOW CHEST OF DRAWERS WITH A TILTABLE MIRROR on it so it can double as a dressing table. (see: *lowboy, tallboy*)

duck dive: To dive like a duck, i.e., SURFACE DIVE. (see: *honey pot/bomb, belly buster*)

duck itch: a RASH that develops as a result of contact with a water-borne parasite that infests some of New Zealand's southern lakes.

It has just left its snail host and is looking for a duck to grow up in. Look for warning signs.

duck shoving: 'I'm sorry, madam, this office does not deal with your problem — you have to go to the under-clerk's office two miles in that direction ...'

'I'm sorry, madam, this office does deal with your type of problem but your specific problem is a special case and you have to go to the under-under-clerk's office, two and a half miles in that direction ...'

'Yes, madam, you are in the right place, but you should have come earlier, it is 4 : 31 p.m. and we are closed ...'

'Good morning, madam, can I help you ...' 'I'm sorry, madam, our Mr Campbell handles these things and and he is on his annual fortnight's vacation. You should have come yesterday.'

PASSING THE BUCK. (see: *fortnight*)

dummy: a baby's PACIFIER; also, A FOOL. (see: *clot*)

Dundee cake: A FRUIT CAKE only lightly specked with fruit.

dunny: (see: *toilet, toilet paper, loo, bog, grot, lav*)

duplicate bridge: The boards are likely to be made of board but the rules are the same and you are more than welcome at any club (some will require you to provide your own partners). If you want to meet some Kiwis, I recommend this method.

duster: When you were a kid did your teacher ever give you the job of taking the BLACKBOARD ERASERS outside and beating them together creating great interesting clouds of chalk dust? Things are no different in New Zealand, except they are called dusters. This term is also used for dustcloths.

dustman: the man who collects the garbage bins (the GARBAGE COLLECTOR), usually at a dead end run, since the job pays, not by the hour but rather a fixed number of streets must be covered. As a result of working at this accelerated pace, they are usually finished between noon and one o'clock (starting at 8.00 a.m.) Some hopeful authors have found this a healthy job that allows them time to write while surviving. Others find it provides more time for their own homes or for drinking with their mates.

dux: (A) From the Latin dux, meaning leader or guide. This is the title given to the top scholar of the top class (7th form) in high school; he or she is the equivalent of the American High School VALEDICTORIAN.

(B) *Dux:* A popular brand of toilet cistern.

E

ear bashing: This enterprise is traditionally accomplished with tongue and tonsils rather than fists, but is no less painful for all that. Ear bashings range from a bollicking to anyone riding his favorite hobbyhorse. TALKING TO EXCESS. (see: *bollicking, ear wagging*)

ear wagging: a gentler (see:) *ear bashing*. Often used to refer to NAGGING it can also refer to any RUNNING OFF AT THE MOUTH.

easies: GIRDLE.

East Cape: The area known as the East Cape consists of the peninsula that forms the northeastern bulge of the North Island plus the area immediately inland from that bulge. Statistics (1986 census) show a population of 53,968 homo sapiens, 2,935,000 ovis aries (baa), 420,000 bos taurus (moo) and 11,000 domesticated (farmed) cervidae (deer). Spectacular scenery around East Cape, beautiful empty beaches, and the motorcamp in Gisborne includes the old jail, whose cells you can occupy for a small fee. The major metropolitan area surrounds and includes the city of Gisborne, 32,238 pop. (1986). (see: *North Island*)

eh: (pronounced as 'ay' in 'hay') Used as 'DON'T YOU AGREE?', e.g., Hot today, (over 50° F), eh? Frequency of use decreases with years of schooling and increases as you go north, reaching a maximum in the Auckland area. It may come from the Maori word, ei.

eiderdown: a FEATHER filled QUILT. New Zealand is well known among aficionados for its down-filled sleeping-bags. These quilts are made by the same people and are very popular in a country where many consider it unhealthy to heat bedrooms at any time of the year. (see: *central heating*)

electric blanket: This electric blanket is under the sheets, not on top of them, and is found on nearly every bed in New Zealand. This is very important in houses that are usually inadequately heated by U.S. standards. (see: *air conditioning, backwards, false friends*)

11'ses: An adopted English custom, practiced by a very limited proportion of the population. SOCIAL DRINKS ON Sunday MORNING.

English sunbathing: The risky and risque exposure of one's ankles (possibly even the whole leg below the knee) to the rays of the sun while ensuring the rest of one's body is swathed in thick layers of woollen clothing. I suspect it has something to do with the English climate, but it does take newly arrived Poms some time to adjust. (see: *Pom — Pommie*)

entree: This is the COURSE BETWEEN the SOUP and the MAIN COURSE. Somehow in the United States, the term main course has disappeared and entree has taken its place. Entree means entrance, so the name makes more sense in New Zealand than it does in the United States.

eryagawn: 'Eryagawn mate? Beaut day. Let's go'n (go and) sink a few' HOW ARE YOU going (doing) ... (see: *owsidgawn, gidday, mate, beaut, sink a few*)

exotic trees: Any trees not native to N.Z. Hence, N.Z.'s extensive pine forests (Pinus Radiata) are exotic forests.

extension lead: You use this, not for your dog, but for your electric heater. It's an EXTENSION CORD. (see: *fire*)

F

face flannel: A FACE CLOTH. You probably won't find one of these in your hotel room, nor will your host be likely to issue you one, should you stay in a private home; although both will be lavish with various kinds of towels. It's not that they aren't used in New Zealand, because they are. I can only speculate that it's like a toothbrush, so intimate an item that you are expected to carry your own.

(to get your) face re-arranged: An offer occasionally made in the heat of an argument. The re-arrangement is accomplished using a closed fist as a tool. (see: *dial, knuckle sandwich*)

facial eczema: A fungal infection that does liver damage to sheep and then produces facial blisters which make the animals go wild with discomfort when exposed to direct sunlight. There is no cure and it's hard to avoid, since the spores live in the grass (in hot damp conditions) the sheep eat.

faculty: In the U.S. the faculty of a university consists of the teaching personnel. In New Zealand universities are divided into subdivisions called faculties which correspond to those called COLLEGES in the U.S. For example the Faculty of Arts and Music, the Faculty of Science, the Faculty of Medicine, etc. The teachers are referred to as the staff or academic staff. In line with the trend toward increasing the levels of management in N.Z., at least one university has regrouped its faculties into 'Divisions' (see: *Uni, varsity, college, false friends*)

fags: Nothing queer about these. It is a U.S. 1920's expression, considered a bit archaic but still in current use in N.Z. and Australia. CIGARETTES. (see: *false friends, sheila*)

fair dinkum: This one is a loan from the Aussies and means 'IT'S REALLY TRUE', or 'IS IT REALLY TRUE?' depending on context. (see: *Aussie*)

fair go: A fair go is a FAIR CHANCE. There is even a TV program, with this name, devoted to redressing the wrongs suffered by individuals at the hands of businesses or government. (see: *gizago, ombudsman*)

Fairydown: A brandname for a down filled comforter or quilt that has become a generic name for such quilts. (see: *Snowtex, Clayton's, Witches-Britches, hoover, lux, Lilo, Biro, Kleensack, Twink*)

false friends: These probably don't mean what you think they do. (see:)

air conditioning	*copper*
Associate Professor	*corn*
award	*cot*
bastard	*cotton*
bathroom	*cove*
be away — be away laughing	*cracker*
Belgium	*crib*
behind	*crook*
(kitchen) bench	*Dairy*
bicultural	*Democratic Party*
bike	*differences*
billion	*dirt box*
bird	*dissertation*
biscuit	*drench*
bloody	*electric blanket*
bog	*entree*
bonnet	*fanny*
book	*fencing*
boot	*flaming*
bowling	*flash*
bubble	*flat*
bushwhacker	*flog*
buttercup	*(have a) flutter*
cabbage tree	*football* or *footie*
can I heat up your tea / coffee	*freezer*
cane	*garden*
calico	*gallon*
canoe	*gallops*
century	*gas*
Chair	*girdle*
cheek	*globe*
cheeks	*guts*
cheerios	*guernsey*
cinnamon	*hard case*
college	*hill*
chippies	*hockey*
come again	*homely*
comparisons	*Honours*

hooker	range
hot dogs	rattling good fit
house	reader
hurray	redskins
in the pink	ring
jerk	robe
jelly	root
Lecturer	rubber
lemonade	rug
lift	scoff
lusty wench	script
manure	skip
match	sister
mate	sixpence
matron	(a) slip
mark	slippers
mean	sod
messages	soldering iron
metal	spider
mighty	station
misunderstanding	stone
momentarily	strides
muslin	solicitor
naughty	straight away
next (Tuesday)	stuff
Normal school	Sunday papers
not really	suspenders
(a) park	swept up
physician	swish
pluck	T-bone
prawn	table a motion
privates	tablespoon
period	television license
pet	thanks
pimp	thesis
proms	tip
pudding	togs
pulley	too bad
punt	toot
punter	trots
put down	you shouldn't have done that!
quite	vacuum tube
raging	valve
Randy	varsity

villa	white pointer
wardrobe	wicked
wetback	Woolworths
wetback destructor	wops

family benefit: New Zealand PAYS its residents FOR HAVING CHILDREN. This isn't the stated intent of the law which is designed to ensure that there are funds for the necessities of life for a child but it is the effect. Every child resident in New Zealand is in receipt (via his parents) of a stipend which can be collected in fortnightly instalments or 'capitalized' to the tune of about $3,000 for the downpayment on a house.

fancy: 'I fancy that bird.' I LIKE (WANT, DESIRE) that girl. (see: *bird, got tickets on*)

fancy boy: GIGOLO (see: *bit on the side, toy boy*)

**fanny: One of the no-no words. This refers specifically to the FEMALE EXTERNAL GENITALIA. People will be very shocked if you talk about patting someone on the fanny. Use backside or bum instead, but not fanny!

I'll never forget the first time I used that perfectly ordinary phrase while lecturing to 250 University freshmen. The shocked silence that greeted my 'humorous' sally puzzled me until I was able to ask a friend shortly after the lecture. It did give me a red face and a peg on which to hang my next lecture on cultural relativism. (see: *backside, bum*)

*fart arsing around: GOOFING OFF. (see: *puddle around, muck around*)

Father Christmas: You know, that jolly old man with the red suit, 12 tiny reindeer etc. Elsewhere he may be St Nicholas, or SANTA CLAUS. In New Zealand he is Father Christmas. Perhaps this is recognition of the usual proximate source of those wee guifties. (see: *Christmas, wee*)

Father's Day: The FIRST Sunday IN SEPTEMBER as contrasted with the first Sunday in June in the U.S. Mother's Day is the same in both countries (2nd Sunday in May). My dad got a shock when I telegraphed a Father's Day greeting in the September of my first year in N.Z. I got a bit of culture shock in return when his reply informed me that it wasn't Father's Day in the U.S.

fed up to the back teeth: Did you ever wonder where one was FED UP to?

Feed *Moose*: A sign prevalent on New Zealand roadsides. Moose is the name of AN ANIMAL FEED. Evidence indicates that there are no living wild Moose in New Zealand although some were introduced into Fiordland early this century. They don't seem to have adapted. (see: *Peerless Sheep Nuts*)

feeder: This device is designed to prevent toddler members of the human species from soiling that portion of their garments located between their chins and their knees. For an adult this would be called a napkin (usually serviette in N.Z.) for a toddler it is a BIB. (see: *napkin, serviette*)

fencing: (A) One of the most highly skilled and physically demanding jobs on a New Zealand farm is SINKING FENCEPOSTS AND STRINGING FENCING WIRE. In fact, there are individuals and firms that specialize in this, but every cocky has occasion to do some of his own fencing.

(B) Don't let me mislead you, as with every other sport except gridiron, there is an active federation of sports clubs in New Zealand that fence with foils rather than hammers, nails and wire strainers. (see: *cocky, number 8 fencing wire, waratah, wire strainer, gridiron, primary products, false friends*)

filled roll: A SANDWICH usually made from a hot dog or hamburger bun. It invariably includes a slice of red beet, potted meat and lettuce. Unless you are fond of beets, try something else. (see: *beetroot, bread roll*)

fillet: Pronounced 'fill it' — it means the same as the word you pronounce 'fill eh'. (see: *T-bone, butchery, dear*)

Fiordland: The west coast of Southland. An area carved with fiords as spectacular as any in Norway. Unless you take a special yacht trip around this coast it is only really accessible at two points; from Manapouri, where you will also see the power station buried deep in a mountain and looking like a 'Star Wars' set, and from Milford Sound, the terminus of the Milford track. (see: *Southland, Otago, South Island*)

fire: There are coal, wood, gas and electric fires. The tricky one is the last. An ELECTRIC HEATER is called an electric fire and the adjective is often left off. (see: *torch*)

fish and chips: Breaded and battered fillets of fish deep fried and accompanied by an order of french fries, all served up (to go) wrapped in a sheet of brown or cream newsprint quality paper (it is regrettably no longer legal to use newspaper). Traditionally one does not open the package but rather tears off a corner and (preserving the heat) burrows in, like a worm into an apple, eating each delicious morsel as your fingers reach it. Cheap, inelegant and usually very good, this takes the place of an American's hamburger and fries. It is, in my opinion, generally better than the latter. (see: *hamburger, hot dogs, chips, shark and tatties, greasies*)

fish slice: You don't cut fish with this, you turn them. As a matter of fact the deft also use it to flip flapjacks; a SPATULA.

fit as a trout: 'Old Sam is as fit as a trout, he walked five miles yesterday just to sink a few with me.' Old Sam is IN GOOD SHAPE, he walked five miles yesterday just to drink a few beers with me. (see: *sink a few*)

fizzler: 'It's a fizzler!' It's a FAILURE. As are most things that fizzle out.

fizzy drink: A SOFT DRINK is a fizzy drink. Rather more descriptive isn't it? (see: *lemonade*)

flag it away: To GIVE UP. 'I can't solve this problem!' 'Flag it away then.' (see: *give it a miss*)

flagon: A HALF imperial GALLON BOTTLE OF DRAFT BEER. (Now 2.25 liters). It is customary to buy a couple of flagons from the bottle store to take home; much as an American might pick up a six pack. (see: *gallon, half g, bottle store, beer, draught, pissed*)

flake: As in 'flake out'. Go to SLEEP.

flaming: This means DAMN. 'Sam's a flaming bore.' 'Then the flaming tire went flat.' 'Where were you the whole flaming day?' Let's see, something that is damned goes to hell. Hell (except for Dante's bottom floor) is a very hot, even flaming place. Cussing at one remove. (see: *ruddy, bloody*)

flash: (From flashy but without the negative connotations). EXPENSIVE—ELEGANT. 'That's a flash restaurant.' *Dead flash* is the superlative of flash. A most or VERY UPMARKET place. If a bar has carpet on the floor, it used to earn this appellation; nowadays it requires rather more cachet to do so. It also refers to an activity traditionally practiced by otherwise naked men in raincoats. (see: *swept up, swish*)

flat: The shape of the earth before the discovery of New Zealand. Use this term instead of APARTMENT. Apartment is a chic word that no one ever uses in casual conversations. Friends who live in the Jerningham Apartments (a high-rise co-op. and one of the 'in' places in Wellington) always say that they 'have a flat in the Jerningham Apartments'. (see: *false friends*)

(going) flat out: Does not mean resting on your back, indeed just the opposite — WORKING VERY HARD. 'I can't talk now, I'm flat out trying to finish this by midday.' I have a feeling this has something to do with putting your accelerator flat to the boards. (see: *midday, accelerator, flat tack, flat to the boards, go/going like the clappers*)

flat tack: FLAT OUT. He was going flat tack down the highway. He was going very fast down the highway. Your gas pedal is (flat) to the floor and your tachometer is wound up to its maximum. This term now refers to other forms of activity as well, e.g., running, horseback riding, writing, cooking, etc., etc. (see: (going) *flat out, accelerator, flat to the boards, go/going like the clappers, gas*)

flat to the boards: Literally, to push the gas pedal flat against the floor. It refers to GOING AS FAST AS YOU CAN. This is used both for motorized vehicular transportation and most any other activity. (see: (going) *flat out, flat tack, petrol, gas, go/going like the clappers*)

flicks or (less commonly) **flea house:** The MOVIES (some move, some flicker). One generally books (reserves) a seat and dresses in one's best, especially on Friday or Saturday night. The best seats are in the dress circle (balcony). With some exceptions, this is not a theatre. Theatres serve another purpose.

The movies are subject to censorship by a governmental agency in N.Z. The resulting bowdlerized versions are then classified as follows:

G — 'General Exhibition' (e.g., Bambi)

GY — 'Recommended for persons 13 and over' (e.g., Ben Hur, Star Wars)

The above classifications do not have the force of law. The following classifications do have the force of law, and both the theatre proprietor and the minor concerned are liable to prosecution for violation.

R = Restricted

R13 = Only persons over 13 years of age admitted

R16 = Only persons over 16 years of age admitted

R18 = Only persons over 18 years of age admitted

R20 = Only persons over 20 years of age admitted

(see: (the) *Gods, Patricia Bartlett, X-rated, dress circle, theatre, Opera House, Concert Chamber, Town Hall*)

flog: To STEAL or to SELL. A salesman may flog (sell) you a car while a thief may flog (steal) the hubcaps. Car theft is comparatively rare in New Zealand — at least one make of motor vehicles (like my first N.Z. purchased vehicle) didn't even (then) have locks on their doors. (see: *nick*)

(have a) **flutter:** LAY A BET; usually on the GG's. (see: *divy, punt, punting, GG's, trots, gallops, punter, T.A.B., false friends*)

florin: Now it means a twenty cent piece. It used to mean 24 pence but decimalisation changed everything to 10's. On July 10th, 1967 New Zealand gave up the attempt to produce mathematical geniuses by forcing the discipline of learning the pounds, shillings and pence system on all inhabitants and settled for U.S./Canadian mediocrity, and incidentally comprehensibility, by adopting decimal coinage; dollars and cents. In 1990 the dollars remain but the cents do not, as one and two cent pieces are being phased out of circulation. They now cost more to make than their face value. (see: *quid, not the full quid, as silly as a two-bob watch, ten bob each way, decimalisation, metrication, pound, shilling, sixpence, penny, bob*)

fly cemeteries — dead fly biscuits: a very thin flat cookie that comes in sheets and appears to be 90% fruit and 10% pastry — good but gooey. (see: *biscuit, scone, cookie, Fruit Fingers*)

flyswat: This is a noun, not a verb. A FLYSWATTER.

football or **footie:** This could be SOCCER, in which you can use anything but your hands, i.e., feet, shoulders, head. The ball resembles a basketball and rules resemble those for ice hockey. The term more often refers to RUGBY FOOTBALL played by the usual (Rugby League) rules (whatever they are), Rugby Union rules, or Australian rules, all of which resemble our football without the protective clothing. We don't play football, we play gridiron. (see: *hockey, gridiron, All Blacks, try, false friends*)

footpath: The part of the roadway intended for feet; the SIDEWALK. (see: *walking, kerb, Footrot Flats*)

Footrot Flats: The imaginary district in which N.Z.'s favorite native cartoon characters live. A wide cast of bucolic characters, led by Wal and Dog (Dog's name is N.Z.'s most closely guarded state secret) are well worth getting to know. Scratch a Kiwi and you are going to find some relatives on the farm or some recent forebears there. It has been suggested that the depictions of what really happens on a sheep farm would be too strong for American's tender stomachs. I disagree, this one would be a hit if syndicated in the U.S. Like *Peanuts* this comic strip often uses its animal and human characters as allegories to poke fun or gently elucidate the predicaments in which we all find ourselves as we cope with living. Easy to identify with and very funny!

fortnight: You probably know (if you read historical novels) that this is an archaic term for a period of TWO WEEKS. What is hard to realize is that this word is part of the living everyday language in New Zealand, used, without exception, in place of saying two weeks. If you think it is strange to hear, wait until you use it for the first time, nervously awaiting the incredulous laughter that never comes. However once you are used to using it you will be extremely reluctant to give up its convenience.

fossick — fossick about: to SEARCH for or look for something. 'I'll go fossick about in that rubbish heap I call an office, and see if I can find those papers for you.' (see: *rubbish*)

4 and a half: GALLONS OF DRAFT BEER in a metal keg, available from your local hotel. Enough for yourself and one or two mates. For a real thirst rent a mini-tanker. (see: *gallon, beer, draught beer, hotel, mini-tanker*)

(a) **4×2:** is a 2 × 4 inch piece of wood. Surprising how hard it is to accommodate to this one. (see: *backwards*)

Fowl House: The MICHAEL FOWLER civic Centre in Wellington, named after a former Mayor. (see: (the) *Beehive*)

Fred Dagg: The stage name of a New Zealand comedy figure. A STEREOTYPE of the N.Z. FARMER, he is popular with many segments of the community including many of the farmers he characterizes. The role is most often used to lampoon Government figures, political parties and anyone else whose dignity could do with a bit of deflation. Alas Fred has been successfully seduced by the prospect of more money (paid in HARDER CURRENCY) and a bigger audience and has moved to Australia. This is a not unusual pattern among successful N.Z. entertainers (and other ambitious and talented Kiwis; the superstars tend to go even farther afield than Australia). There are no legal barriers to Kiwis working in Australia or Ockers working in New Zealand. (see: *dag, cocky, kiwi, Ocker, O.E.*)

free walk: On at least two of New Zealand's most famous hiking trails (the Routeburn and the Milford Track), you can go either by sponsored (escorted) walks or ON YOUR OWN. If you are doing it on your own, you carry your own food, in addition to the rest of your gear, and spend the nights in marginally less comfortable accommodation. On the sponsored walks, the guide carries the food and cooks, you are responsible for carrying only yourself, your sleeping bag, your personal and tourist paraphernalia. Rumor has it that the Dept. of Conservation which currently operates these hikes is going to be directed to sell a lease on the concession to operate them. Privatisation is a watchword of the Labour government. (see: *tramping, privatisation, Labour Party, Labour government*)

freezer, or **freezing works:** This is the place where New Zealand's major exports are converted from meat on the hoof to fastidiously prepared sides or whole carcases for overseas consumption. A SLAUGHTERHOUSE for export lamb and beef. This is one of the kingpins of the economy and everyone knows it. However, like every other industry in the country the freezing works have been hit by 'restructuring' which means that fewer works, and workers, are doing what used to be done by many more firms and workers. (see: *freezing workers, abattoir, works*, (the) *season, primary products*, (the) *chain, gemel, restructuring, dole, false friends*)

freezing workers: These men and women have one of the hardest, most monotonous and best paid jobs in the country; slaughtering stock for export. For most it is seasonal work, and they work for about nine months and then take a less demanding job for the remainder of the year or just rest up for the next season. The industry is plagued with strikes (called industrial unrest) as the beginning of 'the season' is a point where these workers have the entire nation's prosperity in their hands, and they know it. For most, the money is the only thing that keeps them at this otherwise unrewarding job and any opportunity to sweeten the pot is important. If a farmer has to hold on to stock past optimal slaughtering time it puts on fat; this lowers its value in an industry where U.S. customers (for example) demand lean meat. In addition, the animals waiting for slaughter are eating up the feed being saved for wintering over breeding stock. This means that the farmer must either kill breeding stock, reducing the number s/he will have to sell in the subsequent year, or buy in expensive winter feed from someone who has it to spare. On the other side, the Freezing Works have contracted with shippers to have refrigerator ships (or container ships with capacity for running the containers' cooling systems) pick up the prepared meat on specific dates. If these dates are not met, the ships sail without that portion of their load. This has two effects; firstly when the meat is ready there are no ships to carry it, and secondly it arrives at traditional markets too late for its usual sale (e.g., England for Christmas season dinners). A wharfies' strike can have the same effects on shipment, if not slaughter. (see: *freezer, primary products, traditional markets, wharfies, industrial action,* (the) *British disease,* (the) *season, overseas funds, terms of trade,* (the) *chain, C.T.U.*)

french letter: A prophylatic device. (see: *rubber*)

fresher: FIRST YEAR UNIVERSITY STUDENT (freshman). (see: *Uni.*)

Friesian: During World War I the British Empire (which included New Zealand) was understandably upset with its Teutonic neighbors. One of the consequences of this annoyance was that the large black and white splotched cattle called HOLSTEINS after a German State, were renamed for the Dutch province across the border where they could just as easily have originated. Americans were either not so mad at Germany or, more likely, weaker on geography, and didn't change the name. (see: *Belgium*).

frighteners: (A) Frighteners are GOONS USED by people like loan sharks TO INTIMIDATE slow payers. I don't know whether this happens in N.Z. or not but the term is English and well understood here.

(B) This term has generalized to other contexts; heard on the radio 'didn't this report put the frighteners on the union?'.

fringe: This fringe is not on a surrey but on a head. BANGS are still popular as a part of many ladies' hairdos down under. (see: *minge*)

68

fruit, *Fruit Fingers*: FIG NEWTONS by any other name do taste as sweet. (see: *fly cemeteries, biscuit, cookie, scone*)

fruit machine: Pull that lever (pronounced lee-ver) and watch the rollers spin; 3 lemons, too bad. A ONE ARMED BANDIT by any other name costs just as much. These are becoming more and more common in New Zealand. Sports clubs, for example, are finding them a good fund raiser. You, as a visitor may not have access to them but don't despair, the T.A.B., Lotto, Instant Kiwi, and Post Office Bonus Bonds will be happy to take your wagers and your money. (see: *T.A.B., Bonus Bonds, Lotto, Instant Kiwi*)

fruiterer: This is the person who sells you your fresh fruit and vegetables, a FRUIT AND VEGETABLE VENDOR or, as the English would say, GREENGROCER. The majority of such vendors in New Zealand are Chinese family businesses, many families having started as market gardeners after the New Zealand goldrush was over. Most of their stores do sell a few things besides fruit and vegetables. For instance I buy my Chinese whiskey at the fruiterers.

full stop: Is what you put at the end of a sentence, a PERIOD (the punctuation kind). (see: *period*)

G

gallon or **Imperial gallon:** It's bigger than the U.S. gallon (even the variety used in Texas). An Imperial (British Empire) gallon is 1.19 U.S. GALLONS. Note that your fifth of whiskey is $\frac{1}{5}$ of an Imperial gallon. This means that you are constantly trying to recalculate. Petrol (gas) is $4.14 (Jan 1990) a gallon! Wait a minute, that's bigger than a U.S. gallon, $\frac{4.14}{1.19}$ = $3.48 per U.S. gallon (still a lot). My mate Barry gets thirty miles to a gallon from his bucket of bolts. Let's see, that's $\frac{30}{1.2}$ = 25 m.p.g. U.S. Good, but not as good as it sounded. Since this definition was originally written, New Zealand has gone metric (1980) and liquids are sold in liters. Why then talk about gallons? Well, anyone over 30 is likely to slip into this terminology, especially when talking about the fuel efficiency of his or her vehicle. The price of petrol (Jan. 1990) per liter is 91.9¢, still the equivalent of $3.48NZ per U.S. gallon [Which, by the way makes it $2.09 per U.S. gallon in Jan. 1990 U.S. dollars.] (see: *litre, petrol, gas, metrication, bucket of bolts, false friends*)

gallops: That vulgar variety of HORSE RACING in which the rider actually sits upon the horse. The most popular of the kinds of racing in New Zealand, where racing is one of the most popular pastimes. No matter how small, every community seems to have a racetrack although it may only be used once or twice a year. (see: (have a) *flutter, GG's, beer, T.A.B., trots, punt, punter, punting,*)

gaol: JAIL, same meaning and pronunciation — different spelling. (see: (in the) *nick, nett, programme, boob, boobhead, 'Words'*)

garden: Does not refer only to the sections of your YARD which have been dug up and planted with veges or flowers but refers to the grass as well. Most Kiwis seem to have a keen interest in gardening and their yards are beautifully kept. (see: *false friends*)

garden gnome: a PLASTER OF PARIS version of one of the seven DWARFs brightly painted and placed in the front yard for the appreciation of passers-by.

gas: This is a (see:) *false friend*, if you are thinking of the liquid fuel that you put in your motor vehicle. That fuel is called petrol and is purchased from a petrol station. Where it is dispensed from petrol bowsers. Gas refers to the methane you generate internally (see: *break wind*), to LPG (Liquefied Petroleum Gas) which is used as a vehicle fuel and to run stoves in caravans and remote residences and it refers to NATURAL GAS which is piped all around the North Island for industrial and domestic (heating, cooking, refrigerators) use. In the South Island LPG is often gassified and reticulated to urban consumers although this service seems to be on the way out, with appliances being converted to bottled LPG. It wasn't very long ago that every town, of any size, had its 'Gas Works' where coal was turned into coal gas and this coal gas was piped into households exactly as natural gas is now. In these towns you will see tall tanks which have an outer tank like an upsidedown open tin can that slides over an inner tank like a rightside up, slightly smaller open tin can. The coal gas went inside this structure and the pressure of the sinking lid (outer tank) provided the pressure to feed the gas through the pipes to homes and industry. (see: *LPG, bowsers, petrol, Motunui synthetic petrol plant, North Island, South Island*)

gasbag: An adult (usually female) who releases wind from her lungs, vibrating the vocal chords, during a large proportion of each day; a CHATTERBOX.

gave him the boot: FIRED HIM. (see: *sent down the road, get the boot, auroraed*)

G.B.: GREAT BRITAIN. This notation is most often seen as an oval bumper sticker identifying automobiles from the British Isles through an internationally agreed system. (see: *U.K.*)

gemel: The BAR on which CARCASES in a freezing works HANG BY their hind legs. (see: *freezing works, freezer*, (the) *works, abattoir*, (the) *chain*, (the) *season*)

gen: NEWS. 'What's the gen Sam?' 'The bloody government is going to devalue again, that's what.' (see: *bloody*)

gentleman's residence: You will often see this description in the real estate section of New Zealand newspapers. The gentlemen referred to were of the Victorian era and favored two-storied houses, preferably of brick or stone, with high ceilinged rooms and quarters for at least one maid. (see: *villa, property, section*)

(the) GENTS: The MEN'S ROOM.

(to) get down on: Does not mean to 'to go down on', although there are similarities. 'I'm getting down on that tin of biscuits at the rate of knots.' 'I'm EATING that jar of cookies very quickly.' (see: *tin, biscuits, rate of knots*)

get in behind: (A) An instruction to working dogs that has become a national in-group joke. In general usage it says in a humorous way, if used in the sense of get in behind me, KEEP YOUR (SUBORDINATE) PLACE. (see: *dogs*)

(B) If on the other hand it is an exhortation to members of a sporting team by spectators or a leader of any sort refering to a policy or an ongoing activity, then it means ACTIVELY SUPPORT WHAT IS GOING ON.

*get one away-get it away: To become 'the beast with two backs'. (see: *have it off, shag, stuff, root, on with,* (a) *naughty*)

get stuck into: 'Get stuck into the roast' or 'get stuck into that job'. Used in the sense of 'BEGIN VIGOROUSLY'.

get the boot: Getting a boot in the backside would seem to be an effective way to accelerate someone's progress whom they have sent down the road or FIRED. (see: *sent down the road, gave him the boot, auroraed, backside, restructuring, dole*)

get the strap:

The authority for corporal punishment in schools is contained in section 59 of the Crimes Act 1961. This provides:

> "Domestic discipline—(1) Every parent or person in the place of a parent, and every schoolmaster, is justified in using force by way of correction towards any child or pupil under his care, if the force used is reasonable in the circumstances.
>
> (2) The reasonableness of the force used is a question of fact.
>
> This power to punish a child is not unlimited—its use must be within the limits that the courts regard as reasonable or moderate in the circumstances. If corporal punishment is excessive in nature or degree, it is regarded as an assault and a criminal prosecution and a claim for damages may be brought against the teacher. ... various considerations must be regarded when determining what is reasonable punishment, such as: the

nature of the offence; the apparent motive and disposition of the offender; the influence of his example and conduct upon others; the sex, size and strength of the pupil to be punished. Neither the Education Act 1964 nor ... 1969 deal specifically with corporal punishment. However, a board of trustees may make any bylaws it thinks necessary or desirable for the control and management of the school. Such a bylaw could set out the rules thought desirable to control the use of corporal punishment in the school. Finally, it should be noted that a Crimes Bill currently being considered by the Minister of Justice would, if enacted, have the effect of abolishing corporal punishment ... "

The preceding represents an abridged version of an opinion provided by the Legal Section of the Ministry of Education: Te Tuhuhu o te Mutauranga on February 14, 1990.

Note: It has now (Aug. 1990) been enacted and some schools are trying to get around the prohibition by inviting parents to administer the school-mandated corporal punishment. (see: *cane*)

get the wind up — windy: I get the wind up when faced with a deadline. Most drivers who have been drinking get windy when they see that flashing red light. Anxious, worried or AFRAID. (see: *put the wind up*)

get your knickers in a twist: This is to GET UPSET, as indeed you would be if the underwear you were wearing got all knotted up. 'Calm down, Sam, don't get your knickers in a twist, we'll get it all sorted out.'

gets on my wick: 'That TV ad gets on my wick.' 'That TV ad IRRITATES ME.' (see: *gets up my nose*)

gets up my nose: 'He gets up my nose.' 'He IRRITATES ME.' (see: *gets on my wick*)

GG's: RACE HORSES on whose noses you can lay a bet. (see: (have a) *flutter, punt, punting, trots, gallops, punter, T.A.B., false friends*)

gidday: 'Gidday mate', a traditional greeting. Now heard more often in the country than the city, it means 'GOOD DAY friend'. (see: *eryagawn, owsidgawn*)

gig lamps: Originally used to refer to the two headlight-like lamps used at night to illuminate the road before a horse and carriage. The similarity in appearance has, as gigs get scarcer, shifted the meaning of this term to refer to the GLASSES you wear (I used to wear) on the end of your (my) nose. From a slightly later era of transportation comes another term for these glasses, i.e., goggles.

gink: (North Island) 'Have a gink at that'. LOOK at that.

girdle: (A) The well known foundation garment.

(B) The GRIDDLE on your stove. (see: *false friends*)

Girl Guides: The local version of GIRL SCOUTS right down to the cookies.

give blood: One gives it for free and gets it (when needed) for free in New Zealand. Such a system only works when a substantial portion of the community is willing to support it. This used to be called 'doing one's civic duty'. The fact that it works in New Zealand is a most favorable comment on the country.

give it a go: (A) HAVE A TRY at it. 'I don't think I can do it.' 'Come on, give it a go.'

(B) Give something a chance. 'It won't work.' 'Give it a go, we'll see.' (see: *gizago*)

give it a miss: 'Would you like to go fishing with me?' 'I've got a headache; I'll have to give it a miss.' DECLINE THE OPPORTUNITY TO PARTICIPATE. see: (*flag it away, give it a go*)

give me the go by: Give me the COLD SHOULDER.

give them arseholes: (A) Administer a defeat to our opponents. BEAT EM!

(B) 'He really gave me arseholes for doing that.' CHEWED ME OUT. (see: *bollicking*)

give way: A less degrading traffic sign than one which commands you to YIELD. (see: *road works*)

give us a hand: It's the royal me. 'Give us a hand' is 'GIVE ME A HAND', and more likely to be a polite order, than a request.

gizago: 'If you can't solve that problem gizago.' Give us a go, meaning LET ME TRY. (see: *fair go, give it a go*)

glad rags: a very commonly used term for PARTY CLOTHES.

glasshouse: If your tour guide says he is going to show you a glasshouse, it's not Hester's residence, but a GREENHOUSE.

Gleneagles Agreement: Prior to the 1977 meeting of the Commonwealth heads of government in London, representatives of five of these states got together in an hotel (called Gleneagles) in Scotland to work out a formula that would allow N.Z. to participate in Commonwealth sporting activities (particularly the 1978 Commonwealth Games in Canada) without objection from her sister states (see: *All Blacks*). The ostensible purpose of this meeting was to work out a 'Commonwealth Statement on Apartheid in Sport', however, as N.Z. was the only country under fire from the other Commonwealth nations for sporting contact with South Africa, the compromise was pointed at N.Z.

The representatives at Gleneagles were Trudeau (Canada), Manley (Jamaica), Yar Adua (Nigeria), Jumbe (Tanzania) and

73

(see:) *Muldoon*, (New Zealand). Paragraphs 3 and 4 (of 6) of the statement read as follows:

'Mindful of these and other considerations, they accepted it as the urgent duty of each of their governments vigorously to combat the evil of apartheid by withholding any form of support for, and by taking every practical step to discourage, contact or competition by their nationals with sporting organizations, teams or sportsmen from South Africa or from any other country where sports are organized on the basis of race, colour or ethnic origin.

They fully acknowledged that it was for each government to determine in accordance with its laws the methods by which it might best discharge these commitments. But they recognized that the effective fulfilment of their commitments was essential to the harmonious development of Commonwealth sport hereafter.' (Keesing's Contemporary Archives Aug 12, 1977, p. 28507).

Unfortunately, like everything else, such a formulation is subject to interpretation. The opponents of South Africa have put the emphasis on paragraph 3. These opponents include the present 1990 Labour government who have put considerable pressure on N.Z. sporting bodies to cease all contact with South Africa. As a Western democracy N.Z. does not go as far as many African states would like and deny passports to Kiwis intending to go to South Africa. This interpretation has proved acceptable to the African members of the Commonwealth and they demonstrated this by turning out in force for the 1990 Commonwealth (formerly Empire) games in Auckland after boycotting the last (1986) games in Edinburgh.

As this is my own forum I'll put my 2 cents worth in. I'm in favor of sporting contacts with South Africa under the following conditions: Teams which go to South Africa should be racially mixed and chosen by merit and they should only play teams chosen the same way with the same racially mixed composition! In my opinion change will not come about from total refusal to deal with South Africa but rather a combination of the carrot and the stick. 'We will play if you meet our terms,' rather than 'we won't play until you change your whole society'. Evolution not revolution is, in my arrogant opinion, the way to go. (see: *tour, Springbok tour*)

globe: That's the thing that lights up when you flip the switch. A LIGHT BULB usually has a bayonet base rather than the Edison screw base you are used to, but don't worry if you brought screw type

74

lamps over, the bulbs are now available from specialty lamp shops. (see: *switches, hot points, false friends*)

glory box: Did you ladies have a HOPE CHEST as a girl? (see: *bottom drawer*)

gnashers: Gnashers are what you use to chew your food (TEETH). (see: *choppers*)

goals: It is commonly stated that: 'A Kiwi's aim in life is two cars, a bach, and a boat.' Vast quantities of beer are taken for granted. (see: *bach*)

go bush: Someone who leaves his usual haunts, friends and possibly family, most often precipitously and usually for the wilderness, has gone bush. The civilian version of AWOL. The Australian equivalent is to go walkabout.

go for a burn: TAKE A SPIN in a motor vehicle.

go/going like the clappers: To proceed with speed or to GO LIKE HELL. (see: (going) *flat out, flat tack, petrol, gas, flat to the boards*)

(to) **go rude at:** To exercise the fine art of the INSULT with respect to someone. (see: *rude*)

God stiffen the crows: GOD FORBID.

(the) **Gods:** In a live theatre the seats nearest heaven are called 'the Gods' and are the least expensive. Therefore impecunious students sit in 'the Gods.' This is in curious contrast to movie theatres where the best seats are considered to be those on the mezzanine level. As a result new movie theatres are usually built without ground floor seats. (see: *dress circle, flicks, theatre, false friends*)

God Save The Queen: This is the British national anthem, Her Majesty's theme song and the tune is exactly the same as that of 'My Country 'Tis Of Thee' Or, to be fair, the music for 'My Country 'Tis Of Thee' was more probably borrowed from 'God Save The Queen'. (see: (the) *Queen*)

Godzone: This is Godzone country and don't let nobody tell you different (God's own). The foregoing being understood Godzone is often used as a synonym for NEW ZEALAND. 'How long have you been in Godzone?'

(it) **goes like a bomb:** Usually refers to a car, but any mechanical device can 'go like a bomb'. Strangely enough this means that it is GOING WELL. (see: *go like the clappers, worked a treat*)

goggle box: Sometimes without the g. Idiot box or TELEVISION SET to you. You will see some familiar faces. Col. Potter runs his new (stateside) V.A. hospital, and Dolly Parton also struts her stuff. (see: *telly*)

Golden Shears: New Zealand's championship sheep shearing contest. Held in Masterton (north-east of Wellington) each year, it is a very major event for the whole country. Points are awarded, not only for speed, but also for a clean job; nicking the hide is not allowed. The participants show incredible skill, shearing about 20 sheep in an hour. If you read *The Mayor of Casterbridge*, you will find that in Hardy's day, it took the same time to do two sheep. (see: *shearing gang, sheep, blows, rowsie, wide comb, primary products*)

Golden Syrup: a brand name SUGAR SYRUP (*Karo Syrup*) ubiquitous in Kiwi kitchens. It is like maple syrup without the maple. Used for baking and general sweetening. A less common, but just as traditional use for *Golden Syrup*, is at stag parties where the prospective bridegroom is first covered with a layer of shoe polish (*Nugget* is preferred), then a layer of Golden Syrup is applied and this is liberally sprinkled with dots of multicolored, hard sugar, cake decoration called 'hundreds and thousands'. (see: *hundreds and thousands*)

(a) **gong:** HONOUR (see: *Honours*)

good God!: IS IT REALLY TRUE? 'Good God! you didn't really say that to your boss!'

good on yer — good on you: A term of approbation. Means, roughly, GOOD FOR YOU.

goosegogs: a slang term for CHINESE GOOSEBERRIES or KIWI FRUIT. A major export item and delicious. This term also refers to the original gooseberry, a grape-sized fruit. (see: *Chinese gooseberries, Kiwi fruit*)

gormless: Someone who is gormless is WITHOUT CHARACTER. A nerd is gormless. (see: *berk*)

gorse: Those bushes by the roadside covered with pretty yellow flowers are the farmer's bane. Originally imported from Scotland for use (here as there) as hedges and fences, these thorny bushes adapted to New Zealand's climate with a vengeance. Each winter in its native clime, the gorse freezes and this inhibits its spread. In the milder New Zealand winters, the gorse hardly slows down and much of the effort of low country farmers and vacant lot owners is directed at removing this 'noxious weed', often under considerable pressure from local government. Removal isn't easy. Gorse is very hardy. If you burn it, the roots regenerate the plants. Defoliants work, but only if they are strong enough to kill everything else too, and poison the soil for a time. Digging up the roots does work, but it's expensive. Enjoy the pretty yellow flowers!

go round: 'Go round to Sam's place and borrow his spanner.' 'GO OVER (around) to Sam's place and borrow his wrench.' (see: *spanner, come round*)

got tickets on: 'I've got tickets on that bird (car, job, etc.) Means, I've GOT MY EYE ON (I desire) that ... (see: *fancy, bird*)

Governor-General: Every British Commonwealth country has a direct representative of the British monarch who acts as a TITULAR (meaning all show and little power) HEAD OF STATE in Her Majesty's absence. This office is a descendant of the position of Viceroy, (Vice meaning in lieu of and roy meaning royalty). He/she opens and closes Parliament, gives speeches written by the Government in power and opens new buildings. In other words, he/she takes on many of the ceremonial duties performed by the U.S. President while leaving the administrative and legislative ones (the real power) to the (see:) *Prime* (first) *Minister*.

About ten years ago the Australian Governor General actually exercised one of his putative powers (dissolving Parliament) and raised such a hue and cry that if his party ever gets back into power they are likely to either abolish the office or strip it of any remaining shreds of power. (see: (the) *Queen, Crown*)

G.P.O.: GENERAL POST OFFICE. The central post office of any town. It is also the point from which mileages between communities are calculated on N.Z. Automobile Association maps. The AA is going to have to find a new marker since the post office has been 'restructured' which means that over 400 post offices (something like a third of the total) have been closed in the name of economy and many small towns are left without. (see: *New Zealand Post, AA*)

graduation ball: This is the SENIOR PROM at a high school or university. (see: *ball, ball gown, spray*)

grammar school: An old established and usually prestigious HIGH SCHOOL (e.g., Auckland Grammar). This was the old name for a high school in England where they were originally established to, primarily, teach Latin and Greek. (see: college, school)

grass grub: In an economy that has a large pastoral element, anything that destroys pasture is (a) important and (b) very undesirable. Grass grubs are BEETLE LARVAE which can and do leave 50¢ sized bare spots all over a field, making it resemble a mouldy swiss cheese. A constant battle is waged against these beasties. One weapon in this battle is the use of the female sex attractant (pheremone) to persuade all the adult males to mate with thousands of polystyrene beads scattered around. This not only wears them out, but makes it virtually impossible to find a female with whom to mate.

grazing the long acre: When you have used up all the feed in your own fields you can always do the taxpayer a favour and let your sheep trim the grass between the roadside and your fence.

greaseproof paper: WAXED PAPER.

greasies: a derogatory name for breaded and deep-fried FISH AND FRENCH FRIES. Let me assure you they are rarely greasy and often delicious. (see: *fish and chips, shark and tatties, chips*)

green fingers: It may be adequate in North America for a home gardener to have a GREEN THUMB but in New Zealand, it is green fingers that make the garden bloom.

greengrocer: another name for the FRUIT AND VEGETABLE VENDOR (see: *fruiterer*)

greenstone: NEPHRITE JADE native to New Zealand and favored by the Maori for making ornaments (see: *tiki, Maori*) and various kinds of warclubs. You can still find large chunks of this in the mountain and glacier country, if you are lucky. I recall an incident in which a boulder located by some trampers made them all richer by several years' pay. (see: *tramping*)

gridiron: A bunch of big men get dressed up in all kinds of funny protective clothing, divide into two groups and fight over a piece of inflated pigskin. When their frustration level gets really high they kick it amazing distances. In case the description doesn't ring any bells, this is the New Zealand name for the AMERICAN version of FOOTBALL. (see: *football* or *footie, All Blacks*)

grill: one does not BROIL anything in New Zealand; one grills it instead. In consequence, you can't buy a 'broiler chicken', the closest thing would be a 'roaster'. If you think you have been offered a 'broiler', make sure they didn't say 'boiler'. A menu may well have a section that says 'Grills' referring to steaks and chops cooked over or under a hot element.

grizzle: GRIPE, complain bellyache, etc. Also 'grizzle guts', a nickname applied to a chronic bellyacher. (see: *whinge*)

*grot: (Not for use in polite company.) (see: *toilet, toilet paper, lav., loo, bog, dunny*)

*grunds: MALE UNDERWEAR, independent of its state of cleanliness.

GST: Goods and Services Tax. A SALES TAX or value added tax imposed on almost all transactions outside of the financial services and housing areas. Currently this adds 12.5% to practically every bill. It was introduced along with a major flattening of the income tax structure which gave large benefits to higher income earners and minimal benefits to the lower end of the income scale. (see: *Inland Revenue*)

guard's van: That funny little red car at the rear of the train. No one here has ever heard of a CABOOSE. As a State Owned Enterprise, charged with making a profit, the New Zealand Railways Corp. has just eliminated the 'guards' from all freight trains. (see: *Railways Corp. N.Z., State Owned Enterprise*)

(a) **guest of Her Majesty:** An involuntary occupant of a prison cell. (see: *wooden aspro, been inside*)

gum digger: Many years ago, a major industry, particularly in the Coromandel Peninsula, was digging up the solidified sap of the Kauri tree. This 'Kauri gum' was exported for use in the manufacture of linoleum, paints, etc. Unusually beautiful lumps of this transparent golden gum were kept as ornaments, particularly those with insects embedded in them (as in amber). In this degenerate age, the men who dug for Kauri gum have long gone, but their name lives on largely as an adolescent's familiar and somewhat derogatory reference to the family DENTIST. (see: *B.D.S., murder house, Kauri, gumboots*)

gumboots: Calf high RUBBER BOOTS characteristically worn by farmers. Don't let that fool you, however, nearly everyone in the country down to the five-year-olds has a pair stashed away somewhere for muddy and/or rainy conditions. I'm told these originated as protective footwear for the men who dug Kauri gum; hence gumboots. (see: *gum digger, Wellingtons, Southland slippers*)

gummies: (see: gumboots)

guernsey: A guernsey is a football shirt, and before you double up with laughter at the the thought of a football shirt being named after a cow, think of what you call it (jersey). Both of these are the names of Britain's offshore (Channel) islands from which we got both the cattle breeds and the garment styles. (see: *football* or *footie, jersey, false friends*)

guts: the commonest use of this term would be in a phrase like 'he's a guts'. This means HE STUFFS HIMSELF WITH FOOD, or in other words, 'he is always gutsing himself'. We have a more general counterpart slang term in 'greedy guts'. (see: *false friends, what the guts is*)

gym boots: (North Island) or gym shoes (South Island); the New Zealand name for BASKETBALL SHOES (see: *sand shoes*)

H

haberdashery: The NOTIONS DEPARTMENT of your local department store. 'Buttons and bows' plus a few things Bob Hope didn't mention, like needles, thread, etc. (see: *manchester, cotton*)

hacked off: 'I'm so hacked off with this job that I'm ready to blow it and piss off to the West Coast.' 'I'm so MAD AT (ANGRY WITH) ... (see: *blow it, piss off, slack me off, West Coast*)

haere mai: The warm and cheerful Maori WELCOME.

hairgrips or **hair clips:** BOBBY PINS. You have to admit the Kiwis are more logical than we are on this one. (see: *clothesgrips* or *clothespegs, bottling, cement block*)

hairdressers: There are no barbers in New Zealand, only hair-dressers. Some cater to men and some to women (more and more unisex shops are springing up). You are likely to get a surprise when you go to the men's hairdressers. You are most likely to find the kind of BARBERSHOP you remember from your youth (or do you go back to the days of 4-part harmony?).

When I first came to New Zealand in 1970 the cost of a haircut was 50¢. Now I'm afraid the range is around $7.50 to $25.00, as Kiwi barbers try to cope with inflation and the fall-off in business brought about by longer hair and infrequent haircuts.

haka: CEREMONIAL DANCE OF THE MAORI. The traditional way to express feelings. There is a haka for birth, one for marriage and for death. A haka for happiness, for sorrow, for victory and for defeat. Not to mention damn near anything else. (see: *Maori*)

not/isn't **half bad:** PRETTY GOOD.

half cut: What you are after half a bottle of brandy. More than half DRUNK. (see: *pissed, skinfull*)

half g: Now superceded by its metric equivalent (2.25 liters). This is the standard sized bottle for taking home draft beer from the hotel. If there are only one or two of you, then 2–3 of these would be standard. Oh, yes, a half g is HALF AN IMPERIAL GALLON bottle, almost always containing draft beer. (see: *flagon, peter, gallon, hotel, bottle store, beer, pissed*)

half pie: SORT OF. 'Well, he half pie asked me to marry him.'

hamburgers: A cow of a different color. I can't tell you why they are different (excepting the ubiquitous beetroot garnish) but, except for the slightly less ubiquitous *McDonalds*, they are. (see: *hot dogs, bread rolls, beetroot, mince*)

hand brake: Another automobile word that's different. The EMERGENCY BRAKE that you use for parking a lot more often than you use it for emergencies. (see: *bonnet, boot, accelerator, windscreen, mudguard*)

(a) **handle of beer:** Beer (or other beverage) served in a pint or half pint glass that has a mug style handle. (see: *beer, jug*)

hang one on (someone): PUNCH someone. (see: *bunch of fives*)

hangi: A MAORI BARBECUE, except that the food isn't barbecued. The day before your hangi, you must dig a pit 4–6 feet deep. Then go down to the riverbed (with your expert adviser) and select a dozen or so round cantaloupe sized rocks. These must be of a very special variety so that they won't crack with the heat. Store these in the bottom of your pit. Early next morning, build a roaring fire over the rocks and let them get red hot. Rake out the ashes and build up a cone-shaped wall of dirt around the pit. Put in baskets of pork, chicken, kumara, veges, fish wrapped in leaves, etc. Pour water over the hot rocks. As the steam rises quickly complete the dirt dome over your pit; enclosing rocks, food and steam. About 8 hours later open the pit and eat well. You and 30 or 40 friends that is! (see: *kumara, veges, rock melon*)

hard case or hard shot: Not a tough guy in the sense of being a criminal, but rather someone with the courage of his or her convictions. A STRONG CHARACTER with equal emphasis on 'strong' and 'character'.

A Kiwi lady, who I was proud to call my friend, used to dance until 1 p.m., manage several rental properties and always had at least two lawsuits going at the same time, would be described as a hard case or hard shot. Oh, yes, I almost forgot, at the time she was doing all this she admitted to having passed her 70th birthday, a 'short' time before. (see: *bushwhacker, false friends, Kiwi*)

hard grafter: The man you want to hire! Gung-ho all the way — this is the Stakhnovite of New Zealand. A HARD WORKER. Chances are you can't hire him — most of this rare species work for themselves.

hard yakker: HARD WORK. (see: *hard grafter*)

has the makings: (A) 'He has the makings of a good worker.' He SHOWS PROMISE of being (becoming) a good worker.

(B) The INGREDIENTS for a roll your own CIGARETTE.

have a bar of it: HAVE A PIECE OF THE ACTION. 'He won't have a bar of it.' He won't have anything to do with it.

have a go: If you never have a go, you'll never know if you could have done it. (for 'it,' read: ride a horse, jump from a plane, marry a millionaire, make a million on your own, write a book. Fill in your own fantasy!) TRY.

have a look in: is to HAVE A CHANCE. 'The election was a farce. Bazzer gave such a good speech Sam didn't have a look in.' (see: *Bazzer*)

*have a slash: A strictly male term for URINATING. (see: *caught short*)

(you) have him: YOU'VE BEATEN HIM (in some sort of contest). (see: *good on you*)

*have it off: COPULATE. (see: (a) *naughty, get one away, shag, stuff, root, on with*)

have me on: PUT ME ON — an attempt to bamboozle. (see: *don't come the raw prawn with me*)

Hawke's Bay: Just south of East Cape, on the east coast of the North Island, it was named by Captain Cook for the man (Sir Edward Hawke, First Lord of the Admiralty) who gave him his command. A rich farming region, it had a 1986 population of 140,709 people, 6,106,000 sheep, 480,000 cattle and 31,000 domesticated (farmed) deer. The major metropolitan area consists of the twin cities of

Napier and Hastings which, with their satellite towns, had a 1986 population of 107,060 people. An area with beautiful beaches, deserted by the standards of the rest of the world, and other tourist attractions such as Napier's Marineland, small but very well done. (see: *North Island*)

hazelnuts: The nut of the hazel tree; a FILBERT to you.

head prefect: New Zealand high schools have an internal discipline system manned by the students themselves. These teenage cops are called prefects and in semi-military hierarchy, the top student cop is the head prefect. The closest American equivalent would be a CHIEF SCHOOL MONITOR or the gold badge in a school patrol. My wife still fumes about the head prefect at her (all girl) school who used to hide behind a gate and pop out hoping to catch girls who had their gloves off, i.e., 'out of uniform'. Got your buttons done up, soldier? (see: *school uniform*)

headmaster: A male school PRINCIPAL. This is a position of considerable autocratic authority in New Zealand, very much like being the captain of a ship. (see: *headmistress, head prefect*)

headmistress: A female school PRINCIPAL. This is a position of considerable autocratic authority in New Zealand, very much like being the captain of a ship. This term would be more likely to be used in an all girls' school with the headmistress of a mixed sex school being more likely to be called the principal. (see: *headmaster, head prefect*)

hells bells and buggy wheels: You lose so much when you shorten things. (see: *my eye (and Bessie Martin)*)

hessian: This is very fancy stuff. Screen printed it is used to cover the walls in some of the most elegant homes. Perhaps we would do the same if it had an elegant name in North America. Unfortunately we call it BURLAP.

hill: A central Otago term for anything under 7000 feet. In the rest of the country the locals are likely to use this word in approximately the same way you do. (see: *loopies, Otago, false friends*)

hoardings: It sounds like what a Kiwi miser would squirrel away, but it isn't. Hoardings are BILLBOARDS and other places where ads and notices are placed.

hockey: A very popular game (especially for the girls) in New Zealand. Also, from your point of view, a very false friend. This is not North American Ice Hockey. Instead it is the original game played on the open field. As the original, they can call it just hockey; while we are forced to add the adjective. (see: *curling, false friends*)

hogget: A hogget is a young sheep between 10 months of age and roughly two years of age when they become a two tooth. When you buy N.Z. lamb in the U.S. it is indeed lamb but most of the non-N.Z. lamb chops you buy there are much too big to be lamb and are probably hogget. Hogget is slightly less tender than lamb but, to my palate, tastier. (see: *lambing, two toothed ewe, sheep, primary products*)

home and hosed: 'I never thought Bazzer would pull off that deal but he did. He's home and hosed.' '... He has SUCCEEDED and tied up all the loose ends.' I suppose if you run a successful race and get home to a cooling and cleaning shower under the garden hose then you could be described as home and hosed at the end of this process.

homosexuality: A strictly male activity in New Zealand, according to the law. It appears that Queen Victoria said 'Women don't do that sort of thing!' and there's no point legislating about something that doesn't happen. The 'Homosexual Law Reform Bill' has taken the legal sting out of these activities, however, they are still considered rather dubious by a large segment of the population and the advent of AIDS (largely confined to this segment of the community) hasn't helped. (see: *sod, bugger, poncey, twee, camp as a row of pink tents, poof*)

honey pot/bomb: For those who have travelled in the Far East, this term will conjure up odoriferous memories of night soil. Not so in New Zealand. Here it is the name of that swimming pool spectacular, spectator drenching dive, you know as a CANNONBALL dive. (see: *belly buster, duck dive*)

Honours: (A) The Queen's Birthday Honours List. The N.Z. government rewards the faithful, the enterprising, the good and the brilliant by nominating them for:

> K.B.E. (Knight Commander of the Civil Division of the Most Excellent Order of the British Empire)

> Knight Bachelor of the Most Excellent Order of the British Empire (called Sir but doesn't rate any initials.)

> O.B.E. (Officer of the Civil Division of the Most Excellent Order of the British Empire; the Beatles got this one. It is also known by the rude or jealous as 'Other Bugger's Efforts'.)

> M.B.E. (Member of the Civil Division of the Most Excellent Order of the British Empire)

Most Kiwis who are honored get one of the above. However, there are also Knights and lesser orders of the Garter, of the Thistle, Bath, of the Order of St Michael and St George, the Royal Victorian Order, the Order of Companions of Honour, etc., etc., etc. (see: *Queen's Birthday, rude, bugger*)

(B) A four year university degree program that requires good grades to enter and extra work plus the extra year (ordinary Bachelors degrees are three years). This degree, if earned 'with distinction', can allow a student to proceed with a Doctorate without getting a Master's along the way. (see: *Uni, varsity, false friends*)

hoo-ha: When the streaker came by everyone made a great hoo-ha over a little nothing. FUSS. (see: *Patricia Bartlett*)

hooker: A RUGBY term referring to a front row PLAYER whose job it is to hook the ball out of a scrum with his foot and get it to a waiting team mate outside this organized pileup. So don't look shocked when that husky young man you've been talking to in the hotel tells you, with some pride, that he is a hooker. (see: *All Blacks, football* or *footie, scrum, hotel, false friends*)

hooley: A hooley is a WILD PARTY. This can be a good thing, or a bad one, depending on whether you are a guest or a neighbor.

hoon: TURKEY (human variety). This expression is largely confined to the southernmost part of the South Island. (see: *prawn, drongo, larrikin, Southland*)

hooray: (pronounced hurray): A Canadian lass, new to New Zealand, was mortally offended when, as she was leaving a party, several people said 'hooray'. It was much later that she discovered that in New Zealand, this is a FRIENDLY GOODBYE. It may derive from the Maori phrase for welcome 'Haere Mai'. (see: *cherry bye, false friends*)

hoover: Just as the everyday word for all brands of facial tissues in the United States has become *Kleenex*, originally the name of one brand, so has *Hoover* become an everyday name for VACUUM CLEANER in New Zealand; also independent of brand name. (see: *Biro, Snowtex, Clayton's, Witches-Britches, lux, Lilo, Fairydown, Twink*)

*Hori: A patronizing name applied to a Maori. (see: *Pakeha, Maori, coconut*)

Horowhenua: This local government region covers a small segment of the southwestern coast of the North Island just above the Wellington region. The largest population center is Levin with 18,962 people (1986 census). The entire region has 53,592 people, 201,000 sheep, 87,000 cattle and 3,000 farmed deer.

hostel: That's the University DORMITORY (heaters are on 7–9 a.m. and 6–12 p.m.) and New Zealand winters are cold! Brr!! Also no heat in the loo. (see: *billet, loo, central heating*)

hoot: If you think that this is nothing as in, 'I don't give a hoot.' Then you have another think coming. For those Kiwis who have been of mature years for a very long time, hoot is a synonym for MONEY. (see: *false friends*)

hot dogs: A banger (SAUSAGE) ON A STICK covered with batter, and then dipped in tomato sauce. Not one of your gastronomic delights. Something called an 'American Hot Dog' has recently made it onto the scene and certainly looks like what you would buy at the ball game. (see: *tomato sauce, bangers, hamburgers, bread rolls, alpine sticks, cheerios, false friends*)

hot pies: Sorry to disappoint you, no chance of a piece of hot apple pie. These are SAVOURY PIES, meat or mince. (see: *meat pie, mince pie, savouries, steak and kidney pie*)

hot points, power points or just **points:** ELECTRICAL OUTLETS (220 volt, 50 cycle). Note that each usually has its own switch. Note also that these switches, like light switches, are ON when they point downwards and OFF when they point upwards. Forgetting can be a frustrating experience. (see: *switches, mains, backwards*)

hot water cylinder: In most New Zealand homes, the HOT WATER TANK is located in the closet that doubles as a linen cupboard. This warm, dry place is good not only for airing the washing but also for germinating bean sprouts, making yoghurt, etc. An ecologically sound way of using 'waste' heat, considerably older than New Zealand's ecology movement. (see: *air the washing, Califont*)

hotel: (A) licensed hotel — a place 'licensed to sell spirituous liquors'. One requirement of the licence is that accommodation be provided (except for a new innovation called a tavern). This accommodation is, in most cases, a very secondary thing; with the profits being made from pumping up beer from the vast vats under the establishment. In country places the rooms are often permanently booked by local bachelors with jobs that are subject to transfer, e.g., the constable. Normal closing time for such establishments is 10 p.m. (weekdays); however, this regulation is often honored in the breach, particularly in more remote districts where the hotel is the sole public gathering place. I have been told of a hotel on the West Coast, where the constable was resident, that followed a strict tradition. At 10 p.m. the innkeeper would (under the uniformed constable's watchful eye) call 'time, gentlemen, please'. Everyone would drink up and leave. Meanwhile, the constable would go upstairs and change into civvies in time to come back down to the BAR and join the rest of the male community. Which had, of course, returned to the bar with the departure of the constable's 'official' presence.

(B) private hotel — provides food and accommodation, often in a homelike atmosphere. Does not sell booze. (see: *beer, booze barn, public bar, lounge bar, six o'clock swill, bottle store, boozer, West Coast, constable*)

hottie: Remember when you were a kid (assuming that was some time ago) and you caught a cold? Your mother used to bundle you into bed with a HOT WATER BOTTLE for company. This tradition has not died out in New Zealand and most homes will boast at least one hottie and a knitted wool bag to put it in while in use. This bag makes it much nicer to cuddle into than the unadorned rubber would be.

house: Means what you think it does, but is also used in place of BUILDING when that building has a formal name, e.g., New Zealand House is the building which houses the New Zealand Embassy in London. (see: *false friends*)

Housie: The local version of BINGO. The cards are smaller, and usually blackout is the only game played. Many hotels have a Housie night at least once a week, and there are people who travel from game to game playing every night of the week.

hu hu grub: The EDIBLE LARVAL form of a moth found in downed and decaying trees. A Maori delicacy in the days before effete Pakeha ways took hold. They are, of course, traditionally eaten alive. In a quick survey of friends and acquaintances, I was only able to find one who would admit to having eaten (not enjoyed) this tidbit. He had to eat them as part of a 'survival' exercise when serving with the Territorials. (see: *Maori, Pakeha, Territorials, puha*)

humpty: Pull your easychair up by the fire, put your feet up on the OTTOMAN, relax and read that good novel you've been saving for a cold and rainy winter's day like this one. (see: *pouf, scats*)

Hundreds and Thousands: You will, on occasion, be offered frosted cakes or cupcakes with TINY MULTICOLORED BITS OF CANDY scattered like glitter over the surface. These bits of candy are called Hundreds and Thousands. (see: *biscuit, cookie, Queen cake*)

huntaway: A huntaway is a NOISY (barking) WORKING DOG used to drive sheep, cattle or recently, deer to new paddocks. Generally these dogs are used for gross control such as pushing a flock out of one area into another. Strong-eyed dogs are used for fine control. These dogs are one of the major reasons for the success of New Zealand's pastoral economy, as one man and his dogs here, tend to easily do the work that three shepherds (with or without dogs) do elsewhere. (see: *strong-eyed bitch, dogs, dog trials*)

I

I'm easy: This doesn't imply that your virtue is of an extremely fragile nature. Instead it means I'm happy to do WHATEVER YOU SUGGESTED. (see: *knock me up, false friends, I'm not fussed*)

I'm not fussed: 'Where should we go to dinner?' 'I'm not fussed, anywhere you like.' I DON'T CARE. (see: *I'm easy*)

ice blocks: Usually refers to ICE CUBES (North Island) but the term is also used for POPSICLES (shaped much like a *Good Humor* bar). (see: *quenchers*)

ice cream soda spoon: ICED TEA SPOON. (see: *spider*)

iced buns: This term refers to New Zealand's closest approximation to coffeecake. Sort of a HOT DOG BUN WITH PINK ICING, thinly SPRINKLED with COCONUT on top. Not a winner. (see: *bread roll*)

icing sugar: When your American recipes call for CONFECTIONER'S SUGAR, use icing sugar. (see: *cinnamon*)

I didn't come down in the last shower: I'M NO GREENHORN.

I'd rather you didn't!: It is STRICTLY FORBIDDEN!

I hear what you're saying: I UNDERSTAND you (but I don't necessarily agree with what you say).

in a tick: 'I'll be with you in a tick'. I'll be with you in a SECOND or a tick of the clock.

industrial action: The union is out on STRIKE. It has been suggested that New Zealand has the British disease. If so, this is confined to a few unions with clout and militant leaders. The ones you are most likely to hear about are the wharfies and the freezing workers. However, government policy, which has scrapped compulsory arbitration is making even the most complacent unions contemplate industrial action. (see: (the) *British disease, industrial unrest, wharfies, freezing workers, award, demarkation dispute, C.T.U.*)

industrial unrest: The union is THREATENING TO STRIKE, or the industry has had a series of strikes and more are anticipated. (see: (the) *British disease, industrial action, wharfies, freezing workers, award, demarkation dispute, C.T.U.*)

Inland Revenue: INTERNAL REVENUE. They take a rather larger bite in New Zealand than in the United States particularly at the lower end of the scale. However, in some ways you get more for it. For instance, Public Hospitals are free to New Zealand residents and medical bills and the cost of prescriptions are subsidized to varying extents. There has been something of a rundown in the public health service over the past five years as a reduced amount of (inflation adjusted) government funding has forced local health boards to cut back on services. A breakdown of the (April '89) income taxation structure appears below. However, you should take into account that almost all transactions now attract a 12.5% sales tax equivalent (GST) when comparing the figures below with what you are used to.

Yearly Taxable Income ($)	% Tax	Actual Tax
6,000	19.5%	1,170
10,000	19.9%	1,987
15,000	22.3%	3,337
20,000	23.4%	4,687
24,000	24.0%	5,767
30,000	24.6%	7,387
38,000	27.0%	10,267
40,000	28.5%	11,398
50,000	30.9%	15,448
60,000	32.5%	19,498
80,000	34.5%	27,598
100,000	35.7%	35,698

(see: *IR 12, P.A.Y.E., GST*)

Instant Kiwi: A scratch and win instant lottery operated by the government, at one remove (operated by the Lotteries Commission, who report to the Department of Internal Affairs) to raise money for various 'good causes', e.g., supporting sports and culture. P.S. To collect your money you must unscramble the following letters 'ikiw' which makes this a game of 'skill or knowledge' rather than chance unless you are a kiwi. (see: *Kiwi, Lotto, Bonus Bonds*)

Insurance Companies: that sounds perfectly reasonable doesn't it? Then why are they INSURANCE AGENCIES on the other side of the Pacific?

inter-island: There are inter-island ferries, inter-island power transmission and telephone cables, etc., etc. The two islands in question are the South and North Islands of New Zealand but this is so well understood that no one would ever think to mention the fact. (see: *South Island, North Island*)

Intermediate: (A) The FRESHMAN year of a University Science Degree is called the Intermediate Year. If it is an Arts degree the first year is called a prosaic Stage I. (see: *Uni, Varsity*)

(B) JUNIOR HIGH SCHOOL (see: *school, college*)

in the hand: 'You want me to talk that sheila into going to the party with us? It's in the hand (EASY). Just watch me.' (see:*sheila, *piss in the hand, piss in, not a problem, be away — be away laughing*)

in the pink: It means in fine physical condition, just as in the U.S. but it also is used by sheep farmers to refer to ewes who have just had the excess wool removed from their genital region to allow easier entry for the ram. Ladies, be careful who you say this to. (see: *tupping, false friends*)

inverted commas: New Zealanders never put QUOTATION MARKS around quotations; instead, they put inverted commas. Same thing, different name. (see: *full stop*)

IR 12: N.Z. Inland Revenue form 12, the equivalent of a U.S. Internal Revenue form W2. (see: *Inland Revenue*)

Is that you?: 'Is that you Louis?' Heard when someone telephoned me, when I open my front door with the key, and in almost any other circumstance when the odds are 99 – 1 that it is me, but visual confirmation is not available. Actually I have heard the phrase used with a wondering lift at the end when a lady friend who had changed her hairdo (drastically) met another mutual friend. HELLO. (see: *Are you there?*)

Iwi: Maori TRIBE. The word can also mean 'the people' (see: *Iwi Authority, Maori*)

Iwi Authority: New administrative structures set up by Maori tribes because Iwi Authorities are having the funding and many of the responsibilities formerly handled by the now defunct government Department of Maori affairs 'devolved' down to them. These include housing programs, Maori land development and social and economic development. All of this is in accord with the 'principles of the Treaty of Waitangi' which guaranteed to each tribe the ownership and management of its natural resources unless they wished to sell these to the Crown. (see: *Iwi, Maori, Treaty of Waitangi, Crown*)

J

jam: Boil up your fruit, do not strain out the pulp, add your syrup and cook again. Spreads beautifully on bread (see: *jelly, bilberry, money for jam*)

jandals: Terms which will not be understood are: GO-AHEADS, FLIP-FLOPS, ZORIS. These are (primarily) purchased at a New Zealand-wide chain of stores, in addition to shoe stores, called *Para Rubber* stores, and are all made of rubber.

January: Summer vacation time — all factories shut! Almost all wholesalers shut! Many retailers shut (at least part of the time)! Your boss, your secretary and your cleaning service on vacation. Relax and enjoy it. You aren't going to accomplish anything that involves others anyway. The sun is shining and the summertime beaches are inviting. (see: *Christmas, school holidays, seasons*)

jerk: A jerk is STUPID and possibly not very nice. (see: *clot, no hoper, berk, thick, clueless*)

jelly: 'Ice cream and jelly and a punch in the belly.' The logic of children's rhymes is beyond me. I think you have to grow up in a culture to understand this sort of thing.

    (A) jelly is JELLO. (see: *false friends*)

    (B) jelly is also STRAINED JAM (see: *jam*)

jersey: Any warm SWEATER whether jumper or cardigan. Called jerseys from the isle off the northern coast of Great Britain where the style originated. (see: *jumper, cardigan, guernsey, twin set and pearls*)

(Hamilton) jet boat: This is one of the best examples of Kiwi ingenuity. Parts of New Zealand have a boating problem similar to that of the Florida Everglades. In swift flowing mountain streams, there is often only 4–6 inches of water at spots, while other areas are comfortably manageable. In the still waters of the Everglades, this was solved by removing the protruding outboard motors and mounting aircraft propellers on the tops of flat bottomed barges; a solution clearly impractical for swift flowing mountain streams. So a man called Hamilton, living in the mountains near Mt Cook (N.Z.'s highest) applied the same principle that propels squid and jet aeroplanes. Water is sucked in toward the front of the engine and squirted forcefully out the back. These boats go upwards of 35 m.p.h. and, at speed, draw no more than 4 inches of water. It is the only kind of boat that has gone through the Grand Canyon going upstream. If you are in Queenstown, take the Shotover River Jet Boat ride. Disney would have been green with envy, it makes Adventure Land feel awfully artificial, yet it is so undemanding that my son, at 3, loved it. (see: *concrete yacht*)

Jnr: One of the banes of my life (see: *loo*) is this abbreviation for junior in New Zealand, as Jr. is in the United States. Furthermore, no one seems to understand why you feel this should be part of your (my) name when Sr. is 10,000 miles away. grr!!

Joe Bloggs — Joe Pakipaki from **Opanaki:** Is the non-existent 'ordinary' Kiwi (JOHN DOE).

joker: ... then this joker comes out and tells me that my credit's no good so I hauls off and pops him one. GUY. (see: *bloke*)

jolly dee: O.K. Husband: 'I'm off to visit the Ballaghs.' Wife: 'Jolly dee.' (see: *right oh, righty oh*)

judder bar: When you are driving down the road and come to a point where the powers that be want to ensure that you slow down, whether you wish it or not, you will find asphalt or concrete ridges placed transversely across the road a short distance (up to 30 cm or 12 inches) apart. These SPEED BUMPS make your vehicle, and your teeth, judder.

jug: (A) Remember those vats of beer under the hotels? Well, when it is pumped up to the bar it usually gets hosed into one of these ONE LITER PITCHERS. (see: *beer, hotel*)

(B) A hot water jug (POT) used to make the vital ingredient for endless cups of tea.

jumble sale: A more descriptive phrase than a WHITE ELEPHANT SALE. These are most often held for the benefit of a church or school. The goods sold are usually donated by parishioners or parents.

jumper: Not an athlete, not a Calveras county champion (frog, to those who haven't read Mark Twain for a while), but a warm woolly knitted PULLOVER or SWEATER. Since Kiwis kept their thermostats at 68° F or lower by choice, long before it became fashionable in the rest of the world, jumpers indoors and out are very popular clothing. (see: *cardigan, central heating, jersey, twin set and pearls*)

junket: Made with milk, and an enzyme called rennet that causes milk to clot this (thin) yoghurt textured dessert is an acquired taste. If you are a yoghurt fan you might give this a cautious try. With fruit flavorings, or a sprinkling of nutmeg, junket is a favorite of children and the preference lasts into adulthood. (see: *Marmite* and *Vegemite*)

just like a bought one: HOME BUILT or home repaired and (hopefully) WORKING WELL. (see: *Do you think it would pass in a crowd?*)

K

K's: KILOMETERS or kilometres to a Kiwi. New Zealand is surprisingly quickly learning to think in metrics. (see: *metrication*)

kack: (A) MUCK
(B) EXCRETORY PRODUCTS

kack-handed: The not very nice Kiwi way of saying SOUTHPAW. I have heard it suggested that the first word in the phrase has something to do with the use for which the Arabs reserve their left hands. (see: *kack*)

kaka beak: This beak isn't on a bird but rather the beautiful, red, pointed BEAK SHAPED FLOWER on an ornamental garden plant.

kai: Maori word for FOOD which has come into general use. (see: *Maori, tucker*)

Karitane yellow: At one time most of the pediatric nurses in N.Z. were trained by the Karitane organization. One of the anal biproducts of infants is the yellowish residue of digested food. The color of the residue is identified as Karitane yellow. (see: *Plunket Society, manure*)

katipo spider: LATRODECTUS KATIPO is about an inch across and has a large egg shaped middle with a red stripe down the center. Closely related to the black widow, it is, as far as I know, the only poisonous, land living, member of the animal kingdom in New Zealand. Not a usual beach companion, they do appear in bunches when you find them. Don't play with that nice red striped spider, you may, (unlikely) see on a sandy beach anywhere north of Christchurch. (see: *snakes, spider, weta*)

Kauri: When Captain Cook first explored New Zealand in 1769 he wrote an enthusiastic report for the British Navy. This report concerned neither the planting of colonies nor the mineral wealth of New Zealand. What Cook was selling the Navy were these ruler straight, incredibly tall HARDWOOD TREES. Just the thing for the thousands of masts needed by a world girdling sailing ship fleet.

Later, the gum (sap) from these trees became a major export item, going into varnishes and linoleum. The wood, especially the heartwood, of the Kauri was valued for building and fine furniture. As with any such item in a frontier economy, it eventually became scarce and the trees are now protected pending the centuries-long tasks of regeneration and reforestation. One of the best places to see these today is the Coromandel Peninsula (look east from Auckland on your map). (see: *gum digger, Thames Valley*)

keen: *A GOOD KEEN MAN* is the title of one of the excellent and hilarious books by Barry Crump. He is New Zealand's ethnic author where Pakehas are concerned. His stories are usually in rural settings of the 1930's and 40's but the flavor remains the same. Keen tends to mean REALLY INTERESTED OR SHARP. 'I'm keen to get to that new trout stream.' 'He is a good keen man.'

keep your hair on: DON'T GET YOUR BOWELS IN AN UPROAR.

kerb: The CURB between the sidewalk and the street. (see: *footpath, 'Words'*)

kindy: (KINDERGARTEN) These are attended by children 3 – 5 years of age who usually come five half days per week. As kindy's are free and other preschool education costs (and most kindy teachers are better qualified than their counterparts in playcentres and creches, although this is changing for the better), there are waiting lists, often very long, for places and many children don't get in until age 4. The teachers are trained at Colleges of Education (see: *College of Education, playcentre, creche, Teachers College*)

kip: A kip is a NAP or a short sleep.

Kiri Te Kanawa: She is one of the world's leading operatic divas. It doesn't hurt that she is beautiful in addition to having a trained voice that most of her competitors would kill for. So why is this 20 year plus resident of London, who is so much a part of the scene there that she was chosen to sing the aria at the wedding of Prince Charles and Lady Di, in this dictionary? Well, she was born and raised in NZ and she and Sir Edmund Hillary are the two Kiwis who their fellow countrymen are most likely to recognize by name, and in her case by photo as well. This is true, even if you include current and past Prime Ministers in your list of well known Kiwis.

I should point out that in a fit of chauvinism I have left off her title, for she is a Dame which is the female equivalent of being a Knight and one should address her as 'Dame Kiri', just as one would call the 'conqueror' (along with the Sherpa, Tenzing Norgay) of Everest, 'Sir Edmund'. (see: *Honours, Prime Minister*)

kitchen tidy: Sounds like a housemaid; refers to the plastic GARBAGE CAN with a foot operated lid found in every kitchen. (see: *rubbish*)

kitchen whiz: A FOOD PROCESSOR or *Cuisinart*.

Kiwi: (A) A flightless relatively sightless, nondescript, nocturnal, brown bird that spends most of its time grubbing in the dirt for a living.

(B) The national symbol of NEW ZEALAND. Most CITIZENS are proud to call themselves Kiwis. Sound strange? Remember the Bald Eagle is a fish eater, known (by its handlers) for its bad breath. It's the spirit that counts.

Kiwi fruit: Brown and hairy on the outside, bright green on the inside and about the size and shape of an egg. After a night of chilling in the fridge, (don't say ice-box, New Zealand went from counting on the coolith of the evening to refrigerators with no intervening steps, so no one knows what an ice-box is) the Chinese gooseberry makes my favorite breakfast. I just slice off the widest end and scoop out the rest with a teaspoon. Highly recommended. (see: *goosegogs, Chinese gooseberries*)

*Kiwi grace: (before meals): '2,4,6,8, bog in don't wait.' Not heard at the most refined tables. Not heard at moderately refined tables. (see: *bog in, bog*)

knackered: If you are knackered you are BEAT and no wonder. A horse knacker was traditionally the person who took the old broken down horses and converted them into dog food and glue in the knacker's yard.

Kleensak: The brandname/generic name for a ubiquitous large doublewalled RUBBISH BAG. (see: *Snowtex, Clayton's, Witches-Britches, hoover, lux, Lilo, Fairydown, Twink, Biro*)

knees up (Mother Brown): A 'knees up' is a PARTY. This comes from the 1950's English song whose first line 'Knees up, knees up, Mother Brown' can be heard when the middle income — middle aged get middlin' sloshed (in large group settings).

knickers: (A) Oh, this one will take you back; about a generation. Ladies underwear, PANTIES. (see: *sheila, Witches Britches*)

(B) Also used as a swearword for those for whom 'darn' is a bit too strong.

knitting pins: KNITTING NEEDLES. (see: *clothesgrips* or *clothespegs, hairgrips* or *hair clips*)

knock up: A sweet little old lady from New Zealand arrived in San Francisco, checked into her hotel room, and just before retiring for the night said to the flabbergasted young man at the front desk, 'Please knock me up at 8 a.m. Good night.' All she was asking for was a MORNING CALL.

knuckle sandwich: What you offer the obviously hungry individual who has stepped on your toe, spilt beer in your lap and implied that you have canine ancestry on your mother's side. A PUNCH IN THE FACE. (see: *to get your face smacked in (rearranged), a bunch of fives, dial*)

kumara: A SWEET POTATO-like root vegetable introduced into New Zealand by the Maoris. Like most other root crops, it looks unattractive in its raw state, but you can prepare it in any way that you would an ordinary potato and it will taste better in 90% of those preparations. (see: *Maori*)

L

Labour Party: No I haven't misspelled it. Lots of words pick up an extra u in New Zealand. Officially called the New Zealand Labour Party to differentiate it from other parties of the same name around the globe. This is the second, and more socialistic (but see the next entry), of New Zealand's two major parties. This party has close ties to the C.T.U. (New Zealand's A.F.L.-C.I.O.) but this proved of scant help to the unions when the Labour government took a distinctly (Milton) Friedmanesque approach to the economy. (see: *Labour government, New Labour Party, National Party, Values Party, Social Credit Political League, Potty Party, Parliament, C.T.U., industrial unrest, industrial action, 'Words'*)

Labour government: The present (1990) Labour government, now in the last year of its second (3 year) term in office is a contradiction in terms. The Labour Party is socialistic in philosophy, this government appears to be, in economic policy, somewhat to the right of Margaret Thatcher and Ronald Reagan. This has led to a poorly papered over split between Party and government. Voters have been deserting the party in droves but the organized labor movement sticks with it on the grounds that the National Party (despite never having dared to put in right wing economic reforms anything like as drastic as those the Labour government has introduced) is saying that the reforms don't go far enough. (see: *Labour Party, National Party, New Labour Party, C.T.U., dole, industrial unrest, restructuring*)

ladies a plate (gents a crate): It's a party (invitation) with the female guests providing the food and, most likely, the male guests providing the drink. (see: *B.Y.O.B.*)

lambing: That SEASON (spring) of the year when all good farmers are out helping their ewes give BIRTH, hopefully to a pair of twin baby LAMBS apiece. (see: (the) *season, hogget, two toothed ewe, sheep, primary products, cocky, seasons*)

lamb's fry: In a butchery this is LAMB'S LIVER, which can be fried up with onions to make a delicious dish. (see: *butchery*)

land agent: There are those who would feel this term is equivalent to road agent; however, s/he is merely your friendly, hard-working REAL ESTATE AGENT.

Lange, David: Prime Minister of New Zealand 1984–1989, made a name for himself as an antinuclear proponent on the world stage. Presided over the most radical restructuring of New Zealand's economic life and social structure since World War II. Left office and became Attorney General after a bitter political row with his Minister of Finance who had drawn up the basic restructuring plan, and after Lange had swapped his lovely wife for his lovely speechwriter. (see: *A.N.Z.U.S., Rogernomics, restructuring, State Owned Enterprise, Minister of Finance, Prime Minister*)

larrikin—larrikinism: A larrikin is a WILD YOUNG MAN. Larrikinism is what such a young fellow might engage in: VANDALISM. (see: *yahoo, yob-yobbo, hoon*)

last post: Trumpet solo played on military posts as the flag is lowered for the evening (TAPS). (see: *reveille*)

late night: Between government regulations and union rules shopping hours in New Zealand are severly restricted. It has long been a tradition that people should work a 40 hour week with their weekends free and this applies to (see:) *shop assistants* as well as the rest of the work force. One concession is usually made to the fact that most people are otherwise employed during 9–5.30 shop opening hours. This concession is called a late night (SHOPS OPEN 9 A.M. TO 9 P.M.) and each shopping area holds one per week. Friday night is the usual time but in larger centers Thursday and even Wednesday nights are the late nights for peripheral shopping areas who profit from being open when they have no competition from the central shopping district. Saturday morning is now also a regular shopping time in larger population areas as it has been for a long time in resort areas. The current government is talking about total deregulation of 'shop trading hours' and some cautious Sunday shopping experiments are underway. One bar to this is time and a half wage payments for Saturday and double time for Sunday. Employers and government are cautiously circling this (appropriately) sacred cow. (see: *shop, dairy*)

laughing at the floor: To return whatever you have ingested to the outside of your body through the oral rather than the anal orifice. (see: *Technicolor yawn, chunder, driving the porcelain bus, talking to the big white telephone, *spew, *puke*)

laundrette: LAUNDROMAT.

lav: (see: *toilet, toilet paper, loo, bog, dunny, grot, bathroom*)

lay-by: Yes, we have it in New Zealand, too. The LAY-AWAY with time to pay at your friendly department store. (see: *hire purchase, on the never never*)

leading hand: Another way of saying FOREMAN. (see: *charge hand*)

Lecturer — Senior Lecturer: Academic rank roughly corresponding to ASSISTANT-ASSOCIATE PROFESSOR in the U.S. (see: *Professor, Reader, Associate Professor, Chair, false friends*)

leg-in: A leg-in section is a HOUSING LOT that is located away from the road and BEHIND ANOTHER HOUSE or houses. These are often the quietest and most pleasant, but they are very hard for first-time guests to find.

legless: So DRUNK that you have lost so much control of your legs that you might as well not have them. (see: *pissed*)

leg up: It used to refer to helping someone mount his horse; 'let me give you a leg up.' Now it refers to HELPING someone GET AHEAD in a job or recreational activity.

legal age for drinking: 20 YEARS. For voting it is 18 years, for sex, it is 16 years. Doesn't reflect your priorities? Why not? Why should it? (see: *age of consent*)

lemonade: If it looks like 7UP or SPRITE and tastes like *7UP* or *Sprite*, then it is lemonade. What you think of as lemonade is lemon cordial. *Sprite* is now available by name in N.Z. but it is still lemonade. (see: *cordial, fizzy drink*)

lever: Pronounced (leever), same meaning, different sound.

licensed hotel: A hotel that can legally indulge your taste for a drop of liquid cheer. (see: *hotel, beer, boozer, booze barn*)

lie back and think of England: Wedding night advice. Despite most expressions of nationalism having transferred to the concept of New Zealand as a nation, this one hasn't changed. (see: *home, have it off, shag, get one away, stuff, root*)

lieutenant: Pronounced leftenant — same meaning, same spelling.

lift: ELEVATOR. (see: *false friends*)

Lilo: Another of those brand names that has become a generic term. In this case it refers to an AIR MATTRESS. I've been told of an American family who thought their daughter had been asked to take a piece of lino to put under her sleeping bag on a campout. They obtained, and carefully cut to size, a piece of kitchen linoleum. It's a pity that teenagers, particularly female ones, have such an enormous capacity for embarrassment (see: *Biro, Snowtex, Clayton's, Witches-Britches, hoover, lux, Fairydown, Kleensak*)

lines: I will not talk in class
I will not talk in class
I will not talk in class
I will not talk in class
I will not talk in class
I will not talk in class
I will not talk in class
I will not talk in class
I will not talk in class
I will not talk in class
I will not talk in class
etc., etc., etc.

litre: A litre (U.S. liter) is a metric measure (see: *metrication*) of liquid volume. It is equal to 1.057 U.S. quarts or .88 Imperial quarts (see: *gallon*). Beer and petrol are now, by Government fiat, sold by the litre which initially confused everyone including salespeople. Now it is only old fogeys like me who have problems conceptualizing how much liquid is in a litre. (see: *beer, jug, half g, 'Words', metrication*)

littlie: A CHILD. Older children are prone to refer to younger ones as littlies. (see: *oldies*)

local rag: The best quality paper has some old rags in its manufacture. This is your HOMETOWN NEWSPAPER. Like the U.S. and unlike the U.K. (United Kingdom = Great Britain), there are no national daily papers, each region and town of any size has its own. (There is now one exception, very much a business oriented daily.) Local news takes priority in the small town papers; and plurality in the city papers. (see: *U.K., Sunday papers, Saturday papers*)

lollies: What the kids badger for. CANDY of any kind.

lolly scramble: Originally an activity engaged in at kid's parties where double handfuls of candy are thrown on the floor and the kids scramble for them. Rather like what happens when someone finally succeeds in busting a pinata.

The term now has wider application, as describing any kind of undignified attempt by groups of people to 'get theirs'. The competing promises of opposing political parties at election time has been described as the 'election time lolly scramble'. (see: *lollies*)

loopies: In the resort areas of New Zealand (particularly Central Otago), the residents and the transient workers have a name for those of us who only come to sun, ski, climb or boat. I haven't been able to find the origin of this ungenerous appellation for TOURISTS and I'm not sure I want to. (see: *Otago, hill*)

long batons: Extra long police billys (clubs) designed for crowd/riot control. These were first used in N.Z. on the occasion of the 1981 rugby tour by the South African national team, the 'Springboks' and gained a reputation of being very vicious weapons. (see: *Red Squad, Springbok tour, tour, touring, All Blacks, test, side, Gleneagles agreement*)

long-nosed pliers: NEEDLE NOSED PLIERS. There are a large number of differences in tool names, only a few of which are recorded herein. (see: *bastard, spanner*)

loo: Bathroom (Gardez loo.) Kiwis can't figure out why we call a room without a bath a bathroom. The TOILET or loo occupies its own little room in most places, and it is quite difficult to sell a house where the toilet is in the bathroom. In some older houses (40–50 years or more) you may have to go outside to get to a perfectly modern toilet (without heat) while bath and sink occupy the 'bathroom' in the house.

   The term 'loo' is used more by women than men and both sexes usually say toilet. 'John' may be understood in context but is not used by your hosts. The grosser types refer to this convenience as the 'grot'. (see: *toilet, toilet paper, lav, bog, grot, dunny, bathroom, caught short*)

look the dead spit: 'Beaut baby! Looks the dead spit of his dad!' JUST ALIKE. (see: *beaut*)

lorry: This word is rapidly being replaced by TRUCK as American influence spreads, but you will hear it.

Lotto: Playing the NUMBERS (GAME) may be a Mafia monopoly in New York, but it is a government sponsored national mania, indulged in on a weekly basis, in New Zealand. The profits are used for 'good causes' which pleases the government who, through the Lotteries Board, are the real operators of this enterprise and who benefit by having to put less money into those activities funded by the profits. (see: *Instant Kiwi, Bonus Bonds*)

lounge: The lounge of your home is most definitely not for lounging. This is your LIVING ROOM, most often treated as a formal parlor for entertaining visiting strangers or other visitors of high status. The real day-to-day living goes on else where in the house.

lounge bar: This used to be, and still is in some places, the 'Ladies and Escorts Bar'. Unlike the public bar, genteel ladies can drink here and unlike the public bar, seats are provided. In most pubs, now, the public bar is smaller than the lounge bar. (see: *public bar, hotel, licensed hotel*)

lowboy: A short man? A low character? A juvenile delinquent? A subservient lad? A low CHEST OF DRAWERS without a mirror on top. (see: *tallboy, duchesse*)

LPG: LIQUEFIED PETROLEUM GAS. In the North Island natural gas is reticulated directly from the Maui field to homes and industries. The South Island has no such convenient source and has to have its gas imported from the north under pressure so great that it liquefies and consequently occupies minimal space. It is used to run some automobiles in both islands as well as doing most of the jobs that electricity might otherwise do. I hear that *Volvo* is developing a practical electric car for the 90's so the 'as well as' may well have to be removed in the next edition. (see: *gas, Motunui synthetic petrol plant, North Island, South Island*)

LSZ: A traffic sign which is an acronym for Limited Speed Zone. The M.O.T. tells me that this means that you can go 100 km per hour unless adverse conditions obtain. If adverse conditions are present then the limit becomes 50 km per hour. Examples of such conditions are ice, snow, rain and pedestrian traffic. (see: *M.O.T.*)

Ltd.: Written after a company name it is a shortened form of the word limited. This means that the liabilities of the company are limited to the assets of the company and that the shareholders are not liable for the company's debts. Inc. or incorporated in the U.S. means the same thing, the company is a legal entity, in and of itself. (see: *DIC Ltd.*)

lusty wench: Teenage argot for the GIRL NEXT DOOR, attractive, desirable but respectable. (see: *town bike, scrubber*)

lux: (A) TO VACUUM one's carpet

(B) a VACUUM CLEANER. This, like *hoover*, is a corruption of a brand name. In this case, *Electrolux*, which appears to be the most widely used vacuum cleaner in New Zealand. (see: *hoover*)

M

mac or **macintosh:** (A) a RAINCOAT or slicker. Very important, especially in the winter. A 'plastic mac' is a plastic raincoat. (see: *flash*)

(B) a waterproof, plastic or rubber sheet placed between the bottom sheet and the mattress on the beds of those (usually extremely young or extremely old) who have imperfect bladder control.

mai mai: There you are, crouching, cold, wet (?), and expectant in your little hut among the reeds next to your favorite lake. Duck season is about to open and you await the sunrise and the game in your DUCK BLIND.

main centres: In New Zealand there are traditionally four 'main centres', even though some 'provincial centres' are threatening to overtake the smallest of these in size. The 'main centres' are, from north to south (1986 census), AUCKLAND (area pop. 820,754), WELLINGTON (area pop. 325,697), CHRISTCHURCH (area pop. 299,373), DUNEDIN (area pop. 106,864). (see: *'Words'*)

mainland: This depends where you hail from. If you're from the North Island, then there isn't one in N.Z. South Islanders know, and will tell you that they live on the mainland. Stewart Islanders, however, haven't yet developed such delusions of grandeur.

The story goes that the god Maui sat on the South Island and fished the North Island out of the sea. That should be pretty conclusive, but the North Islanders say that they have the bulk of the population and the $$. The South Islanders say that they have the bulk of the land. It all boils down to where you live. I live in Dunedin, so a clear and impartial reading of the evidence makes it clear that the South Island is the mainland. (see: *pig island, North Island, South Island, Stewart Island*)

mains: This is what you plug your TV into. The ELECTRIC WIRING in your house. (see: *hot points*)

maize or **Indian corn:** That's what you think of as CORN. To a Kiwi, it is a very specialized type of grain. (see: *corn*)

make a fist of it: MAKE A GOOD JOB OF IT.

Manawatu: Local government region extending from coast to coast in the center of the lower North Island just south of Wanganui and Hawkes Bay. Palmerston North is the main population center with 67,405 people (1986 census). The regional population (1986 census) is 115,500 people, 4,013,000 sheep, 440,000 cattle and 15,000 farmed deer. It is a good place to live. Take it from one who has 'been there and done that.' (see: *North Island, Wanganui, Hawkes Bay*)

manchester: In the industrial revolution, the city of Manchester specialized in mass production of things made of cloth. As a result, the manchester department of your local New Zealand department store sells the sheets, towels, etc. The DRY GOODS counter. (see: *drapers, mercers*)

manure: Refers to ANY FERTILIZER, not necessarily animal wastes. To manure is to SPREAD FERTILIZER. (see: *aerial topdressing, super, false friends*)

Maori or **Maaori:** (pronounced Mawri or Ma-o-ri). NATIVE NEW ZEALANDER. Well, in some ways, no more native than you are. These Polynesians retain records of their first landings in New Zealand and any group with such good memories is no more a native of New

Zealand than you are of North America (unless you are an American Indian). They are the majority of the only non-pale types you will see, most of the rest are other Polynesians from New Zealand's island neighbours. [Is someone who lives 3,000 miles away a neighbour?] (see: *coconut*); Maoris are copper-coloured, with curly black hair. Note this well because it is usually the only detectable difference between the Pakeha (which see) and the Maori. Their speech is identical and so are many of their customs. Here, integration used to work so well it usually wasn't even noticed. There is now, however, an upsurge of nationalistic feeling among a vocal group of Maori, particularly in the North Island and racial tensions have arisen where long dormant. (see: (the) *Treaty of Waitangi, Waitangi Tribunal, Waitangi Day, Bastion Point, Iwi, bicultural, Pakeha*) p.s. They haven't eaten anyone for 100 years or more.

*Maori holiday: Like other socio-economically disadvantaged groups, the Maori is the butt of a number of jokes. (How many Irish, Polish, or Black jokes do you know?) A Maori holiday is THE DAY AFTER PAYDAY. Maoris do not, as a group, have the middle class (Protestant) ethic. That is the idea that work is an end in and of itself. This reminds me of story about a New York executive who was driving through the Appalachians when he spotted an Indian under a tree. He stopped and, after some preliminaries, the following conversation ensued:

> (NY) 'Why don't you come to the city and get a job?'
>
> (I) 'What's in it for me?'
>
> (NY) 'Well, once you get to be an executive you can take Wednesday afternoons off to play golf or just sit under a tree.'
>
> (I) 'I see! Anything else?'
>
> (NY) 'You can get from two weeks to a month off each year, with pay, to visit beautiful spots like this one.'
>
> (I) 'That's nice. Anything else?'
>
> (NY) 'When you get to 65 or so you can retire and buy a house in one of those beautiful spots and just relax.'
>
> (I) 'Under a tree like this one?'

(see: *Maori*)

Maoritanga: Maori CULTURE.

marae: I'm told this used to refer specifically to the open (ceremonial) ground in front of a Maori meetinghouse. In common usage today, it refers not only to this ground but the meeting house itself and any auxiliary space or buildings.

marching girls: One of New Zealand's less comprehensible phenomena. Imagine teams of 10 to 50 pre-pubescent (and early post) little and mid-sized girls, dressed like the baton-twirlers that accompany High School bands, wearing busbies like the guards at Buckingham Palace. Now remove the batons and train them to march and countermarch like a crack military drill team. The country is overrun with their like. Every hamlet has its team, and please note, this is 'voluntary fun'.

mark: (A) This is the cry that goes up from rugby fans when the ball is caught by the defending team inside their own 22 yard line. (see: *rugby, football* or *footie, false friends*)

   (B) What one does to exam papers and assignments: correct them, grade them. End of year marking seems interminable.

market garden: A small farm that raises vegetables for sale, i.e., a TRUCK FARM. (see: *greengrocers*)

Marlborough: The north-eastern corner of the South Island. It's major city is Blenheim (1986 pop. 22,681) and the most striking feature is the Marlborough Sounds, a collection of peninsulas and islands that combine relatively untouched forests and beaches with a very comfortable climate. If you have the time, a cruise (probably starting at Picton) in this region is highly recommended. Now for the obligatory statistics (1986 census); people 38,225; sheep 1,690,000; cattle 115,000 and 9,000 domesticated (farmed) deer. (see: *South Island*)

Marmite and **Vegemite:** FLAVOURED and fortified YEAST EXTRACTS, which are used like peanut butter as a SPREAD on bread. Popular tradition has it that *Marmite* is flavored with beef and *Vegemite* is flavored with some sort of vegetable extract. Careful examination of the labels on these containers in my local dairy suggests that if this is indeed true, then the manufacturers are keeping that portion of their recipes a secret. Why, you might ask, did I look at it in the dairy rather than purchasing it? Friends, this is an acquired taste! Kiwis, on the other hand, have been known to scour grocery stores abroad frantically searching for this concoction, and if they fail, they write desperate letters to New Zealand requesting CARE packages of *Vegemite* or *Marmite*. I might add that most Kiwis view the idea of a peanut butter and jelly sandwich very much the way I view a *Marmite* sandwich, but at least I have tried *Marmite*. (see: *sandwich, dairy*)

marrow: If you see marrow on a menu, it isn't bone marrow, it's SQUASH. (see: *runner beans, swedes, beetroot, veges, butternut, buttercup*)

match: A match can indeed be the familiar red-headed flammable object, but, it is more likely to refer to the meeting of two sports teams on the playing field. A GAME. (see: *test*)

mate: 'Me mate' is not the lady to whom I am wed, but rather my FRIEND. (see: *cobber*)

mate's rates: If you happen to be a plumber, storekeeper, paperhanger, etc., mate's rates is what you charge your friends, considerably DISCOUNTED from what you charge the general public. Of course, this works both ways; when you need their services you, too, pay mate's rates. (see: *mate, do a foreigner*)

Maths or to do Maths: MATHEMATICS. To do maths is to undertake a course of study in this subject.

matron: This term always conjures up, for me, a vision of a stout, dignified, married lady of middle years. Wrong again! This is the title of the SUPERVISING NURSE (if female) at a hospital. The ones I am privileged to know tend to be lean, energetic, and of indeterminate age. (see: *sister, false friends*)

M.B. Ch.B.: Bachelor of Medicine and Surgery. This is the degree held by our local family DOCTOR. Note he does not have a doctorate. M.D.'s either come from overseas or, if local, have earned the M.D. as a higher (research) degree in medicine. M.B. Ch.B. is a six-year degree. The first year of this is an undergraduate university year and the rest, medical school training. (see: *B.D.S.*)

me: 'Me house', 'me car', 'me wife', 'me property'. MY house, etc. A passing fad among middle class men in their 20's and 30's who appear to think they are proclaiming unity with the manual workers.

mean: A mean man could be a very pleasant chap. He does, however, have one failing, or virtue if you are inclined that way. He is MISERLY. (see: *false friends*)

meat and two veg: The STANDARD Kiwi MEAL; consisting of a generous serving of meat and two kinds of vegetable. (see: *veges*)

meat pie: A (3 – 4 in. diameter) pastry shell filled with chunks of meat and vegetables. These can be very good, however, a close relation that looks very much the same (mince pie) does not receive the same endorsement. Unfortunately, the latter has largely driven the former out of the shops. Much as bad money is said to drive good out of circulation. (see: *mince pie, dressed pie, pea, pie and pud, pie cart, savouries*)

Meccano set: ERRECTOR SET.

mercers — mercery: An establishment which purveys men's clothing to the general public for considerations of a pecuniary nature. A MENSWEAR STORE. This term has lost popularity in recent years, but is still used in provincial centers. (see: *drapers*)

messages: 'I have to go do my messages.' 'Have you done your messages?' Sounds very strange until you learn that messages are ERRANDS.

metal: It isn't metallic at all. Metal just means GRAVEL. Usually it means the gravel under the wheels of your car. Roads come in grades I, II, Metal and Dirt. I and II are sealed. (see: *seal, pavement, false friends*)

metrication: This was the process of shifting from measuring in imperial units (feet, inches, gallons, etc.) to metric units (meters, centimeters, liters, etc.) New Zealand built up to this slowly but when M day came it was drastic. In timberyards, the foremen went around all of the men, took away their folding rulers (marked in inches and sometimes also meters) and replaced them with metric rulers. The day after, I had occasion to go into a timberyard looking for a 6 ft by 4 ft sheet of plywood. All I got was a helpless shrug from the yardman and a request for the metric dimensions as he had no way of converting my requirements.

metric measure	U.S. measure	
kilometre	.62	miles
metre	1 yard, 3.37 inches	
centimetre	.39	inches
millimetre	.04	inches
hectare	2.47	acres
litre	1.057	quarts
millilitre	.27	fluid ounces
metric ton	2,205.07	lbs.
kilogramme	2.205	lbs.
gramme	.035	ounces

U.S. measure	metric measure	
mile	1.610	kilometres
yard	.914	metres
foot	30.480	cm
inch	2.540	cm
acre	.450	hectare
gallon	3.785	litres
quart	.946	litres
pint	.473	litres
pound	454.000	grammes
ounce	28.350	grammes

Note that the U.S. liquid measures above do not correspond to the Imperial measurements that go by the same names. If an

Kiwi talks about pints, quarts or gallons, he/she is talking about Imperial measures. (see: *gallon, decimalisation, 'Words*)

mighty: 'How was your trip?' 'Mighty!' How was your trip? TERRIFIC (marvelous)! (see: *boomer, false friends*)

Mikhail Lermontov: To paraphrase a former Prime Minister 'New Zealand is the only country to sink a Russian ship since WWII.' On 16 February 1986 a N.Z. harbour pilot misdirected a Soviet cruise ship, full of Australian tourists, into some rocks. A skindiving tour firm is currently trying to get permission to take underwater tourists through the wreck.

milk: Milk has been pasteurized in New Zealand since World War II, when pasteurization was begun as an aid to the Allied war effort (many U.S. soldiers were getting violently ill on Kiwi unpasteurized milk) but is only sometimes homogenized, thus unless you want to use the 'top of the milk' for something special, you must shake the bottle before opening. Milk is sold in glass 600 ml bottles, one liter cardboard cartons and two liter plastic bottles with built in handles. (see: *top of the milk*)

milk bar: A combination of NEIGHBORHOOD mom and pop store combined with the LOCAL ICE CREAM PARLOR. It will typically sell dairy products, canned goods, fresh vegetables, ice cream, milk shakes, magazines, newspapers and paperbacks. This store is usually open seven days a week and often 14 hours a day. Many young couples get their start in business by running one of these for a few years (without a break at weekends, evenings, or much in the way of holidays). (see: *dairy, milk bar cowboy*)

milk-bar cowboy: The teenager polishing his macho image at the local ice cream parlor since he's too young to go to the hotel. The ice cream parlor and the corner dairy are often one and the same place; unlike the U.S. where the drug store doubles as the ice cream parlor and the equivalent lout used to be called a DRUG STORE COWBOY. (see: *legal age for drinking, hotel, dairy*)

milk coffee: If you want coffee with milk added, do not ask for coffee with milk, for you will get COFFEE MADE ENTIRELY WITH hot MILK, which, I'm told, is quite a lovely drink in midwinter if you like hot milk. (see: *white coffee / tea, tea*)

milk shed: the place where one of New Zealand's foremost primary products passes from bovine to man. These are sophisticated, shiny clean, modern structures designed to elicit maximum co-operation from the cows and allow one or two people to milk massive numbers without help. The actual milking is done with suction cups that feed into hoses and from there into a central reservoir. A smooth, efficient and profitable operation. (see: *milk treatment station*)

milk tokens: New Zealand has retained that distant memory of North American childhood, the milkman. He does, however, drive a truck rather than having the familiar well-trained horse. In some places, there is a problem, in that placing money in milk bottles on your front doorstep isn't always safe. It has occasionally been known to disappear. Consequently each milkman coins his own PLASTIC MONEY; good only for buying milk from him. You purchase this money from your local corner dairy (see: *dairy*) and put it in the milk and cream bottles. (see: *milk*)

milk treatment station: The milk comes from the milk shed on individual farms and is then collected by truck and taken to a (usually co-operatively owned) MILK PROCESSING PLANT where it is pasteurized, and in large part made into butter, cheese and milk powder for export. (see: *milk shed, milk*)

mince: (mincemeat). No one will threaten (in so many words) to make this out of you. Nevertheless, you better ask for steak mince if you want HAMBURGER MEAT (ground beef). Otherwise you will not be understood. Hamburgers per se retain the name but unfortunately the addition of beets, as garnish, and ground mutton doesn't enhance their flavor. (see: *mince pies, hamburgers*)

mince pie: A soupy concoction of mince (hamburger) inside a slightly leathery wheaten crust, usually about 3 inches in diameter. Not recommended. Only around Christmas is this term likely to mean what you think it does. (see: *mince, meat pie, steak and kidney pie, savouries, hot pies*)

****minge:** from fringe perhaps? This term refers to the short and curly pelt which is found in the pelvic triangle of homo sapiens. This particular term usually refers to the female of the species. (see: *short and curlies, privates, crutch — crutching, fringe*)

mingy: A cross between MISERLY and dingy — it refers not only to people but to objects. For instance 'that's a pretty mingy piece of pie she sold you'. That's a pretty small and tattered piece of pie she sold you.

mini: Mini as in skirt, alas seems to be a past fad (they were so much shorter in New Zealand than in the States at the height of the fad that I had trouble adjusting to the idea that this was a cultural norm rather than a series of aberrant individuals). However, a Mini is a CAR manufactured by *Austin* of England. It is comparatively inexpensive, easy to repair and, while small, appears larger on the inside than it is outside. A thoroughly good idea. Unfortunately, like the *VW* beetle it is no longer available as a new car. (see: *Yank tank*)

mini-Budget: When the government decides that it made inadequate provision for income and/or expenditure in its annual Budget statement, a mini-Budget is announced with new taxes and other financial changes. Usually these are black Budgets. (see: *Budget, black Budget*)

mini-tanker: a 100 (Imperial) GALLON CONTAINER OF DRAFT BEER, these can be rented for your private parties at appx. $9 per Imperial gallon and you only pay for what you drink. (see: *gallon, beer, 4 and a half, draught beer*)

Minister of Finance: This is the SECRETARY OF THE TREASURY except that s/he must be an elected Member of Parliament before s/he is eligible for appointment to this post. The Minister of Finance is usually the second most powerful governmental position in the country. (see: (The) *Budget, Rogernomics, Prime Minister*)

Ministers: these come in two varieties, both noted for their loquacious habits; Ministers of religion and Ministers of the Crown. The latter group are MEMBERS OF THE CABINET and include their leader, the Prime Minister. Who, you might ask, is 'the Crown'? This is the Queen of New Zealand (who bears a suspicious resemblance to Queen Elizabeth of Great Britain) as represented by Her Governor-General. (see: *Queen, Governor-General, Prime Minister, Crown*)

Ministry of Works lure: Warning: devoted fishermen, especially fly fishermen, should not read this item without medical help standing by with massive doses of tranquilizer! First, you set up your net downstream, blocking most of the channel and then you take your M.O.W. lure (a stick of DYNAMITE) and throw it in upstream. The dead and stunned trout accumulate in the net. Not sporting, what? The Ministry has changed its name, the lure has not. (see: *Works Corp., nickel spinner*)

misunderstanding: This is the general euphemism for PERSONALITY CLASHES. If you come into a place in a trouble-shooting capacity and are told that Mr X and Mrs Y have a misunderstanding about issue Z, this does not mean that a clear explanation of the other side will clear up the misunderstanding. Instead it tends to mean that they understand each other perfectly well and have a fundamental disagreement, or that they just can't stand the sight of each other. (see: *false friends*)

mixed grill: grilled sausages, chops and perhaps a bit of beef served with veges and chips. This is also a common meal at home for many Kiwis. (see: *grill, veges, chips*)

momentarily: 'She's gone around the corner momentarily.' 'She's gone around the corner FOR A MOMENT.' In the U.S. this usually means in a moment, e.g., 'We are momentarily expecting news of the birth'.

moggy or **mog:** A name used to refer to a cat in N.Z. and, I am told, a calf in Scotland. Somehow it changed referent in the long sea voyage. (see: *cat, pet*)

money for jam: Once all your expenses and reasonable needs are covered, any cash left over is money for jam, GRAVY, icing on the cake. In the hard world of England's industrial revolution, bread was the necessary 'staff of life'. Jam on your bread was pure luxury.

M.O.T.: MINISTRY OF TRANSPORT. In New Zealand, the police and the Traffic Officers are two completely different non-interchangeable organizations. Traffic Officers are empowered, only, to deal with motoring offences. The police take care of crimes. Cars (usually black with a white stripe around the middle and marked M.O.T.) with red lights on top, give tickets. Unless you are driving reck- lessly the (white) ones with two blue lights on top, aren't interested (Police). This may soon change as there are rumblings in both major political parties about amalgamating the two forces. (see: *pointsman, warrant of fitness, Labour Party, National Party*)

mother, king and country: MOTHER, FLAG, and APPLE PIE.

motor: A motor is a MOTOR VEHICLE or a vehicle's engine. (see: *false friends, motor car, motor along, really motoring*)

(to) motor: To MOVE QUICKLY whether by vehicle or some other way, e.g., 'he really motored through that work'. (see: *false friends, motor along, really motoring*)

motor along: MOVING RIGHT ALONG. This can refer to any sort of mechanized or unmechanized movement and it can also refer to getting on with one's work even if it involves no locomotion at all. (see: *motor, really motoring*)

motorbike: This is what a bikie rides. A MOTORCYCLE. The local price of these will set you back on your heels. Three wheeled motorcycles are working vehicles on nearly every farm, having turned out to be cheaper, faster and much less trouble than dobbin. (see: *bike, push bike, bikie*)

motorcamps: *KOA* would love these. A place to pitch your tent, park your trailer, and often a very, very simple cabin in which to spread your sleeping-bag, i.e., CAMPGROUND. Most of these are operated by local municipalities. They are cheap, clean and simple. Not for those who want the *Hilton*, but a marvelous way to meet Kiwis. One word of warning; don't try to stay in one during school holidays unless your nerves are much better than mine. (see: *school holidays*)

motor car: What other kind of car is there these days, I ask? An AUTOMOBILE.

motorway: FREEWAY, autobahn, autostrada, etc., two or more lanes of limited access, usually divided, highway. There are short stretches of this near 4 or 5 major centers. The word, however, is unique; your synonyms will usually not be understood.

Motunui synthetic petrol plant: As far as I know, no one else in the world, since WWII, has found it cost-effective to change natural gas to the kind of gas that runs cars. This pioneering plant uses gas from the Maui offshore natural gas field to make about 35% of N.Z.'s automotive petrol. Many cars can't use the gas produced as it requires/would require further processing to work in high compression engines. (see: *LPG, bowsers, petrol, Taranaki*)

mountain oyster: Unlike the beautiful Bluff oysters, these do not come in shells. They are the GONADS of RAMS.

M.O.W.: THE (former) MINISTRY OF WORKS AND DEVELOPMENT. It has been restructured and renamed. (see: *Works Corp., restructuring*)

mozzie: They don't carry yellow fever but they sure do bite. Local wisdom has it that the best way to kill a MOSQUITO is to clap it between two pieces of wood. The term and the killing method are both Australian imports.

M.P.: Not a military policeman, but a MEMBER OF PARLIAMENT. (see: *Parliament, boys on the hill, shadow cabinet ministers, P.M., caucus, conscience vote*)

muck around or **muck about:** 'He's been mucking about with that car for two months now and he still hasn't gotten it running.' FOOLING AROUND. (see: *fart arsing about, puddle around*)

muck in: DIG IN and get the job done. (see: *buck in*)

mudguard: This intrepid private servant protects you from the dreaded ... Well it is really the body shop's favorite, the FENDER of your car. (see: *accelerator, bonnet, boot, hand brake, panel beaters*)

mug: SUCKER.

Muldoon, Robert D. G.C.M.G. C.H.: The controversial, blunt spoken ex-leader of the more conservative of New Zealand's two major political parties (the National Party). This statement should be tempered by the realization that while the National Party is the more capitalistic of the two major parties the current (1990) Labour government (as distinguished from the Labour Party) is far more capitalistic than either major party or than the previous (Muldoon) government.

Sir (G.C.M.G. is 'Knight Grand Cross of the order of the Most Distinguished Order of St Michael and St. George') Robert is an advocate of closely regulated and often subsidized, private industry. He was nicknamed 'Piggy Muldoon' as a result of his tax gathering efforts when he was the Minister of the Treasury. An astute, if often abrasive, politician, he decided 'if you can't lick 'em, join 'em' and when approached by a toy manufacturer who wished to put out a line of 'Piggy Banks' which are hollow busts of himself, he agreed. (see: *Labour government, Labour Party, National Party, P.M., Prime Minister, boys on the hill, Honours, Minister of Finance*)

mum or **mummy:** MOM.

murder house: At most large schools, and for each collection of small ones, there is a small prefabricated building set slightly apart in which you can find one or more School Dental Nurses who do all of the preventative, and most of the corrective dental work (free) for the children in their schools. Complex problems are referred to a dentist, whose fees are paid by the Ministry of Education if s/he can handle the problem. If it has to be referred to a specialist, e.g., peridontist, orthodontist, then the parents have to pick up the tab. Some children, unlike you and I(?) consider a visit to the SCHOOL DENTAL CLINIC an unpleasant necessity, at best. Hence the name. I should mention that this is changing. My 6 year old enjoys his visits (but he doesn't have any cavities). (see: *B.D.S., gum digger*)

muslin: Not the sturdy cotton fabric you would use for backing quilts, lining tote bags, etc. Muslin in New Zealand refers to thin cotton GAUZE of the sort you would use for bandages. (see: *hessian, false friends*)

muster: (A) Roll out the chuckwagon boys, it's ROUND-UP time. Usually (but not always), it is sheep that are being rounded up. (see: *runholder, station, high country station, sheep, primary products*)

(B) A gathering of soldiers. (see: *up to muster*)

mutton dressed up like lamb: The human variant on an old hen (or rooster) bedecked in the feathers of a spring chicken.

muttonbird: The SOOTY SHEARWATER or puffinus grisens is a petrel (type of seagull). The name muttonbird presumably derives from a similarity in taste between muttonbirds and old sheep (see: *mutton*) I must admit to having chickened out, so far, on this one. The majority of my muttonbird eating friends claim it is greasy and ghastly, a minority claim it is delicious. There seems to be no middle ground. It is the chicks, harvested just before they can fly, that are taken for food and oil. In fact, the copious oil from these birds was once the staple lamp fuel in the South Pacific.

my eye (and Bessie Martin): An expression most often heard in Southland, it means fat chance, or MY FOOT, or I don't believe a word you say. Outside of Southland, my only encounter with this phrase was on a television historical adventure program, called *The Onedin Line*.

nana or **nanna:** (A) Pronounced like banana, it means GRANDMOTHER. This is baby talk that lasts into maturity.

(B) A shortened form of the word BANANA. (see: *do your bun / scone / nana*)

nappies or napkins: This is always good for a laugh — usually at me. One simply does not go around asking for a DIAPER in the best restaurants. A napkin is a diaper. A serviette is what you must ask for when you want a napkin.

(to) **nark:** to irritate or to RIDE. 'If you don't quit narking me about that $5 I'll stuff it down your throat'. (see: *take the mickey*)

National Party: The less socialistic of N.Z.'s two (socialist) major parties. This party is thought of, by Kiwis, as the equivalent of the Republican Party in the U.S.A. As far as economic policy goes it is actually considerably to the left of the left wing of the (U.S.) Democratic Party. Its economic policies are also rather to the left of the (1990) Labour government although to the right of the Labour Party. On the other hand, many of its non-economic policies are right wing, somewhere between the center and Senator Goldwater. The National Party was clearly the dominant party until the early eighties having run the country for 23 of 34 years since the second World War. However, the Labour Party has now (1990) been the party that supplies the personnel who make up the government for one and $2/3$ three year terms. The National Party looks like it will be elected to be the next (starting somewhere in October 1990) government, by default, as a result of considerable disquiet in the country produced by the Labour Government's economic restructuring that has, among other things, produced record post depression rates of unemployment. (see: *Labour government, Labour Party, Social Credit Political League, Democratic Party, New Zealand Party, restructuring, dole*)

national programme: The YA radio network that carries news, commentary, drama, and music (at the level of show tunes); with a blessed absence of commercials. A subsidiary of Radio N.Z. Ltd. (pronounce the z, zed). (see: *Radio N.Z. Ltd., concert programme, Television New Zealand, State Owned Enterprise, wireless, television license, TV3, zed, Ltd.*)

National Service: The N.Z. term for the military DRAFT. There hasn't been any compulsory National Service for at least the last 20 years and the armed services currently (Jan. 1990) have an 18 month waiting list of eager volunteers. (see *dole*)

natter: 'Let's have a natter about that'. Let's have a TALK about that.

(a) **naughty:** To have CARNAL KNOWLEDGE of a member of the opposite sex. My, how the terminology doth change, while the behavior remains relatively constant. (see: *shag, have it off, get one away, root, on with, false friends, bit of crumpet*)

neateh: neat, eh? AIN'T IT THE BERRIES? or GOOD ISN'T IT?

neither use nor ornament: Evocative isn't it? I'd hate to be described this way.

Nelson Bays: This region consists of the northern western corner of the South Island. Its major city is also called Nelson and has a metropolitan population of 44,593 (1986 census). An area of mild climate, beautiful beaches, apple orchards and the inevitable 837,000 sheep, 105,000 cattle, 11,000 domesticated (farmed) deer and 69,648 people to look after their welfare. (see: *South Island*)

netball: A version of OUTDOOR BASKETBALL played mostly by women. Seven to a side, no dribbling, no backboard.

nett: Net, as in profit. (see: *goal, programme, 'Words'*)

New Labour Party: This party represents a recent schism in the Labour Party. The N.L.P. (headed by a former Labour Party President and M.P.) sees the unabashedly capitalistic economic policies of the Labour government as an anathema to the socialistic principles that theoretically guide the Labour Party and accuses them of having traded purity for power. They see the Labour Party as unable to control the Labour government (true) and the Friedmanesque policies of the government as totally unacceptable. It may well be that this schism will put National in power at the October 1990 elections as a similar schism in National's ranks helped put Labour M.P.'s in government in the 1984 elections. The polls (Feb. 1990) have them at about 3% of the committed voters. (see: *N.L.P., Labour Party, Labour government, Muldoon, restructuring, M.P., New Zealand Party*)

New Zealand Christmas tree: A beautiful green tree with lovely red flowers that bloom in the middle of summer, i.e., at Christmas time. Its other name is the POHUTUKAWA. (see: *seasons*)

New Zealand Post Ltd. or N.Z. Post: They have taken our wonderful post office cum bank cum telephone company cum lottery shop cum government agency (e.g., place where you could collect your tax forms and pay your automobile license fees) and turned it into three profit making corporations. One of these, the bank, has been sold to private enterprise (Australian) and there are rumors about the sale of the remaining two. New Zealand Post is the post office remnant after 400+ post offices around the country were closed; often leaving small towns, and most suburbs of larger ones, without a post office (other than a local store authorized to sell stamps and envelopes and weigh and mail parcels) or a bank for many miles (in at least one case, an hour's drive, most of the way over unpaved roads). (see: *restructuring, State Owned Enterprise, Telecom N.Z., Bonus Bonds, Postbank, Labour government*)

New Zealand Party: In the 1984 elections there was a segment of the economically right wing portion of the National Party that was disgusted with the socialist and interventionist policies of the long serving National government of Sir Robert Muldoon. Initially the activists in this group appeared to consist of one determined, noisy, rather unpleasant, and very wealthy man named Bob Jones. Mr Jones set out to topple the Muldoon government by setting up a splinter party that attracted the economic conservatives from the National Party. As an added touch he advocated a foreign policy which was somewhat to the left of what the Labour Party dared say in those days. From its founder's point of view this party exceeded his expectations, not only serving as a major factor in toppling the Muldoon government and removing Sir Robert from the leadership of the National Party, but leading to the election of a Labour government that appears to have adopted almost all of the New Zealand Party's domestic and foreign policies. For a while the New Zealand party appeared to retain a life of its own even after being abandoned by its founder, however, it now appears to have been re-absorbed by the two major parties. I would like to know how Bob Jones was able to call the exact (20%) level of devaluation of the New Zealand dollar that the Labour government was 'forced' to make when taking office; considering that he made this prediction long before they took over and no one else was talking about even half that much. Smart fellow!

In 1990 the Labour Party has developed its own splinter group, the N.L.P. (New Labour Party). It remains to be seen whether this group will be as successful in taking enough of the Labour vote to topple Labour in 1990 as the New Zealand Party was in toppling National in 1984. (see: *Labour Party, Values Party, Democratic Party, New Labour Party, restructuring*)

next (Tuesday): Is not the next one but the one after next. If you make a date for next Tuesday your date isn't for tomorrow but for a week and a day away. This one drives me up the wall! (see: *false friends*)

(to) **nick:** is to STEAL. (see: (the) *nick,* (in the) *nick*)

(in the) **nick:** (A) To be in Jail. As people who nick things should be. (see: (to) *nick, gaol, boob, boobhead*)

(B) To be naked. Did they used to strip people who went to jail?

nickel spinner: Another horror story for the devoted fisherman. A BULLET (not necessarily nickel plated) fired at a trout (or any other fish). This almost always misses but it stuns the fish which then floats to the surface to be gathered in. (see: *Ministry of Works lure*)

nifty: CLEVER or EFFICIENT or WELL DESIGNED. 'Mavis had a nifty idea which she executed in nifty fashion, something you wouldn't expect from such a nifty looking bird.'

nightdress: NIGHTGOWN. (see: *nightie*)

nightie: Those frilly NIGHTDRESSES worn by the fair sex and by some members of the unfair sex. (see: *nightdress*)

(a) **night on the tins:** An EVENING and a substantial portion of the succeeding period of darkness SPENT, usually in good fellowship but invariably, IMBIBING CANS OF BEER. (see: *piss up, *piss, on the piss*)

9 o'clock flu: A disease that strikes workers and school children only during weekdays. Weekends are miraculously free of this disorder. (see: *take a sickie, wag school*)

Nippon-clipon: The AUCKLAND HARBOR BRIDGE was once a four-lane bridge (two in each direction). Thanks to New Zealand money and Japanese engineering, it is now eight lanes. The extra four were built in Japan, towed to Auckland and attached to the sides of the existing bridge. No new pilings needed. Clever, what?

N.L.P.: (see: *New Labour Party, Labour Party, Labour government*)

No.: This is the written or printed symbol for number. # will not be understood.

no hoper: A NERD; Someone for whom there is no hope. (see: *clot, thick, clueless, berk, jerk*)

not a problem: I CAN DO that EASILY. (see: **piss in the hand, in the hand, be away — be away laughing*)

no tipping: You will often see signs that say 'no tipping' in the countryside. These do not enjoin you from presenting honoraria to wandering sheep but rather FORBID the DUMPING of garbage at that point. No tipping signs are not seen in places of business because as a general rule Kiwis do not tip (TIP = to insure promptness). A few of the more expensive restaurants, particularly in the Auckland and Wellington areas have adopted this pernicious habit under the influence of overseas visitors, but those of us who live in N.Z. full time would rather *this did not spread!* (see: *tip, false friends*)

Normal School: Unlike the U.S. where Normal School is the old name for Teachers' Colleges, in New Zealand it is the name applied to some PRIMARY SCHOOLS IN WHICH STUDENT TEACHERS ARE TRAINED. (see: *school, College of Education, Teachers College, false friends*)

North Island: New Zealand consists of a large number of islands. The three major ones are (from north to south) the North Island, the South Island and Stewart Island. The North Island is the second largest in area (44,190 sq. miles), has the biggest population of both people (2,438,249, 1986 census) and sheep (34,575,000 in

1986) and boasts climates ranging from sub-tropical in the far north to temperate (mild) as you go further south. Then there is windy Wellington! (see: *mainland, South Island, Stewart Island, inter-island, Northland, Auckland, Thames Valley, Bay of Plenty, East Cape, Waikato, Tongariro, Taranaki, Hawkes Bay, Wanganui, Manawatu, Wairarapa, Horowhenua, Wellington*)

northerly: The WARM WIND from the north. Things are topsy-turvy here with the weather getting warmer (sub tropical even; after all New Zealand is approximately 1000 miles from north to south) as you go north and colder as you go south. Consequently, the northerly is warm and the southerly is cold! (see: *southerly, northern exposure, southern exposure, backwards*)

northern exposure: This is the way you want your HOUSE to FACE, toward the NORTH and the sun. Otherwise, it can be a very chilly place indeed. Because the earth just doesn't tilt far enough, the sun never shines from the south, and with central heating a rarity, the direction of the sun is very important in siting your home. (see: *southern exposure, northerly, southerly, central heating, backwards*)

Northland: This is the northernmost part of the North Island; above Kaipara Harbour and the town (not city) of Wellsford. Northland has 126,999 people (1986 census), 2,050,000 sheep, 1,006,000 cattle and 4,000 domesticated (farmed) deer. Sub-tropical climate, heavy Maori population, beautiful country, superb deep sea fishing, but has a relatively high proportion of rural poor. (see: *city, North Island, Maori*)

no sweat: 'That's no sweat.' I can do that standing on my head, or with one arm tied behind my back. EASY!

nosy parker: Someone who, for no good reason, is interested in everyone else's business, especially yours. A BUSYBODY. (see: *stickybeak*)

not bloody likely: IMPROBABLE IN THE EXTREME. (see: *bloody*)

not half: I SURE AM/IT SURE IS. A somewhat sarcastic comment. 'You sound angry. Not half!'

not on: If something is not on; it is an example of UNACCEPTABLE BEHAVIOR. Another way of saying this is to say that it just isn't cricket. (see: *cricket*)

not really: This means 'I DON'T HAVE THE FAINTEST IDEA'. 'Do you know the way to Purakanui?' 'Not really.' In the United States, this would imply that you had some notion of where the place is and, if you had to, might be able to puzzle out how to get there. In New Zealand, it is likely to mean that you have never heard of Purakanui. (see: *false friends*)

not the full quid: A quid is a pound (£), the currency used in New Zealand until 1967. Something less than a full quid would be a few cents short. If something or someone is not the full quid, they are short of some sense. 'Charlie's not the full quid.' NOT TOO BRIGHT, our Charlie. 'That story the mayor told is not the full quid.' He's HOLDING OUT on us. (see: *decimalisation, ten bob each way, bob, pound, shilling*)

noughts and crosses: TIC TAC TOE. (see: *draughts*)

no way!: NOT ON YOUR NELLIE! I ain't gonna do it!

number 8 fencing wire: The traditional 5 wire fence on New Zealand farms is made with this stuff. In consequence it is one of the things that is always available round a farm when you need to build or repair something. It is said that some cockies can put together a *Landrover*, a tractor and half a milk shed with nothing but a roll of number 8. Wire comes in sizes ranging from 1 to approx. 64, with 1 being the thickest. Number 8 is $5/32$ of an inch or about half the diameter of a pencil. (see: *cocky, Heath-Robinson apparatus, Taranaki gate, waratah, wire strainer*)

number plate: This is the LICENSE PLATE on your car.

N.Z.R.: NEW ZEALAND RAILWAYS. A government department that has (like so many others) just changed its name and become a corporation, albeit a state owned one. (see: *Railways Corp. N.Z., State Owned Enterprise*)

O

o(h): What you call the number that is 1 less than 1, especially when talking to a telephone operator. ZERO. (see: *telephone dials*)

Ocker: Hunters of wild Auks in the Antarctic Wastes. Well if you believe that you are reading this at approximately the same unreasonable hour that it was written. An Ocker is an AUSTRALIAN. (see: *Aussie, Oz*)

odd bod: An extra person or one who differs from the norm but not in any inappropriate way. 'We've got nine for dinner, where are we going to put the odd bod?' 'Seven people chose the steak, and two odd bods decided to have chicken instead.' (see: *bod*)

odds and sods: ODDS AND ENDS.

O.E.: OVERSEAS EXPERIENCE. Something almost all tertiary level educated Kiwis, and many others, want to get a bit of before settling down to start a career and raise a family in New Zealand. As a result young Kiwis are to be found as bar staff in London, Nannies in New York and ski instructors in Colorado among many other things and places. Most seem to come back, all the better for their broadened horizons. Much later in their professional careers they may leave once again, having reached the top rung of available ladders in a country of three and a third million people.

(to come) off the turnips: a Southland expression referring to SOMEONE FRESH FROM THE FARM. (see: *Southland*)

offsider: ASSOCIATE. Could be partner, usually subordinate.

oh yeah: Various meanings ranging from 'IS THAT SO' to 'WHO CARES'. (see: *wouldn't have a clue*)

old boy: MALE ALUMNUS of an educational institution, usually a high school. (see: *old boy network*)

old boy network: originally referred to the unofficial line of communication between graduates of the same (exclusive) high school. The term is somewhat more plebeian now, referring to any unofficial lines of communication between old friends, often bypassing the mechanisms designed to ensure that everyone is treated the same. (see: *old boy*)

old identity: someone who's been around a long time. 'An old Wellington identity'.

oldies: ANYONE OVER 21, when a teenager is talking. People with teenagers often find themselves referring to themselves and their contemporaries as 'oldies'. (see: *littlie*)

ombudsman: New Zealand has an OFFICIAL who is CHARGED WITH evaluating and if necessary, REDRESSING WRONGS done to individuals by central, and local, government. If you have a beef, you document it and send it to the ombudsman. It's a brave (and foolish) government department that attempts to flout his rulings.

on the back foot or **caught on the back foot:** (A) When a sports team is LOSING a game it is on the back foot.

(B) When you are found to have failed to complete work you promised for a particular time you have been caught on the back foot.

on the trot: 'George is always on the trot.' George is always PURPOSEFULLY ACTIVE.

on remand: To be in gaol or mental hospital, AWAITING TRIAL. (see: *gaol*)

on the fiddle: Engaging in malfeasance, usually of a pecuniary nature. A bureaucrat who takes money under the table for giving someone preferential access to government services would be on the fiddle. (see: *theft as a servant*)

on the full: When a ball is caught before it touches the ground, it has been caught ON THE FLY.

on the game: The game is PROSTITUTION.

on the ice: A drink that is on the ice doesn't necessarily, or even probably, have ice in it, but rather it is being REFRIGERATED.

on the never-never: Purchasing ON TIME PAYMENT. (see: *hire purchase, lay-by*)

on the pig's back: Perhaps because pork is New Zealand's most expensive domestic meat, to 'live on the pig's back' is to LIVE very WELL indeed.

*on the piss: 'He's on the piss, in fact he's been on the piss for four hours.' He's DRINKING (usually beer), in fact ... (see: (a) *night on the tins, piss, beer, piss up, legless*)

on the turn: Is not on the mend. Something that is on the turn is JUST ABOUT to go ROTTEN or the equivalent. 'I wouldn't eat those bananas mate, they are on the turn.'

on the tiles: If you have been OUT PARTYING all night you have been out on the tiles.

on with: 'Sally and Sam are on with each other'. They enjoy the benefits of the marriage bed without benefit of clergy. (see: (a) *naughty, have it off, shag, get one away, stuff, root, bit of crumpet*)

on your bike: GET MOVING! This can be an injunction to begin an assigned task or an order meaning 'get the hell out of here'.

(a) oncer: something that is NOT going TO BE REPEATED. 'This offer of a beautiful color TV for only $450 is a oncer. Take advantage of it now or never'. (see: *one off*)

one off: 'This is a one off'. This is ONE OF A KIND or a never to be repeated offer. (see: *oncer*)

O.N.O.: When you see these letters (sometimes printed as ono) at the end of an advertisement, they invite you to make a bid. $500 ono means $500 OR NEAR OFFER.

Op shop: An Op Shop is an opportunity shop. A shop in which you have an opportunity to purchase a used and donated bargain. In the States this would be called a THRIFT SHOP. (see: *shop, bottle shop, chemist's shop, bottle shop, tuck shop*)

Opera House: Most towns of any size have an Opera House. These are used for most kinds of stage performances but almost all have a resident (amateur) opera company which will stage at least one opera each season. (see: (the) *Gods, Dress Circle, flicks, Concert Chamber, theatre, Town Hall*)

other ranks or **O.R.:** This isn't the operating room from M.A.S.H. but you might see a relationship since these are ENLISTED MEN.

orange chocolate chip ice cream: Yummy! Orange colored, orange flavored ice-cream with chocolate chips scattered through it. My New Zealand favorite! [All right, so it isn't blueberry cheesecake ice cream.] New Zealand ice cream is rich (taste, ingredients) and cheap ($).

orange roughy: A singularly ugly deep sea fish that has the flavor and texture of the best lobster. Early in the popularizing of this fish, the oil that was a biproduct of its processing was so much less expensive than fuel oil that the University of Otago used it to run its boilers for building heat. Now the oil, like the fish itself is in demand as an expensive luxury.

ordinary ice cream: VANILLA.

Otago: Have you ever wondered where the 49'ers went when they gave up on finding gold in California? A goodly number of them came to the newly discovered goldfields of Otago (a corruption of the Maori name for one small village). Otago exists on two levels. The relatively flat area near the east coast and the mountain and lake country stretching inland and all the way to the west coast. Dunedin (the old Celtic name for Edinburgh) is the major city (metropolitan area population 106,864 in 1986) and the very large Mc and Mac section of its phone book attests to its Scots heritage, as do the proliferation of pipe (bagpipe) bands in the city and other parts of Otago. The lake country centering around Queenstown is, to my mind, some of N.Z.'s most striking and beautiful country. Otago (Clutha-Central Otago plus Coastal-North Otago) has (1986 census) 186,164 people, 9,342,000 sheep, 302,000 cattle and 25,000 domesticated (farmed) deer. (see: *South Island, Thames Valley, loopies, hill*)

out and about: UP AND AROUND. 'Jim must be feeling better, he's been out and about a lot lately.'

outdoor basketball: the old name for netball. (see: *netball*)

oven tray: COOKIE SHEET. That flat piece of metal on which one bakes cookies. (see: *biscuit, cookie*)

overdraft: The amount by which you have overdrawn your bank account. NEGATIVE $.

overseas funds: Anyone else's currency. New Zealand $ are worth very little overseas. This means that if a company or individual wants to purchase anything from overseas they must obtain some HARD CURRENCY acceptable in the country of origin and at the moment N.Z. buys more than it sells. So please buy New Zealand beef and lamb when you get home! Not only will you save money and eat well but you'll help us pay for such luxuries from the U.S. as Yank tanks and such necessities from the Middle East as petrol. (see: *Yank tanks, petrol, primary products*)

over the moon: 'That's just over the moon.' 'I'm over the moon about her.' That's just TERRIFIC. I think she's the berries.

overstayers: You could be eligible for this obnoxious appellation, although it usually gets hung on Pacific Islanders who have come to work in N.Z. An overstayer is someone who has not left the country when his or her visa expires. New Zealand's economy, while not buoyant by world standards (see: *terms of trade*) is very good when compared with many of her Pacific neighbors. As a result their citizens would prefer to be in N.Z. where there is work, or welfare payments, instead of at home where both are in very short supply. In earlier years the Immigration Department got some indignant headlines by raiding houses before dawn to catch these unfortunates. However, as N.Z.'s own unemployment rate worsens, public sympathy for overstayers wanes. (see: *dole*)

own-your-own: CONDOMINIUM. (see: *O.Y.O.*)

owsidgawn: HOW IS IT GOING? a friendly greeting/inquiry. (see: *eryagawn, gidday*)

O.Y.O.: Refers to an 'own-your-own' flat, or CONDOMINIUM. (see: *flat*)

Oz: Land of, on the other side of the Tasman; AUSTRALIA. (see: *Tasman, Aussie, Ocker*)

P

pack a sad: to GET ostentatiously DEPRESSED. (see: *do a Hollywood*)

paddocks: ALL FIELDS, not just those in which horses are kept. (see: *manure*)

Pakeha: WHITE MAN (or European) in Maori. Weird word, because Maori means man. My own guess is that it means 'the ghost that walks'. After a New Zealand winter, Europeans are pale!
  pa = house; keha = flea — Therefore — House flea? (see: *Maori*)

pale and peaky: This does not mean that you have a fashionable (Victorian era) complexion and have reached the apex of your attractiveness. Instead it suggests that you have a hospital pallor and are feeling distinctly unwell. PALE AND PASTY.

Palmer, Geoffrey: The current (Feb. 1990) Prime Minister of New Zealand. A former professor of constitutional law, he retains some of his academic habits (he actually reads the mountain of papers put in front of him) and mannerisms (Huey Long he ain't). His popularity is standing up better in the polls than is his (Labour) party's and he may well soon be the leader of the opposition after the November elections. (see: *Prime Minister, P.M., boys on the hill, Parliament, caucus*)

panel beaters: In New Zealand, a young man not born to the farm can ensure his financial and social success by entering one of two equally honorable and lucrative occupations. The first is medicine (entered through Medical School) and the second is AUTOMOBILE BODY SHOP work (entered through a 4–7.5 year apprenticeship). On the whole, I recommend the latter, as the responsibilities are slightly lighter and the pay (after apprenticeship) slightly better if you own your own business. (see: *M.B. Ch.B., tradesman*)

(a) **park:** The PLACE WHERE one PARKs a CAR is called a park, whether or not it is in a parking lot, and there are National parks, but city and country parks are not called parks. (see: *reserve, domain, carpark, false friends*)

Parliament: The legislative branch of government in N.Z. It consists of 25 representatives of the South Island, a proportional number of North Island seats (North Island population) ÷ (South Island population) × 25, plus four Maori seats (North, South, East and West and always Labour Party) making a grand total of 97 M.P.'s. (1990). There is only one house (unicameral legislature as in some U.S. states) and no constitution. Theoretically then there is no legal constraint on Parliament preventing it from passing any laws it wishes no matter how liberal or repressive. Somehow this dire possibility never comes to pass. Parliament has only two parties in it (1990), the two representatives of the Democratic party having lost their seats at the last (1987) election. If you listen to Parliament on the radio it quickly becomes obvious that party discipline is much stronger than in the U.S. Congress. This means that the Bills of the majority party pass (always) the Bills of the minority party don't pass (never) and private members' Bills pass (.0001% of the time, i.e., once in living memory). So where are the decisions made? (see: *caucus, conscience vote, Labour Party, National Party, Prime Minister, boys on the hill, shadow Cabinet Ministers, M.P., Democratic Party, Social Credit Political League, Treasury benches, Budget*)

passbook: Your passbook is your BANKBOOK recording your savings account transactions.

patience: (A) A true friend (see: *false friends*), the ability to endure boredom and frustration.

(B) A bad game for those of us without any; SOLITARE. (see: *pluck*)

Patricia Bartlett: Should anyone who knows England well read this, I'll say that she is New Zealand's Mary Whitehouse. For North Americans, she is rather harder to explain for, while there are many local equivalents, I don't know of any national ones. Patricia Bartlett is the founder of 'The Society for the Promotion of Community Standards' — a group who appear to feel that their extremely high personal morality and wisdom enable them to read all new books, view all new movies and decide which of these are safe for the perusal of us weaker types. Pat Bartlett herself is a poised, witty lady who holds her own well when debating with some of New Zealand's more acerbic figures before largely unsympathetic

University audiences. My admiration for the lady does not extend to her cause. New Zealand does have an official film censor and a censorship board for books. These censors, while repugnant in principle, are not too restrictive in current (1990) practice. (see: *flicks, X rated*)

pav or **pavlova:** In the 1920's Anna Pavlova came to New Zealand for the first time and floated across the stage into the Kiwi's heart. As a result (so legend has it) THE NATIONAL DESSERT, a feather light concoction made of egg white, sugar and love was named after her. The best of these to my mind, have a marshmallow texture inside and a very light crust outside. If you aren't lucky enough to have some proud Kiwi housewife to invite you in for a bit of the homemade, then I recommend a commercially made pavlova made by *Cowells*. (These are available in Wellington and Dunedin). By the way, should you visit Australia you may hear a totally unfounded rumor that this delicious confection is really a native born Australian. While a totally objective culinary historian might feel that there is as much truth in this claim as there is in the New Zealand one, like any other resident of New Zealand, I can assure you that this is pure balderdash and that the pavlova was conceived and rose in Godzone. (see: *Aussie, Godzone*)

pavement: The SIDEWALK is called the pavement. A paved road is called a sealed road. 'Seal begins' and 'seal ends' are common signs, indicating that you are about to run out of or into metal. (see: *seal, metal*)

P.A.Y.E.: PAY AS YOU EARN. That portion of your income tax skimmed off your salary before it ever reaches you. (see: *Inland Revenue*)

pea, pie and pud: (rhymes with mud): A full meal, a MEAT PIE with a side order of PEAS and MASHED POTATOES. (see: *dressed pies, meat pie, pud*)

Pebbles: With a capital letter, this is one of the brand names for what are known as *M & M's* in North America. *M & M's* have just arrived on these shores but the name probably won't be recognized if you ask for them. (see: *Smarties*)

peckish: 'Around six o'clock I get peckish, no matter how much I've eaten during the day.' HUNGRY.

Peerless Sheep Nuts: This sign on the side of the road is advertising neither 'mountain oysters' nor the instant answer to virility problems — it is merely one more brand of animal feed. (see: *Feed Moose, mountain oyster*)

penalty kick: An opportunity awarded by the referee to the side that wasn't caught doing something against the rules in a rugby game. (3 points). (see: *football* or *footie*)

pencils: Are the familiar graphite filled (did you think it was lead?) wooden sticks. In this case the difference is a minus not a plus. They usually don't have a built in device for removing the errors you make with them. (NO ERASER.) (see: *rubber*)

penny: A penny is not a cent. Penny is term that refers to the old £ (pounds), s (shillings), d (pence), system that New Zealand used to use. A penny is a large copper coin (about the size of a current 50¢ piece). It is still in use in some lodging houses and motorcamps where they have coin meters on the cooking and/or water heating gas. In these cases, the proprietor will undoubtedly sell you some. A cent, on the other hand is one hundredth of a dollar and was, until 1989, the smallest New Zealand coin in both size and value. One and two cent pieces, like pennies, are no longer being made and are being phased out of use; as their face value is less than the cost of manufacturing them. (see: *decimalisation, pound, quid, bob, shilling, sixpence, florin, motorcamp, gas, LPG, false friends*)

penny-farthing: This is an old fashioned bicycle with an enormous front wheel (often the height of a medium sized man; this is the 'penny') and a small, tricycle sized wheel at the back (the 'farthing'). (A farthing = $^1/_4$ penny.) (see: *decimalisation, penny, farthing, quid, push-bike*)

period: Of TIME or menstruation. This is not a form of punctuation. (see: *full stop, false friends*)

perks: PERQUISITES. Those extra advantages that accompany most jobs such as the ability of department store employees to purchase from their own store at a discount, or a salesman's expense account. I know these are innocuous ones, but I don't want to queer anyone's pitch.

pet: (A) 'This vase is a real pet'. This vase is a real TREASURE. (see: *false friends*)

(B) The furry friend that dominates your household. (see: *moggy, dogs*)

(C) A rather old-fashioned term for what happens in the backseat of a car on lovers lane.

peter: (A) A half gallon BOTTLE OF BEER. (see: *half g, flagon, hotel, bottle store, beer*)

(B) PRISON CELL (criminal and prison officer jargon). (see: *boob, boobhead, gaol*)

(C) CASH REGISTER but I've only heard it used this way in one restricted context (see: *tickle the peter*).

petrol: Petrol is GASOLINE, it comes in Super (96 octane), and Unleaded (91 octane). Petrol is sold by liters. There are service stations with 'self service' pumps but old habits die hard and you are probably going to get helped at these pumps just like the others.

The current (Jan. 1990) prices are (on average): Super: 91.9¢ a liter, or $3.48 per U.S. gallon; Regular: 89.9¢ a liter, or $3.40 per U.S. gallon. If you hear someone talking about gallons or miles per gallon, he is not talking about the U.S. gallon, but rather the Imperial gallon which is roughly ⅕ larger. (see: *gallon, litre, gas, bowsers, Motunui synthetic petrol plant*)

phone box: PHONE BOOTH.

physician: A medical PRACTITIONER specializing in the practice OF INTERNAL MEDICINE. It does not refer to any other kind of medical man. (see: *false friends*)

piddle around or **puddle about:** Fiddle around or POTTER ABOUT. (see: *fart arsing around, muck around*)

pie-cart: A house trailer fixed up as a traveling KITCHEN dispensing meat pies (and often fish and chips, dim sims and anything else that can be fried) through a hatch running the entire length of one side. My favorite pie-cart is in Dunedin. It is called the 'Cafe de Curb'. (see: *meat pie, fish and chips, dim sims*)

pig island: Wild pigs abound in the wilder places of both North and South Islands. It is speculated that they are descendants of swine released by Captain Cook on his voyages of discovery. Despite this illustrious ancestry, neither island seems to wish to claim the name. The residents of both major islands are more than willing to pass the pig island name on to the rival land mass. (see: *Captain Cookers, mainland, North Island, South Island*)

pike out: Usually to quit drinking beer before your friends are willing to admit they have reached their capacity. It can refer to PUTATIVE PREMATURE CESSATION of other ACTIVITIES. (see: *piker, beer*)

pikelets: A small pancake (like a silver dollar pancake) usually served cold, topped with butter, jam or whipped cream to accompany morning or afternoon tea. The English call these griddle scones or scotch pancakes. (see: *tea, scone*)

piker: Someone who gives up when you aren't ready to. 'Sam's a piker, he piked out when it actually came to stealing the Bobby's hat and I had to do it all by myself. Send bail money.' (see: *pike out, Bobby*)

pilchers: BABIES' PLASTIC PANTS (see: *dummy, mac*)

pillowslip: PILLOWCASE.

pimp: A pimp does not solicit for his sister, he rats on her; a TATTLE-TALE. To pimp is to tell on others. This is teenage slang. (see: *false friends*)

pinny: What you wear to keep your clothes clean while cooking or washing up, pinafore or APRON.

*piss: (A) Usually BEER, always booze.

(B) URINE or to urinate just like at home. (see: (a) *night on the tins, on the piss, piss up, beer, pissed, plonk*)

*piss in: SUCCEED. Sam will piss in on that exam (job, race, etc.) (see: *piss in the hand, in the hand*)

*piss in the hand: EASY, usually applied to exams. (see: **piss in, in the hand, not a problem*)

*piss off: (A) An instruction given to someone whose presence you no longer desire.

(B) to MAKE ANGRY.

*pissed, pissed as a newt: DRUNK, bombed, stinko, etc. A Friday and Saturday night enterprise on the part of a segment of the community. This is the only country I've ever been to where beer is delivered in tank trucks (like gas trucks) that hold 3024 Imperial gallons (3599 U.S. gallons). They just pump beer into great vats under each hotel. The Kiwi and Aussie have a great capacity for beer. The first *American Airlines* plane into this area ran out of beer within its first hour of flight. This word is not to be confused with pissed off, which means the same as it does in the States (U.S.A.): angry. (see: *skinfull, half cut, piss, gallon, brassed off, beer, hotel*)

piss up: A PARTY at which fermented beverages and often spirituous liquors are consumed in quantity. (see: (a) *night on the tins, on the piss, beer, pissed, plonk*)

plait: A single BRAID down the back is a not unusual style for long hair. It also refers to other braided things such as plaited belts, etc.

(a) **plaster:** A *BANDAID* by any other name is a plaster. (see: *sticking plaster*)

playcentre: A private co-operative KINDERGARTEN partially subsidized by Government but administered and taught by parents. Some of these parents receive special training to be paid 'playcentre supervisors'. Children usually attend 2 – 3 half days per week. (see: *creche, kindy*)

playing gooseberry: being the third that makes a crowd.

plonk: FIREWATER. (see: *beer, piss, pissed*)

pluck: This is indeed what you do to a dead but still feathered goose (a messy job) and it is what your brave friends have, but it is also what you do when taking a playing card from a deck of them. To 'pluck' a card, is to DRAW a card. (see: *patience, false friends*)

Plunket Society: Formed in 1907 under the leadership of Dr Truby King to cut New Zealand's then abnormally high infant mortality rate, this is one of a number of quasi governmental (finance) volunteer agencies that provide many of New Zealand's social services. Plunket provides pre-natal classes in most centers, and has a building/clinic staffed by specially trained 'Plunket Nurses' in most centers. The nurse will visit the new Mum and baby once a week for the first three post-natal months. During the next three months Mum is expected to bring baby into the 'Plunket Rooms' once a week and after that, one visit a month, at least until age 5, suffices to keep track of baby's height, weight and general health. One tourist note, the cleanest and most convenient 'Ladies' Rooms' in most towns are located in the Plunket Rooms. (see: *Acclimatization Society, caught short*)

pluty: 'a very pluty neighborhood'. A very ritzy neighborhood, or a very WEALTHY one. It is a contraction of plutocratic.

P.M.: It can mean afternoon, but it's more likely to mean PRIME MIN-ISTER. (see: *Prime Minister, boys on the Hill, M.P.*)

pohutukawa: (see:) NEW ZEALAND CHRISTMAS TREE. A weather pre-dictor, like the woodchuck. Maori legend has it that if the red blos-soms appear early (e.g., November) a long hot summer is in store. (see: *seasons*)

pointsman: Traffic COP DIRECTING TRAFFIC. He points — you go. The Road Code provides for special signals to tell him which way you would like to go. You may or may not get your wish. (see: *M.O.T.*)

*pointing Percy at the porcelain: Male URINATION. (see: *caught short, relieving oneself, driving the porcelain bus*)

Pom — Pommie: A ruddy (BLOODY? op. cit.) ENGLISHMAN. Many of the Kiwis you will meet are really Pommies in disguise. Since my ear isn't fine-tuned enough to distinguish the accents, I must discriminate on the volume of beer they drink (less than the native born). Another distinctive trait is calling England 'home' whether they have been in New Zealand 20 minutes or 20 years. They can't understand why Kiwis don't do the same, and Kiwis can't understand why they should. Note, however, that the ambition of almost every young Kiwi (see: *Kiwi*) is to visit England. There are several suggested origins for the word Pom. Most likely it is an acronym for Prisoner On Migration which was stamped on the papers of the involuntary immigrants who were sent from England to Botany Bay in Australia. The term has since crossed the Tasman sea to New Zealand. (see: *pongo, bloody, whinge, Tasman*)

poncey: behavior resembling that expected of a male homosexual. (see: *homosexuality, twee, camp as a row of pink tents, poof*)

pong: to exude odoriferous particles. After a day on the tennis courts or in the glasshouse, I pong. Smell isn't strong enough, STINK comes closer! (see: *glasshouse*)

pongo: An even ruder term for an ENGLISHMAN than bloody pom. (see: *bloody, pom, rude*)

pontoon: If someone invites you to play a game of pontoon don't look at him blankly or get our your diving gear. He is suggesting a game of BLACKJACK, or 21. Check local rules before commencing play (e.g.,

5 cards under pays? Is the 10 the equivalent of a face card for passing the deal, etc.)

poof or **poofter:** (A) QUEER. As in homosexual, this meaning probably comes from a female hair fashion, popular in England in the 1700's. (see: *homosexuality, poncey, camp as a row of pink tents*)

(B) poof can also refer to an OTTOMAN on which you rest your feet. This may derive from that same hair fashion since it involved building up the hair on top of the head into a thick mattress. (see: *humpty, scats*)

poozling: Going through abandoned houses scheduled for demolition and removing the (usually antique) fittings that strike your fancy. Until recently this was a socially acceptable practice (although not strictly legal), however, as demolition contractors catch on to the value of these fittings legal and moral pressure is exerted to discourage the practice. SCAVENGING.

pop in: (A) 'I'm going to pop in on Sam.' I'm going to STOP BY and see Sam.

(B) 'Pop this in the pot.' PUT this IN the pot. (see: *pop out, pop over, pop on*)

pop on: 'I'm going to pop the kettle on (the stove).' I'm going to PUT the kettle ON. (see: *pop in, pop out, pop over*)

pop out: 'I'm going to pop out to the dairy.' 'I'm GOING OUT to the dairy.'

pop over — pop (a)round: 'Pop over some time.' COME VISIT some time. 'Pop around to Uncle Joe's and see how he is.' GO OVER to Uncle Joe's and ...

Postbank: Post Office Bank Ltd. The bank that used to be part of the post office and now belongs to the *Australia and New Zealand Bank*. It still often shares premises with post offices and it is still contracted to the Treasury to sell Bonus Bonds. (see: *N.Z. Post, call, Bonus Bonds*)

(to) **post:** A method of raising and lowering oneself in rhythm with the gait of the horse you are riding so as to ensure a smooth forward progression. The preceding is true but totally irrelevant. In New Zealand to post is to MAIL, the post is the mail, and the postie is the mailman/mailperson. (see: *postie, N.Z. Post, call, G.P.O.*)

Post Office: The POST OFFICE used to be just what it says, but it was also the TELEPHONE COMPANY, the TELEGRAPH COMPANY, a BANK, the place that issued T.V. LICENSES, acted as a LOTTERY AGENT and organizer, did automobile registrations, etc., etc. Probably the agency of the government that had the most frequent contact with the populace. In general it was efficient and popular. How's that for a government agency? Almost all of the preceding is history. Over half of the Post Offices are gone and the functions of the remainder have sadly shrunk. (see: *N.Z. Post, restructuring, State Owned Enterprise, television licence, Bonus Bonds, Postbank, tolls, Prospector's Right*)

postie: That man, or more likely woman, in the grey shorts or slacks riding her bicycle (in flat towns like Palmerston North or Christchurch) or striding up and down hills (Wellington, Dunedin, etc.) with mailbag slung over shoulder. For the men, at least, a jersey (which see) is added to the costume. In case my description hasn't rung any bells, it's your friendly neighborhood MAILPERSON. (see: *post, post office, G.P.O.*)

pot plants: Not necessarily, or even likely to be, marijuana, but any POTTED PLANTS (i.e., plants in pots).

pottle: The South Island term for a SMALL CONTAINER. Originally applied to the little wooden boxes in which berry fruit was sold, it then transferred to the plastic boxes which replaced them. A further extension of the term applied it to small plastic containers of yoghurt and sour cream. (see: *punnet, chip*)

potty: The MINIATURE TOILET upon which very young children are first encouraged to wee and pooh. (see: *wees and poohs, Potty party*)

pound: (A) 454 grams. The unit of measure that you and I, and most Kiwis are used to. However in 1976 N.Z. got completely metricated and we oldies have been confused ever since. The kids don't understand our problem. (see: *metrication, oldies*)

   (B) Before 1967 N.Z.'s monetary unit (one £, equivalent to $2 N.Z.). In 1967 N.Z. got decimalized. This confusion is now largely cleared up as the younger generation becomes the middle-aged generation. (see: *decimalisation, not the full quid, ten bob each way, shilling, bob, as silly as a two-bob watch, false friends*)

possie (pronounced pozzie): A location in space or a POSITION. 'I've got a good pozzie for the races — you can see everything.'

P.P.T.A.: Not a strange version of the P.T.A. but the rather militant SECONDARY SCHOOLTEACHERS' UNION, the Post Primary Teachers Association. (see: *college*)

pram: A BABY BUGGY. A shortened version of perambulator. You will see a series of hooks attached to the front of city buses. These hooks are there so that you can hang your pram on the outside of the bus before getting in with babe in arms. Provides more room all round. (see: *sulky, pushchair*)

prang: That's what you had better not do to the boss's car when you borrow it. BANG UP, DENT or otherwise reduce from pristine glory to mundane mediocrity. Usually used in reference to automobiles.

prawn: An expression largely confined to Southland. It implies a certain deficiency in cognitive skills in the individual so described.

DUMMY. (see: *don't come the raw prawn with me, berk, jerk, thick, Southland*)

prefect: SCHOOL MONITOR. (see: *head prefect*)

press studs: Those SNAPS on your western shirt or your pajama fly. By the way, they don't bother with these on N.Z. pajamas. (see: *pyjamas*)

primary products: New Zealand's economic lifeline. Primary Products are the animal, horticultural and grain PRODUCE of New Zealand farms. Two thirds or more of the overseas funds earned by N.Z. come from the export of this produce. Most of the remainder comes from the forestry industry or from industries like carpet manufacturers that make things from primary products. This is extremely important in a modern country that provides less than 40% of its own oil needs, builds no cars from scratch, etc., etc. New Zealand's best market is the European Community with the U.S. a close second and Canada bringing up 11th place (1987). (see: *overseas funds, sheep,* (the) *works, terms of trade, freezing workers, wharfies*)

primary school: ELEMENTARY SCHOOL (see: *school*)

Prime Minister: The POLITICAL but not the titular HEAD of the N.Z. GOVERNMENT. This position is held by the elected (by his colleagues) leader of the majority party in Parliament. He is also the representative of an electoral district. A strong Prime Minister can pretty well get whatever legislation he likes passed. The present (1990) Prime Minister represents an electoral district in Christchurch. (see: *P.M., boys on the hill, Parliament, caucus, Governor-General*)

private hotel: (see: *hotel*)

privates: (A) The lowest rankers in the army.

(B) That portion of your anatomy whose public exposure could lead to public censure. (see: *short and curlies, minge, crutch — crutching, false friends*)

privatisation: The process of selling off government owned businesses to private enterprise. A notable recent example was Air New Zealand. The progression seems to usually be from government department (subsidiary) to State Owned Enterprise to privately owned business. Often these businesses are so big that only overseas firms can afford to purchase them. (see: *restructuring, Rogernomics, State Owned Enterprise*)

Privy Council: This is not a group meeting in the outhouse, although the name is suggestive.

The High Court in New Zealand isn't the highest N.Z. court and the highest N.Z. court, the Appeals Court, isn't supreme either. Cases can be appealed once more to the Crown or more specifically to the 'Judicial Committee of the Monarch's Privy Council' in

London. Like the U.S. Supreme Court the Privy Council reserves the right to select which of the cases appealed to it will actually be heard. The Judicial Committee of the Privy Council is made of 'eminent Judges of Commonwealth countries'. The apron strings aren't all that slack as yet! (see: (the) *Queen, court, Crown*)

problems: There is a tendency to take professional criticism very personally in New Zealand. One American friend was hired as a consultant to a government department and send around the country to see what she could do to help the various branches of this department. When talking to the people in each new branch she initially would say, 'What kind of problems are you having with . . . ?' This produced an immediate clam up. After much frustration, she hit upon this formula, 'What particular challenges are you facing here?' This immediately elicited the list of problems that she was after.

procession: A procession is a PARADE. Every town in New Zealand finds an excuse for at least one of these each year, complete with floats, queens, brass bands, bagpipe bands, etc., etc. The term also applies to other kinds of parades, for instance, students and staff marching to the graduation ceremony form a procession. (see: *capping*)

Professor: In an American University everyone is a Professor. So much so that Dr is the title of choice. In N.Z. things are very different. Until very recently one wasn't a professor, one was 'the Professor of . . .', in other words the DEPARTMENT HEAD. In these prosperous days a university department may boast two or even three 'Chairs' (one for each Professor) while the lower ranks are Associate Professors-Readers, Senior Lecturers, Lecturers, and Junior Lecturers. Consequently low ranked American academics who reply, to the inevitable status question, that they are Assistant Professors find themselves receiving unwonted deference. (see: *Chair, Reader, Associate Professor, Lecture, false friends*)

programme: PROGRAM. (see: *gaol, nett, 'Words', national programme, concert programme*)

Proms: This has nothing to do with the senior prom. They are instead a series of CONCERTS given annually throughout the country by the New Zealand National Symphony Orchestra. The orchestra is partly funded by the TV license fee paid by everyone who wishes to operate a TV set. (see: *television licence, ball, false friends*)

property: A property is usually a BUILDING, and its surrounding ground. It may be a residence or a commercial building. 'That's a nice property you have there.' 'That's a nice house (building, etc.) you have there.' This usage survives in the U.S. in 'Get off my property.' (see: *section*)

Prospectors Right: Purchased for $90 from the Ministry of Commerce: Energy and Resources Division office, in any major city, this entitles you to:

> (a) 'Enter on unoccupied Crown (i.e., government owned) land and prospect and conduct tests for any mineral'
>
> (c) 'Keep ... samples ... of any mineral found ...'

This is what entitles you to go gold panning in central Otago if you can find any appropriate unoccupied Crown land. It is increasingly difficult to find any gold bearing streams without contiguous claims stretching the length of the banks. It is, however, tremendously exciting when you see your first flashes of 'colour'. (see: *Crown, Otago, Thames Valley*)

P.S.A.: The Public Service Association is the UNION OF (mostly) GOVERNMENT EMPLOYEES (appx. 62,000 members). The 'mostly' is in there because it also covers former government employees who now work for State Owned Enterprises and some people who work for organizations ultimately funded by government, like non-academic university employees. It used to have little need for militancy to protect and enhance the interests of employees. Under the new state sector act and restructuring it has been forced to become increasingly militant and, like all other N.Z. unions, rather less influential than it was prior to the advent of the Labour government. (see: *C.T.U., industrial action, industrial unrest, State Owned Enterprise, restructuring, Labour government*)

pseuds: As in people who taste the label, and not the wine. (see: *ski bunny, varsity bunny*)

pto: At the bottom of a page this means 'PLEASE TURN OVER'

pubbing: My unmarried North Island friends tell me this is the latest term for USING your local watering hole AS A SINGLES BAR. (see: *hotel*)

public bar: No chairs, no women (ladies?), no carpet, scattered high tables, dart board, oceans of beer. This NO FRILLS BAR is found in licensed hotels along with the more luxurious lounge bar. However, 'times they are a changing' and even the most traditional of public bars now has scattered a few high stools around and reluctantly admits those few women who venture in. (see: *hotel, lounge bar, licensed hotel, booze barn, six o'clock swill, tavern, beer*)

public holiday: New Zealand is not deficient in these, and shops observe them religiously. The approximate dates of the major ones are indicated below, however, for some of these (non religious holidays), if they fall on a weekend or midweek they may be moved to nearest Monday or Friday to provide a long weekend.

NATIONAL HOLIDAYS

January 1 & 2	— New Year's
February 6	— Waitangi (N.Z.) day
Easter Time	— Good Friday
	— Easter Monday
April 25	— ANZAC Day
1st Mon. in June	— Queen's Birthday
2nd to last Mon. in October	— Labour Day (not to be confused with the international Labor Day which is May 1st)
December 25	— Christmas Day
December 26	— Boxing Day

Provincial Holidays (celebrated on the nearest Monday)

Wellington	— January 22
Auckland	— January 29
Northland	— January 29
Nelson	— February 1
Taranaki	— March 31
Otago/Southland	— March 23
Hawkes Bay	— A & P Show Day
Marlborough	— November 1
Canterbury	— December 16
Westland	— December 1

(see: *Waitangi Day, ANZAC day, Queen's Birthday, Boxing Day*)

pud or **pudding:** The sweet taste at the end of the meal, whether or not it is a pudding. In fact, DESSERT is most likely to be fruit salad (with or without ice cream). (see: *pav*)

puffed: Tired, BEAT, worn out. 'After running up those twelve flights of stairs I'm puffed.' Descriptive isn't it? (see: *beggared, stonkered, stuffed, buggered, knackered, clapped out*)

puha: A native (Maori) SPINACH. Very tasty with a white sauce. (see: *hu hu grub*)

*puke: REGURGITATE. (see: *Technicolor yawn, *spew, chunder, drive the porcelain bus, laughing at the floor, talking to the big white telephone*)

pulley: (A) A (usually WOODEN) CLOTHES RACK that looks like a horizontal ladder and is suspended from the laundry room or kitchen ceiling and is used to dry washing indoors on inclement days. This is raised and lowered with what you would call a pulley. (see: *hot water cylinder, air the washing, false friends*)

(B) The leverage based device used to multiply your strength when pulling on a rope.

punched out: BEATEN UP. (see: *punch-up*)

132

punch-up: A bout of fisticuffs not bounded by Marquis of Queensberry rules, and often occurring on the eve of the Sabbath in the confines of a place in which spirituous liquors are purveyed. FIGHT. (see: *punched out, get your face smacked in (rearranged), hotel*)

puncture: FLAT tire.

punga: A punga fern is a tree fern. It resembles a small palm tree but can be found in much colder climates than palms. This, like the tuatara, is an ancient form. Much of the oil and coal deposits found around the world were formed from forests of the punga's relatives under the pressure of time and layers of newer growth. (see: *tuatara*)

punnet: In the North Island it is a SMALL open-topped (though often *Saran wrap* covered) BOX OF BERRIES, e.g., strawberries. (see: *strawbs, pottle, chip*)

punt: (A) A BET. (see: (have a) *flutter, punting, punter, GG's trots, gallops, T.A.B., divy, false friends*)

   (B) To kick a ball while it is still in the air.

   (C) A flat bottomed, shallow draft boat that is poled along rather than rowed.

punter: GAMBLER, usually on the horses. (see: (have a) *flutter, punting, punt, divy, GG's, trots, gallops, T.A.B., false friends*)

punting: Not ordinarily poling a boat or kicking a football but rather PLACING A BET. (see: (have a) *flutter, punt, divy, GG's, trots, gallops, punter, T.A.B., false friends*)

pushbike: The kind of bike that you push along by pressing (alternately) upon the pedals. A BICYCLE. A bike is something else again. (see: *bike, motorbike*)

pushchair: A much more logical name for a baby's STROLLER. (see: *pram, sulky*)

pussy: Has no salacious connotations! A pussy is a cat, in fact this the exact equivalent of KITTY. When calling his cat at night instead of calling 'kitty-kitty-kitty' a Kiwi calls 'puss-puss-puss' or 'pussy-woosy-woosy', (if you are like one of my wives, who shall, otherwise, remain nameless). (see: *cat*)

put down: In N.Z. this is done to children rather than unwanted pets. It means to PUT TO BED. (see: *false friends*)

put the hard word on: To INSIST that a difficult DECISION be MADE. Usually used in the context of pressuring someone to grant sexual favors or, 'put their money where their mouth is' in the case of a business deal or an offer of marriage. (see: *on with*)

put the wind up: Much as it sounds that way, this is not a euphemism for eructation. (see: *break wind*) 'The Inland Revenue really put the wind up Sam when they demanded copies of all his receipts for last year.' The Internal Revenue really FRIGHTENED Sam when ... (see: *get the wind up, Inland Revenue*)

pyjamas: PAJAMAS. (see: *press studs, 'Words'*)

Q

(the) **quack:** That practioner of the medical arts to whom you take your ills. DOCTOR. (see: *M.B. Ch.B.*)

(the) **Queen:** That is, the Queen of New Zealand, who just happens to be the same grand lady who is the Queen of England, Ireland, Wales, Canada, etc. She gets out here once every five years or so and walks around so she can be looked at. During her absences from New Zealand (i.e., most of the time) she is directly represented by a surrogate called the Governor-General. (see: *Governor-General*)

Every Christmas she broadcasts her message to the Commonwealth which is seen by most of her subjects. [You must remember that every British Commonwealth citizen is a 'subject' of the Queen.] In the 70's her message invariably started, 'My husband and I ...' This stock phrase became a standing (largely affectionate) joke that was revived every year. Unfortunately someone blew the gaff and in the mid eighties she abandoned this formula and has taken to varying her delivery. (see: (the) *Queen, Governor-General, Crown, God Save The Queen*)

Queen's Birthday: Is celebrated as a PUBLIC HOLIDAY on the 1st Monday IN JUNE. The present Queen was born April 21, 1926, Victoria was born May 24, 1819. So whose birthday is it?

Elizabeth II	April 21, 1926
George IV	December 14, 1895
Edward VIII	June 24, 1894
George V	June 3, 1841
Victoria	May 24, 1819
William IV	August 21,1765
George IV	August 12,1762
George III	June 4, 1738

So it appears that if you are celebrating the 'Queen's Birthday' you are really celebrating either the birthday of George V, a king the world has some reason to respect, or George III, whose reputation rather suffers from history, particularly in the U.S.

In any case a long weekend at the beginning of June makes a nice break in the year and that is probably why the celebration hasn't followed the sovereign's actual birthday. I must admit some personal disappointment at this information as, knowing it wasn't

Queen Elizabeth's own birthday, I'd always assumed it was *The Queen* (Victoria) whose birthday we were celebrating. (see: *public holidays*)

Queen cake: These CUPCAKEs are very hard to find in N.Z. (see: *biscuit, cookie*)

(the) **Queen's Chain:** In the England of the mid 1800's access to most inland waterways was severely restricted by the ownership of the riverbanks by private individuals. New Zealand's founding fathers were determined to avoid this social inequity and established the Queen's Chain, which is a strip of land 100 chain links (66 FEET or 20 meters wide) ALONG the banks of all major WATERWAYS which remains in the hands of the Crown and hence provides all citizens FREE ACCESS for recreational purposes. The Labour government has dropped some hints that they want to give the management of these strips over to neighbouring landowners. This has given rise to the fear that these managers might restrict access. The government says we have nothing to fear. (see: (the) *Crown, privatisation*)

quenchers: I'm not sure what it is that they are supposed to quench but this is the South Island equivalent of the North Island's (see:) *ice blocks* or the American ICE CUBES.

quid: N.Z.'s pre-1967 unit of currency. A New Zealand POUND (£) converted to $2.00NZ when decimalisation came in. (see: *pound, decimalisation, not the full quid, shilling, bob, ten bob each way*)

quite: (A) If you read a letter of recommendation which said: 'He is really a quite brilliant man,' you are likely to think that the individual in question has one or two grey cells to rub together.

A Kiwi on the other hand, would read the statement as 'He is of mediocre intellect.' When used to modify something good, quite means NOT VERY. When used to modify something discreditable, it does mean very. 'Sam is quite a bad sort.' Sam is a very bad man. This is then a subtle and very dangerous false friend, particularly when someone's future rides on your word. (see: *false friends*)

(B) It is also used as an affirmation of someone else's statement. 'Bazzer's a good man.' 'Quite!' (see: *s'story*)

R

Radio N.Z. Ltd.: The corporation which controls New Zealand's three government owned radio networks. Partly funded by the Television License fee, two of these networks are entirely free of commercials! (see: *B.C.N.Z., Television New Zealand, State Owned Enterprise, national programme, concert programme, auroraed, wireless, TV3*)

(a) **rager:** This sounds like someone with a terrible temper. It is a PERSON WHO ENJOYS PARTYING. (see: *raging*)

raging: It could be engaging in a temper tantrum, but it is really PARTYING. (see: (a) *rager, false friends*)

Railways Corp., N.Z.: The government owned, (theoretically) profit making, corporation that owns and operates the railroads. I recommend a trip the length of the country by train. It is one of the most spectacular and least comfortable (with the exception of the crack trains the Silver Fern, and to a much lesser extent the Northerner and the Southerner), ways to see New Zealand. Something you will be happy you have done, but won't repeat. N.Z.R. is noted for its coffee. Your first, last and only sip is said to be a memorable experience. (see: *State Owned Enterprise*)

Randy: I have sad news for those of you with this fine old American name. If you are Randy Murgatroyd Smith and you have always gone by Randy M. Smith the time has come to give Murgatroyd an airing (or at least Randolph). It's no worse to be called Randy in N.Z. than it would be to be called HORNY in the U.S. Kiwis find this overwhelmingly funny, but you won't. Before ignoring this advice (after all you never could stand Murgatroyd or Randolph) imagine how your kid sister would react to a young man who approached her with this line, 'Hello, I'm Horny, what's your name?' (see: *false friends*)

range: If you were home on the range in N.Z. you might find it a trifle warm, as the range is the KITCHEN STOVE. (see: *false friends*)

rapt: Slang for being ENRAPTURED with someone or something. 'I was really rapt by the *U2* concert.'

raspberry bun: A HOT DOG BUN FILLED with BUTTER and COVERED WITH RASPBERRY FROSTING. This is definitely not on the recommended list!

rat bag: To call someone a rat bag is to imply that they have done something of which you disapprove. A MILD REBUKE.

rate of knots: To move at the rate of knots is to move with GREAT SPEED. The phrase can be used to refer to activities other than locomotion. For instance, 'Felicity is getting through that box of chocolate at the rate of knots'.

rattling good fit: In the U.S. this would refer to something that fits well. In N.Z. tradesmen and engineers have preserved what I strongly suspect was the original meaning. A rattling good fit is something that is supposed to fit together with precision and instead FITS SO LOOSELY it rattles. (see: ***cock in a sock, tradesman, false friends*)

rattle your dags: HURRY ALONG there. 'The audible manifestation of locomotion in an uncrutched sheep'. (see: *dag, crutch — crutching*)

Reader: Literacy is assumed, but not required for this position, an academic rank corresponding with a U.S. PROFESSOR (who is not a department head). Another misleading N.Z. name for the same rank is Associate Professor. For those familiar with the English academic system a Reader in N.Z. is not the same as a Reader in England; as it is a teaching position in N.Z. rather than a research title as in England. (see: *Associate Professor, Lecturer, Professor, Chair, false friends*)

really motoring: PROCEEDING with a task or journey AT GREAT SPEED (see: (to) *motor, motor, motor along*)

ready, steady, go: READY SET GO.

redskins: Thought these were an American phenomenon did you? Well you were wrong, N.Z. has BIG RED PEANUTS too. (see: *false friends*)

Red Squad: A special police squad that was formed to control protest and rioting when a South African rugby team came to N.Z. in 1981. They achieved a reputation for excessive brutality among the anti-apartheid protesters/rioters. This reputation was much stronger than that of their counterpart Blue Squad. Part of this was because for the first time since the 1951 waterfront strike the police were seen to be charging people with batons and these weren't the usual police billy but long (riot) batons. Many agreed with their actions and the former head of the Red Squad is now a member of parliament. Many others still nurture a lingering distrust of the police; who feel that they were caught in the middle. Most of those on the receiving end of the batons were middle class people who had never found themselves opposed to the police before and were very shocked to find themselves treated as lawbreakers. The present (1990) government will not issue visas to South African sports teams. (see: *Springbok tour, long batons, tour, touring, All Blacks, test, side, Gleneagles agreement*)

registration day: You may think that this sounds like the day on which you get your dog his collar tag, but it is the day on which your kids (or you) ENROLL(MENT DAY) in University or other tertiary educational institution. (see: *Uni, varsity*)

relief teacher: SUBSTITUTE TEACHER. (see: *relieving, relieving oneself*)

relieving: SUBSTITUTING FOR an EMPLOYEE who usually does a particular job. (see: *relief teacher, relieving oneself*)

relieving oneself: A genteel way of saying one is taking the pressure off one's bladder. If you do this against the back wall of the hotel it loses some of its gentility. (see: *relieving, caught short, pointing Percy at the porcelain, hotel, *have a slash*)

reserve: A reserve is a PARK, usually one located in a town or city. (see: *domain, park, city*)

restructuring: The process of changing an organization or a whole industry so that it runs more efficiently/economically. Unfortunately this almost invariably means that the workforce is reduced. During the decade of the eighties this has happened to nearly every organization (both private industry and government funded activities) in N.Z. with consequent rising unemployment and social unrest. We are told that, as a result of these massive changes, good economic times are almost upon us, but almost seems to always be tomorrow, and tomorrow has yet to come as of August 1990. (see: *dole, auroraed, Rogernomics, State Owned Enterprise*)

retaining wall: A retaining wall (hopefully) retains the dirt behind it. This tends to keep that same dirt from coming down and filling your yard and your home, or the public street. (see: (a) *slip*)

Returning Resident Visa: This used to be called a Re-entry Permit. If you become a resident of New Zealand, but not a citizen, then go to the Department of Labour and Immigration before going overseas on a trip and get one of these, it is good for four years and is reluctantly renewable. They prefer you to apply for citizenship if you are still around after 3 years. (Yes you may hold dual U.S. & N.Z. citizenship, if you are careful to touch all the right bases in the process of acquiring your N.Z. citizenship; be sure to contact the U.S. consulate first, in writing, and tell them what you plan to do and that you 'have no intention of giving up your U.S. citizenship.') If you return to N.Z. without a Returning Resident Visa, citizenship or a new visitor's visa you will find the Immigration folks here can be just as bloody minded as their U.S. counterparts and that is very bloody minded indeed. (see: *bloody minded, bloody*)

reveille: Yes it's still that awful 'You've got to get up in the morning sound' but it is pronounced 're-valley.' (see: *last post, beaut*)

return ticket: This allows you to return, it is a ROUND TRIP TICKET.

Rice Bubbles: *RICE CRISPIES.*

right: Used as an adjective, this adds EMPHASIS WITHOUT MEANING, somewhat as 'real' is used in the United States. 'Sam is a right twit.' 'Sam is a real idiot.'

right oh or **rightey oh:** OKAY. (see: *jolly dee*)

ring: TELEPHONE or call. (see: *ring off, call*)

ring off: N.Z. has recently gone digital phone happy in a big way but in the not too distant past (i.e., within living memory) one turned a crank to get the operator's attention and turned it again to tell her you were done. The crank is gone but this expression meaning to HANG UP the phone lingers on, especially with those of mature years. (see: *ring, call*)

rise: An increase in pay in North America would be called a RAISE.

rissole: It looks like a hamburger, its taste is indescribable but it ain't good.

rock melon: No one will recognize the word CANTALOUPE, but that's what it is.

Rogernomics: When the Labour government was elected in 1984 the Minister of Finance was Roger Owen Douglas. It turned out that he appeared to be the only member of the new government who had a coherent, comprehensive economic policy. As the incoming government found that it had inherited a considerable economic mess this policy was seized upon by the new government as the only answer in sight and applied holus bolus. It so happened that the policy in question was one which would have seemed much more appropriate to a right wing than a left wing party. Composed of equal parts of Friedmanite (Milton) monetarism and laissez faire capitalism, with a concomitant dose of user pays. While both Roger Douglas and the Prime Minister he served and then quarreled with have left their former portfolios the policy marches on, seemingly, still for lack of an alternative. The policy fits the international zeitgeist; Thatcher and Reagan (I don't yet know about Bush) seem a trifle trendy liberal in economic policy in contrast. I'd love to criticize because the results in terms of individual suffering seem to be so great but, like the rest of the Labour government, I can't offer a comprehensive alternative either. (see: *restructuring, dole, auroraed, State Owned Enterprise, Minister of Finance, Prime Minister*)

Roman fingers: High school slang for the digits of a boy who, when juxtaposed to a member of the opposite sex, can't keep his hands to himself. Upon reading the preceding, a lady friend said that it's really the W.H.B. or 'Wandering Hands Brigade'.

*root: (A) Root most often means COPULATE. Therefore Kiwis find an American who says 'I live on route 69' absolutely sidesplitting. (see: (a) *naughty, Randy, have it off, have it away, shag, stuff, on with, bit of crumpet, false friends*)

　　　(B) The underpinnings of a plant.

rough as guts: UNCOUTH.

rough enough: Means CLOSE ENOUGH as in a 'rough enough estimate'.

(a) round: Is a ROUND OF DRINKS, or the purchase by you of one drink for every member of your party. Since it is very impolite to drink other people's booze without shouting your own round it is a good move to buy the first or second round. This enables you to depart gracefully should you find yourself flagging, or wish to depart for some other reason. (see: *shout*)

round the bend — round the twist: This is the corner one is assumed to have turned when your behavior becomes so aberrant that the little men in white coats are called. INSANE.

rowsie: A ROUSABOUT who works in a shearing gang, providing unskilled labour. (see: *shearing gang, sheep, wide comb, blows, primary products*)

R.S.A.: RETURNED SERVICEMEN'S ASSOCIATION. N.Z.'s equivalent of the American Legion.

RSJ: Rolled Steel Joint. The N.Z. name for an T BEAM like those that form the skeletons of skyscrapers.

rubber: Not what you wear on your feet (those are galoshes), not what you wear elsewhere (see: *french letter, false friends*), but the bit of gum arabic that you use to remove your pencilled errors. An ERASER.

rubbish: (A) Substitute this word wherever you would normally use the words GARBAGE or TRASH. Hence a garbage can or trash can becomes a rubbish tin. A garbage dump becomes a rubbish tip, etc. (see: *tin, tip*)

      (B) To 'rubbish' someone is to administer a PUT DOWN, often using ridicule. (see: *take the mickey*)

ruddy: If you are too refined (or inhibited) to say (see:) BLOODY, which rates two asterisks, you can swear mildly by saying ruddy. Euphemisms for swear words themselves become guilty by association.

rude: To a North American rude means impolite. To a Kiwi it usually means LEWD or obscene.

rugby or **rugger:** N.Z. football, 15 men to a side, 40 min. half, 5 min. half time, spiked boots but no protective clothing. (see: *football* or *footie, All Blacks, sprigs, hooker*)

run holder: Does this conjure up images of someone successfully restraining a case of Montezuma's revenge?

    A run holder is the LEASE HOLDER on a cattle or sheep station when the government actually owns the land. (see: *high country station, station, sheep station, muster, cocky*)

runner beans or scarlet runners: These are STRING BEANS which grow (run) up any convenient trellis, tree, chair or anything else that stands still long enough. (see: *marrow, buttercup, butternut, veges*)

S

Saaday: The day after Friday. (see: *gidday*)

St John's Ambulance Service or just **St John's:** The shortened form of the name of the organization that provides 75% of all Ambulance and paramedic service in New Zealand. The full name is the 'PRIORY IN NEW ZEALAND OF THE MOST VENERABLE ORDER OF THE HOSPITAL OF ST JOHN OF JERUSALEM'. This is a direct descendant of one of the religious orders of chivalry ('Hospitalers') that tried very hard to liberate the 'holy land' from the 'infidel'. (see: *Zambuck*)

salesclerk: SALESMAN or SALESWOMAN. (see: *clerk, Are you being served?*)

(the) **Sallies:** Saturday night concerts in the Town square (you can't fault their enthusiasm), good works galore, involved in nearly every worthwhile project designed to help individuals in need in New Zealand. Tamborines, comic opera uniforms and all, the SALVATION ARMY is much more a part of the daily fabric of life in New Zealand than it is in the U.S. They also run a couple of surprisingly good (non-alcoholic) hotels called the *People's Palaces*. These are clean, cheap, and the food is good and they are conveniently located in Auckland and Wellington. Recommended for the budget traveler.

salt and pepper shakers: Another instance where the painstakingly acquired knowledge of a lifetime will totally mislead you. The shaker with one hole (or very few holes) in the top is the salt; the shaker with multiple small holes in the top is the pepper. (see: *backwards*)

sand hill: Those heaps of sand on the beach. A SAND DUNE.

sandfly: The scourge of New Zealand as far as tourists are concerned. Most especially found on the West Coast (of the South Island), these gnat-sized flies swarm like gnats and bite like mosquitoes (the really vicious kind). I recommend the liquid form of an insect repellent called *DIMP*; smear it on all exposed skin surfaces liberally and also put some on reachable surfaces that aren't exposed. Don't let them keep you away from Milford Sound's magnificent scenery, but go prepared! (see: *West Coast*)

sandshoes: TENNIS SHOES. (see: *gym boots*)

sandpit: The SANDBOX in which your children play(ed). This is where your kids go to have a good time and bring you home two shoesfull of sand. It does not refer to the box in which your cat defecates (N.Z. cats go outside and often stay there all night). (see: *dirt box, Charlie Browns, cat, moggy*)

sandwich: Presumably named after the 4th Earl of Sandwich famous in other ways. 'For corruption and incapacity, Sandwich's administration is unique in the history of the British navy.'

James Cook (second European discoverer of N.Z., the Dutchman Abel Tasman is said to have gotten here first) also discovered and named the Sandwich Islands (Hawaiian Islands). Alas, the name didn't stick but his discovery did. The New Zealand sandwich wouldn't, however, be given houseroom by Dagwood. It consists of what you would consider one slice of bread cut down the middle to make two very thin slices. Between these slices is put one miniscule layer of (usually) a single substance such as a thin slice(s) of tomato or *Vegemite* or *Marmite*. (see: *Marmite* and *Vegemite, filled roll, bread rolls, doorstops, Tasman*)

(the) *Sanitarium*: This is not where your aberrant Uncle George has been spending his declining years. It's a company that manufactures and sells 'HEALTH FOODS' (in a nationwide chain of STORES called *Sanitarium stores* or just *Sanitarium*).

Saturday paper: In North American the Saturday edition of any daily paper tends to be the thinnest, least imposing and least worthwhile in terms of classified advertisements. In New Zealand, the dailies don't publish on Sunday, so the Saturday paper is the closest equivalent to a North American Sunday PAPER and has all the ads and some of the supplements. (see: *backwards, Sunday papers, local rag*)

sausage dog: DACHSHUND. (see: *Alsatian, dogs*)

saveloy: A banger (SAUSAGE) in disguise, it looks like a fat red hotdog and is an acquired taste. Not recommended. (see: *bangers, alpine sticks*)

savouries: HOT FINGER FOOD that consists of a pastry shell around meat or some other non-sweet, non-dessert food. (see: *savoury pies*)

savoury pies: Hot meat pies, or bacon and egg pies (the latter, apple pie sized, is the most usual way of serving bacon and eggs). This applies to any kind of non-sweet pie. (see: *meat pies, mince pies, savouries*)

scats: For the North Island this usually refers to thick cushions scattered on the floor to make sitting there comfortable. In the South Island it usually refers to a close relation, the OTTOMAN or footstool. (see: *humpty, pouf*)

school: Is a term that refers to primary, intermediate and secondary schools only. It does not refer to preschool education (see: *kindy, playcentre, creche*) or tertiary education. Note that the ages given below (except that children start school on their fifth birthdays, if school is operating, no matter when it falls in the school year) are approximate. (see: *Normal school, Uni, varsity, Teachers College*)

New Entrants	Ages 5 – 5½
J (junior) 1	Ages 5 – 6
J (junior) 2	Ages 6 – 7
Standards 1,2,3,4	Ages 7 – 11
Standards 5,6 or Forms 1,2	Ages 11 – 13
Forms 3,4,5,6,7	Ages 13 – 18

(see: *college, grammar school*)

School Cert.: Or School Certificate. Those of you from the Empire State will be familiar with the REGENTS EXAMS. School Certificate exams are national examinations taken at age 15 – 16 (end of fifth form) by every student. A student elects the subjects in which s/he wishes to be examined. Results are reported for each subject on a 7 point scale A1, A2, B1, B2, C1, C2 & D. In major subjects (which practically everyone takes) such as English 66% got B2 or better in 1988. Students take more than one subject (up to six) and can repeat the exam in later years. (see: *Bursary, school, college, College of Education, U.E.*)

school holidays: From MID DECEMBER TO THE END OF JANUARY the kids are on holiday. Consequently most families take their vacation in this period. This means that (unless you are on a package tour) you had better arrange accommodation in advance, even to reserving sites at motorcamps. This of course applies to resort areas; the cities are empty. Also public transportation is heavily booked during this period, so plan early. This also applies to the term breaks in May and August when the kids are let off the hook for 2 – 3 weeks, depending on their educational level. (see: *January, Christmas, motorcamps*)

school uniform: Many secondary school pupils wear uniforms. Independent of climate those in public schools seem to wear (for the boys) grey shorts, grey knee socks and grey V-necked sweaters with green trim around the collar. The girls usually wear the same colors but add a skirt, white blouse and a necktie (there's a role reversal for you). From the fifth form on, things are usually a bit classier, with the older boys in blazers, ties and long pants and the girls in a feminine version of the same.

I thought this was terrible until hearing a female American Field Scholar (a U.S. high school exchange student) saying that she liked wearing the uniform since it eliminated the clothing competition between girls which she was used to in the U.S. I've been reduced to a position of ambivalence. (see: *school, college*)

Scobie duck: MUSCOVY DUCK.

scoff: To EAT RAPIDLY. 'If you keep scoffing down your food like that you'll get an ulcer, or give me one.' This term is only rarely used to mean ignore/poke fun at, as in scoffing at the law. (see: *snaffle, snarf, false friends*)

scone: An (when hot) utterly delicious BAKING POWDER BISCUIT. Literally melts in your mouth. (see: *biscuit, water biscuit*) Occasionally used to refer to one's HEAD as in 'use your scone'. (see: *bun, bread*)

Scotch chest: A large chest of drawers with (usually) a single drawer across the top and an arrangement of five drawers filling the next space (two small drawers in a vertical arrangement to the right and left of the center and a square drawer equal in displacement to two of the small drawers, in the middle) and three or four full width drawers below this.

Scotch poke: When playing cards one can cut the deck by removing a set of cards from the middle and putting them on top without disturbing the bottom cards. In the U.S. this is crudely known as a WHOREHOUSE CUT. Makes you wonder about the origin of the term Scotch poke.

scratcher or **grunter:** After a long and tiring day when you finally lay your weary bones to rest, you do it on a scratcher. BEDS can of course be used for other activities.

screw: There are good screws and bad screws. Well, a good screw is a large SALARY, and a bad screw is a small one. The word also means what you think it does, so don't use it loosely, but don't assume it refers to sex if you hear it.

script: A PRESCRIPTION. 'Get the doctor to give you a script for some antibiotics.' The script will cost you a medical practitioners fee, but the drugs themselves are subsidized by the N.Z. government and are usually $5 per item unless the actual cost is less or you are a minor or a senior citizen ($2.00 per item). (see: *M.B. Ch.B., physician, false friends*)

scrubber: An adolescent GIRL WITH ROUND HEELS; teenage slang. (see: *lusty wench, town bike*)

scrum: An orderly free-for-all in rugby which determines which side gets a ball that is in dispute. (see: *hooker, All Blacks*)

seagulls: (A) seagulls occupy the social and economic position in New Zealand that pigeons do in North America; although there are usually a few pigeons around trying to make a living off their leavings. It is seagulls that will panhandle you in the park, swarm over the rubbish tip and provide the only reminder of animal life, other than man, downtown. They are, by large, more aggressive and enterprising beggers than pigeons in that they are most adept at stealing what isn't offered.

(B) A part time or seasonal STEVEDORE on the docks. (see: *wharfies*)

seal: Performing at Marineland in Napier. The performing sea leopard is most impressive. Otherwise short for TARSEALED ROAD. (see: *metal, pavement*)

(the) season: The season is for killing. TIME TO SLAUGHTER all those cattle and sheep that provide steaks and chops for New Zealand and the rest of the world. The season begins October – November, and finishes around June. The further south you go, the later it starts and finishes. Industrial unrest in the freezing works always reaches a peak at the beginning of the season as this is when the freezing workers have the most clout. (see: *freezer*, (the) *works, freezing works, abattoir, works, gemel, primary products, terms of trade*)

seasoned topside: BEEF WITH STUFFING (stuffing reminiscent of your last Thanksgiving dinner). (see: *colonial goose, topside*)

seasoning: (A) The salt, pepper and other condiments that you put on your food to increase its palatability and consequently your family's girth.

(B) The STUFFING that you ladle into your Thanksgiving or Christmas turkey. Stuffing is a rude word, seasoning merely a fattening one. (see: *rude*)

seasons: Backwards of course. Summer is December, January and February, one spends Christmas on the beach. Winter is June, July and August, skiing time; March, April and May are Autumn. (Kiwis find the word Fall peculiar in the extreme) and September, October and November are Spring. (see: *Christmas, January, backwards*)

section: A section is a section of ground or a building LOT. 'You've got a nice section Sam. Grow all those shrubs yourself?' (see: *property*)

see you round like a rissole: The 'like a rissole' is meaningless noise (except that rissoles are usually round). It just means I'LL BE SEEING YOU. (see: *rissole*)

semi-detached: If you live in a DUPLEX it is 'semi-detached'.

sent down the road: To be relieved of the necessity of returning to your place of employment as a result of involuntary separation from your employer. FIRED. (see: *down the road, gave him the boot, get the boot, auroraed, restructuring, dole*)

sent up: Someone who has been sent up hasn't gone to prison. He or she has been successfully MOCKED. (see: *take the mickey*)

service: This is provided by bulls for cows and stallions for mares, resulting in calves and foals. Sheep have another word for it. (see: *tupping*)

serviette: What the gentlefolk use at the dinnertable to wipe their mouths after eating. A NAPKIN isn't the same by any other name. (see: *napkin, false friends*)

sesquicentennial: Sesqui means 1 and $\frac{1}{2}$ times and centennial is 100 years so sesquicentennial is 150 years. 1990 was the one hundred fiftieth anniversary of the signing of the Treaty of Waitangi and this signing is the event which brought the political entity called New Zealand into legal existence. Therefore in 1990 N.Z. had a year long birthday party. Not as big a deal as the U.S. bicentennial but big enough. (see: *Treaty of Waitangi, Waitangi Day*)

shadow cabinet ministers: The members of cabinet are those members of the majority party in Parliament, the legislative branch of government, elected by their colleagues, to run the executive branches of government (like making a Senator, Secretary of State).

The PARTY OUT OF POWER also chooses a spokesperson for each of these areas. These SPOKESPEOPLE are collectively called the shadow cabinet, just as the spokespeople of the majority party (called Ministers) make up the cabinet. (see: *Parliament, caucus, boys on the hill, Prime Minister, Minister of Finance, National Party, Labour Party*)

shag: (A) to juxtapose a male and female of the human species in such a way that species perpetuation may result if deliberate precautions are not taken. (see: *have it off, get one away, stuff, root, on with, (a) naughty, bit of crumpet*)

(B) 'gidday shag', hi BUDDY. (see: *gidday*)

(C) A SEABIRD (cormorant) most subspecies of which have a comical topknot.

shandy: The ladies who don't particularly like alcohol will have a MIXTURE of LEMONADE (*Sprite*) AND BEER when dragged to the hotel. Sounds ghastly, surprisingly doesn't taste half bad. (see: *lemonade, hotel, half bad*)

shank's pony: The old grey mare ain't what she used to be (ON FOOT or SHANK'S MARE).

sharebroker: The man from Merrill, Lynch, Pierce, Fenner and Te Raparaha. Your friendly neighborhood STOCKBROKER.

sharemilker: You own the farm, I own the cows and look after them and milk them, receiving a share of the milk or the profit therefrom. A sharemilker is SOMETHING LIKE A TENANT FARMER.

shark and tatties: Another way of saying (see:) *fish and chips* that emphasizes the usual ingredient of the fish segment. Don't turn up your nose, it's good!

she: Replaces IT in all kinds of sentences. 'She's a good old bucket of bolts.' 'She'll be right, mate.' 'She's a cold one today.' (see: *she'll be right*)

shearing gang: A group of scissor happy barbers who roam the streets searching for Australian collaborators; well no, but it's an

146

interesting fantasy. Try a GROUP OF people (SHEARERS) working for an independent contractor who move from farm to farm shearing the wool from N.Z.'s 67,470,000 sheep. (see: *rowsie, Golden Shears, sheep, blows, wide comb, primary products*)

sheep: N.Z. (in 1986) has 67,470,000 of these (and 3,307,084 people). The Kiwi economy lives off the sheep's chops, wool, and hides; the rest is window dressing. (Well, there are 8,279,000 cattle and 392,000 farmed deer plus horticulture and forestry). (see: *primary products, overseas funds, terms of trade, freezing works, hogget, two-toothed ewe, a lamb is a sheep before you've carried it very far, lambing, shearing gang, wide comb, blows, rowsie, Golden Shears*)

sheep station: SHEEP FARM. (see: *station, run holder*)

sheila: A sheila is a FEMALE of the human species. Ah! You've heard that before; but where? Probably from your grandparents or parents since this description was current in North America in the 1920's and 30's. It is everyday speech, neither laudatory or derogatory, like calling a man a bloke.

I have been told by a modern lady that 'sheila' raises her hackles, 'even if the blokes don't mean to be derogatory' and a recent newspaper article suggests that you would be safer strolling about a war zone than using this word in mixed company in Auckland. (see: *bird, bloke, bit of crumpet, bit of fluff*)

she'll be right mate: It has been argued that this is the N.Z. philosophy. In general it suggests 'everything for the best in this best of all possible worlds', and in specific it means DON'T WORRY, IT WILL WORK OUT O.K. In 1990 the remaining optimists can meet in a phone booth.

shifting: When you transfer your family and worldly goods from one place to another in the U.S. you are MOVING. The same process in New Zealand is called shifting. You might move from one chair to another, but you shift house.

shilling: Occasionally someone will hand you a coin that has shilling written on it, or a friend will ask you to loan her a shilling. This used to be $^{1}/_{20}$ of a pound in pre-1967 currency; now it is a DIME. Don't however, say 'dime' to a Kiwi, they don't savvy the term! You must say 'ten cents'. (see: *decimalisation, pound, quid, bob, sixpence, penny, Kiwi*)

shirty: VERBALLY UNPLEASANT/NASTY. A euphemism used for the similar sounding word meaning: covered with fecal material. 'That shirty workman told me that if I wanted his mess cleaned up I should do it myself.

*shit hot: DAMN GOOD.

*shit stirrer: One who agitates troubled waters. TROUBLEMAKER. (see: *stirrer*)

shoe sizes: I have good news for those of you with big feet! You have smaller feet in New Zealand. In general, New Zealand shoes (made to British lasts) run one size larger than their U.S. counterparts. So if you wear a 13 in the U.S. you wear a 12 in New Zealand. A U.S. 6 is a N.Z. 5, etc.

I have bad news for those of you with big feet! It is damn difficult to get anything but work boots and 1940's brogues in N.Z. size 12's and nearly impossible to find larger sizes.

The ladies may have an additional problem. The British lasts used in New Zealand are designed for feet that are, on average, wider than the U.S. female foot of equal length. In consequence, the ladies may find themselves faced with a choice of too short, or too wide.

shop: (A) The thing you do in a store.

(B) A STORE. One does not go to the store, one goes to the shop, usually the shop on a nearby corner ('the corner shop'). (see: *bottle shop, milk bar, chemist's shop, bottle shop, tuck shop, Op shop, shop assistant, dairy*)

shop assistant: That's the title of the SALESMAN or SALESLADY who assists you to make your purchases. In many cases, particularly hardware stores, their assistance is real and practical as opposed to merely courteously taking your money. These people are also referred to as sales clerks. (see: *Are you being served?, sales clerk, shop*)

**short and curlies: PUBIC HAIR. I wasn't going to include this one, but when the caption 'The Short and Curly Show' appeared on the marquee of the legitimate theatre in Dunedin's octagonal town square, I felt it was truly a term in public usage. This was the name of the annual student capping concert. If it's this public, how can we ignore it? (see: *minge, privates, crutch — crutching, capping, capping concert*)

shorts: Bermuda shorts, knee socks, white shirt, jacket and tie are what the well dressed businessman will wear on a summer day.

shout: A pleasant sound — 'BUY', as in 'I'll shout you a drink' — a most welcome and common phrase in Kiwiland. Shouts are invariably reciprocated and I have been told that shouting a round 'is the best way to get everyone as drunk as possible, as fast as possible'.

It might interest you to know that a 'Yankee shout' means Dutch treat.

— Tight anyone? (see: (a) *round*)

shufti: This one came back from North Africa with those New Zealand troops who did make it back. A shufti is a RECONNAISSANCE.

'Let's take a shufti into town and look over that new store.' (see: *dekko*)

side: Remember as a kid choosing up sides for a ball game? Well, this term survives into adulthood in New Zealand where a ball TEAM is more likely to be referred to as 'the side', rather than 'the team'. There is a subtle distinction here, in that the All Black team comprises all the players, but the All Black side that played Wales, refers only to those players chosen to play against Wales in that particular match. (see: *All Blacks, test, match touring*)

sideboards: Them furry things you (men) wore on the side of your face about twenty years ago. SIDEBURNS.

silly galoot: STUPID IDIOT!

silverbeet: This has nothing to do with what we would normally call beets. It is instead a spinach-like green known in the United States as Swiss chard. (see: *veges, beetroot*)

(corned) silverside: A PICKLED (corned?) RUMP ROAST OF BEEF. Yeah, I know, but that's what my butcher said. (see: *topside, seasoned topside, butchery, T-bone*)

singlet: This esoteric garment is an old-fashioned sleeveless UNDERSHIRT. My grandfather used to wear one every day. In N.Z. they come in two major varieties, white and coloured (one variety). This is worn under one's shirt for warmth. Without central heating warm clothes to be worn indoors become very important. The second variety of singlet is black. This one is the sterotype farmers' uniform worn without an overshirt while doing any sort of hot work, e.g., shearing, mowing, etc. (see: *Fred Dagg, jersey, spencer, vest, shearing gang*)

sink a few: To CONSUME a number of glasses of BEER. (see: *beer, shout, brew*)

S.I.S.: The Security Intelligence Service, NEW ZEALAND'S C.I.A. Deserved or not, they have the image of ham-fisted clowns in trench coats, busy protecting secrets New Zealand hasn't got. The only headline making arrest I can recall was that of a former Permanent Secretary in the Trade and Industry Department who, although no longer working for the Government, was accused of selling trade secrets to the Soviet Union, i.e., he was accused of telling them the lowest price New Zealand would accept for some considerable quantity of meat and wool. Of course, he too, should not have had access to this information but like everywhere else, the old boy network functions very well in New Zealand and it was alleged that the information came to him through that route. He was acquitted. (see: *old boy network*)

sister: This can refer to those of your female relatives with whom you share one or more parents, and it can refer to the black-gowned lady

149

with the white headband who teaches in your local Catholic school; but it is most likely to refer to the (senior) NURSE who binds up your wounds and awakens you at 10.00 p.m. to give you a sleeping pill. (see: *matron*)

six o'clock swill: Prior to 9 October 1967, bars in New Zealand had to close at 6.00 p.m. (now they close at 10.00 p.m., often 12.00 p.m. on weekends and the house bar, for people staying in the hotel, has even more flexible hours). This meant that your average working man had to do his day's drinking between 5 and 6.00 p.m. I've had described to me pubs in which the floor was cement and the front of the bar stainless steel with a bit of a trough at the bottom. After all, if you only have one hour or less to do your day's drinking you don't want to waste time running to the grot. These places were hosed out after six.

As a social necessity then, hotels tended to have Public Bars for this kind of drinking and 'Ladies and Escorts' bars' (now called lounge bars) for more civilized tippling. (see: *public bar, lounge bar, hotel, beer, licensed hotel, booze barn, grot*)

sixpence: Is 5¢. This dates back to the days when there were 12 pence to the shilling and 20 shillings to the pound, the New Zealand unit of currency (pre-1967). Came decimalisation and shillings were easy to handle since there had been 20 shillings in a pound and a pound was set equal to $2.00 — a shilling naturally became 10¢. However, at 240 pence to the pound no such simple conversion was available for the sixpence. 200 divided by 6 is 33.33 but 200 divided by 5 is 40. So by a process of double-think if all 6d pieces became 5¢ pieces and all the pieces fall into place. (see: *decimalisation, shilling, bob, pound, quid, penny, false friends*)

6th Form Certificate: This is a cross between a high school transcript and a HIGH SCHOOL DIPLOMA. Scores on it are given from 1–8 in each subject where 1 is the best mark and 8 the worst. Universities and prospective employers now have to use these to make employment and future education decisions. (see: *U.E., school, School Cert., 6th Form Certificate, Bursary*)

ski bunny: This is a person of either sex who can be found in the ski lodge dressed to the nines but isn't often found on the slopes. (see: *varsity bunny*)

skinfull: Of booze. To be DRUNK is to have a skinfull. Evocative isn't it? Similarly one can have a skinfull of (be fed up with) another person. (see: *pissed, beer, boozer, hotel*)

skip or **mini skip:** A large trash container designed to be lifted and emptied mechanically by a specially equipped truck. Called DUMPSTERS in some parts of the U.S. As a verb, the word means the same as it does in North America. (see: *tip, rubbish, tin, kitchen tidy, false friends*)

skite: (A) BRAG. 'He's always skiting.'

(B) BRAGGART. 'Sam's just a skite. Don't pay any attention to him.'

skivvy: (A) An UNDERSHIRT.

(B) Someone who does MENIAL work.

skungy: 'That's the skungiest looking bloke I ever saw.' That's the most GRUBBY guy I've ever seen.

slack or **really slack:** NOT UP TO SCRATCH.

slack me off — slacked off: ANGER — ANGRY. 'You slack me off the way you go around skiting all the time.' You piss me off the way you go around bragging all the time. 'I've never been so slacked off in my life!' 'I've never been so angry in my life!' (see: *hacked off, skite*)

slap and tickle: An alternative, if not entirely descriptive, phrase referring to the mating rituals of Homo Sapiens. 'A little slap and tickle never hurt anyone.' PETTING. (see: (a) *bit*)

(on the) slate: In the days when paper was an expensive luxury English shopkeepers used to write their CHARGE ACCOUNT(s) on a piece of slate with chalk (remember 'chalk it up to experience!'?). The piece of slate is gone but the request to 'put it on the slate' remains in small shops.

Slikka Pads: green plastic bladders filled with liquid (water?) which can be frozen and then put into a chilly bin to keep your picnic cold. (see: *chilly bin, coolibah*)

(a) slip: This one shows. Slip is short for landslip, a minor landslide or SLIDE. This usually happens, as in the canyons of Los Angeles, when deforested areas get too much rain. (see: *retaining wall, false friends*)

slippers: Ladies' SHOES, especially dress shoes. (see: *false friends*)

slow coach: A correction supplied by one of my son's 5 year old classmates when I called my son a 'SLOW POKE'.

(a) smacker: An enthusiastic and noisy KISS. 'Give us a smacker'. 'Give us a kiss'.

Smarties: One of the brand names for the candy known in North America as *M&M's* ('Melt in your mouth, not in your hand'). The original version has now come to N.Z. but the generic names in widespread use are still *Pebbles* & *Smarties* (see: *Pebbles*)

smokes: CIGARETTES. (see: *ciggies*)

smoko: COFFEE BREAK, also known as morning tea or afternoon tea, it all depends on how you like to spend your breaks.

snaffle: (A) TO GRAB. 'He snaffled every one of those biscuits off the tray before anyone else had a look in'.

(B) to WOLF DOWN what you've grabbed. 'He snaffled his dinner like it was going out of style'. (see: *scoff, snarf, have a look in*)

snakes: There is no other reason to believe that Saint Patrick visited these shores but the total absence of snakes from New Zealand is certainly good circumstantial evidence. This absence has had some interesting results. A clinical psychologist friend calls 'Snake Phobia' the 'New Zealand phobia'. A Kiwi heading overseas for the first time is almost always worried about snakebite, to a certain extent, and otherwise sophisticated New Zealanders, when questioned about their expectations of other countries, surprisingly often come up with a fantasy about being met on the foreign tarmac by a carpet of slithering serpents.

snarf: to GOBBLE, as in eat. 'He snarfed up that steak as if he hadn't eaten for a week.' (see: *scoff, snaffle*)

snooker table: If you see something that looks like a pool table afflicted with elephantiasis, that's a snooker table.

Snowtex: The brand name for something that looks exactly like (in appearance, although much coarser in texture) *Kleenex* right down to the box design. It has, like *Kleenex* in the United States, or *Biro* (ball point pen) in New Zealand, become the word that describes the product as well as a brand name. The Australians have managed to manufacture genuine facial tissue texture tissues but Kiwis have yet to learn what a really soft tissue feels like. Mind you, this means that there are no 'wet strength' problems with the N.Z. variety. (see: *toilet paper, Biro, hoover, lux, Clayton's, Lilo, Witches Britches, Fairydown, Kleensak*)

Social Credit Political League: I don't understand Social Credit's policies. It's no excuse, but neither does anyone else of my acquaintance. Called the 'funny money' party by their opponents, popular wisdom has it that they would pay off the national debt just by printing more money. This has got to be too simplistic to be true. Social Credit is tied for third largest party in New Zealand (at 3% according to the latest, January 1990 polls) with the NLP or New Labour Party. The party currently called Social Credit is a schism of the Democratic party which was in turn a new name for (you guessed it) the Social Credit Political League (see: *Democratic Party, National Party, Labour Party, New Labour Party*)

**sod (you): Sod comes from sodomy and means to SODOMIZE. Not at all a genteel or friendly thing to say; it is an expression usually heard only in the heat of anger. A television comedy show used this as a gag line when an American lady turned up with her initials

S.O.D. prominently displayed on her purse. (see: *homosexuality, bugger, false friends*)

S.O.E.: (see:) *State Owned Enterprise*.

soldering bolt: A soldering bolt is a SOLDERING IRON, a soldering iron on the other hand is a gigantic soldering device. (see: *soldering iron, long-nosed pliers, spanner, bastard*)

soldering iron: This is not the dainty little device that you find in your usual electronic workshop. I've just weighed one in at 2 lbs. It is 2 inches in width in the body and one inch at the top. Some of my technical friends are a little dubious about calling it an iron as it is too small and is electrically operated, they think it is only an iron if it is a bar of steel you have to heat in a furnace. (see: *soldering bolt, long-nosed pliers, spanner, bastard, false friends*)

solicitor: Member of one of the oldest and best paid professions. In England, ATTORNEYS AT LAW come in two varieties. The backroom boys called solicitors, and the courtroom LAWYERS, called barristers. In New Zealand, as in the United States, these activities are usually combined in a single individual known in N.Z. as a 'Barrister and Solicitor'. (see: *false friends, barrister, brief*)

solo parent: divorced, widow, widower, or unmarried mum, if you stay home to look after your kid(s) you are entitled to special payments from the Department of Social Welfare. However, this support can be lost if the Department has reason to believe that you are living with someone in a condition approximating marriage, and they are said to have evolved some elaborate measures which include the number of meals you take with a particular person of the opposite sex and the number of nights his or her car is parked in front of your residence. Social Welfare beneficiaries have been known to object to this surveillance and regulation of their sex lives. Furthermore, they maintain that, as enforced, the rules encourage promiscuity and discourage lasting relationships, as seven one night stands in a week wouldn't break the rules, but seven nights with the same person would.

something to go on with: SOMETHING FOR THE MEANTIME. It could be money. 'I'll pay you Friday but there is something to go on with till then.' It could be work. 'That big assignment won't be ready till tomorrow but here is something to go on with, read pages 21–50 in the Kiwi-Yankee Dictionary'.

Sorry!: This is the standard Kiwi APOLOGY in a stand alone sentence consisting of one word. After I had spent a few months at Virginia Tech., on my last sabbatical, I was informed that the habit had spread to everyone in the laboratory.

South Island: 58,192 square miles. The largest single chunk of land under the New Zealand flag. It has marginally fewer sheep

(32,894,000 in 1986) and a lot less people (863,603, as of the 1986 census) than the North Island. In fact the whole South Island has fewer people than the Auckland area alone. The people (like me) who live there call it the mainland. There is a spectacular range of mountains, called (with startling originality) the Southern Alps, running down the spine of the South Island. This area provides good fishing, gorgeous hiking, skiing and for the more adventurous, exciting, if sometimes hairy, mountain climbing. (see: *Nelson, Marlborough, West Coast, Canterbury, Otago, Southland, mainland, North Island, inter-island, Auckland, Stewart Island*)

southerly: A wind from the south. Sound nice? This is a COLD WIND straight from the Antarctic wastes into your lap. In the southern hemisphere it is the word north that has echoes of sunshine, and summer, while the word south connotes cold, snow, and winter. (see: *northerly, southern exposure, northern exposure, backwards*)

southern exposure: If your house has a southern exposure that means it faces towards the south. This is a no-no! South is from whence the COLD winds blow and where the sun never shines! Design your home with northern exposure and save on heating bills and cold discomfort. (see: *northern exposure, southerly, northerly, backwards*)

Southland: This area is defined in different ways for different purposes. Very roughly it consists of the southern and southwestern part of the bottom of the South Island including, for statistical and administrative purposes, Stewart Island. It has a population of 104,618 people (1986 census), 43,000 domesticated (farmed) deer, 211,000 cattle and 9,314,000 sheep. Rich grazing country, spectacularly beautiful in the west (see: *Fiordland*) and a bit chilly in the winter by New Zealand standards. The principal city is Invercargill (metropolitan area population 52,807 in 1986). (see: *South Island*)

Southland slippers: Much of (see:) *Southland* is farmland and when it rains, venturing outside your farmhouse is a muddy business. So you keep a pair of RUBBER BOOTS on the porch and slip them on and off as you leave and enter the house. (see: *gumboots, Wellingtons*)

spanner: A WRENCH, you know, one of those devices for tightening bolts. (see: *long nosed pliers, bastard*)

spa pool: JACUZZI. Note that *Jacuzzi* is a U.S. brand name that has become a generic term. Before looking this up I thought it was a Norwegian word for a whirlpool bath.

(I'd better) **speed along:** 'I've GOT TO be GOING now.'

speedo: The SPEEDOMETER in your car. If you hear a strange term used by a Kiwi, try to think of a longer word whose contraction it could be. What an incredibly awkward sentence! (see: *veges, beaut, strawbs*)

spencer: An item of LONG-SLEEVED LADIES' UNDERWEAR, usually made of wool. Just the thing for those cold winter evenings indoors. (see: *singlet, undies, Witches Britches, vest, central heating*)

*spew: THROW UP. An important term in the macho beer drinking society of young men. (see: *technicolour yawn, *puke, chunder, drive the porcelain bus*)

spider: An ICE CREAM SODA, usually consisting of a dollop of vanilla ice cream in a Coke. Alternatively it can refer to our eight legged fly eating friends. (see: *katipo spider, false friends*)

splash out: SPEND UP LARGE. 'Bazzer really splashed out on his new car.' (see: *Bazzer*)

split: 'What kind of split do you want with your drink?' What kind of MIXER would you like with your alcohol? (see: *spot*)

spot: A SHOT of alcohol. (see: *split*)

spot on: EXACTLY RIGHT, or hit the spot. 'Your dinner was spot on.' 'Her explanation of the economic situation was spot on.'

spaghetti: Often comes in cans — is found on pizza, on toast for breakfast (a childhood favorite), and in sandwiches.

spray: A spray of flowers is the CORSAGE you take your girl when picking her up for the graduation ball. (see: *ball, ball frock, graduation ball*)

spread myself (thin): What does one reply when a very fat person announces that they have really 'spread themselves' to prepare an especially sumptuous meal? WORKED UNUSUALLY HARD.

Springbok tour: In 1981 an official South African rugby team (the 'Springboks') came to N.Z. Kiwis love their rugby, they are also part of a strongly egalitarian society that takes social justice very seriously. With the tour, the keenest of rugby fans and the strongest opponents of apartheid found themselves opposed to each other in the streets and rioting ensued. The police had to intervene on the side of the rugby fans who were engaging in a legal activity. Many people felt that some of them did this rather over-enthusiastically. South African sports teams will not get visas to visit N.Z. from the present (1990) government. (see: *Red Squad, long batons, tour, touring, All Blacks, test, side, Gleneagles agreement*)

sprigs: The cross between spikes and cleats found on the bottoms of rugby boots (see: *rugby*)

sprog: (A) an INFANT.

(B) any human OFFSPRING ('Your sprog')

(C) 'I'm sprogged'. I'm PREGNANT. (see: *up the spout — up the duff*)

squiz: 'Have a squiz at that'. Have a LOOK at that. (see: *dekko*)

s'story: THAT'S THE TRUTH or you're telling it like it is. 'Sam's a right bastard'. 'S'story'. (see: *quite*)

stamp duty: A TAX on financial transactions, such as cashing a travelers check.

stand for office: It has been argued that the 'pace of life' is slower in New Zealand than in North America. Perhaps this is a reflection of that 'pace' since we must RUN where a (see:) *Kiwi* need merely stand.

stand on your digs: This isn't an archaeological term. It is shorthand for STAND ON YOUR DIGNITY.

standover merchant: Your friendly neighborhood PROTECTION RACKET OPERATOR.

starkers: What a streaker is: STARK NAKED. (see: *in the nick*)

State Owned Enterprise: Many government departments and services like the post office, the railways and the telephone service have been turned into profit-making corporations, still owned by the government but run like a private business. The present (1990) government is in the process of selling off as many of these enterprises as possible to private interests (often foreign) and using the proceeds to retire some of the large national debt, particularly foreign debt. (see: *Post Office, Telecom N.Z., New Zealand Post, Works Corp., Radio N.Z. Ltd., Railways Corp. N.Z., Television New Zealand, Rogernomics, restructuring, auroraed*)

States or **Stateside:** Term used by American expatriates (temporary or permanent, voluntary or military) to refer to the land of Uncle Sugar (Sam to you).

station: There are railway stations, but the word usually refers to a farm or RANCH. (see: *cocky, high country station, false friends*)

steak and kidney pie: —Served hot in a slightly leathery pastry crust, this is a very tasty dish. Highly recommended if you can find it. (see: *meat pie, hot pies, mince pies, savouries*)

step on a crack and marry a rat: The old children's game is different down under; STEP ON A CRACK AND BREAK YOUR MOTHER'S BACK. The N.Z. version doesn't rhyme but at least the person who suffers is the one that stepped on the crack. Equity favors the Kiwi version while euphony favors the North American version. (see: *tig*)

Stewart Island: The smallest of New Zealand's three main islands (674 sq.miles), the least populous, 542 people (1986 census; which is down from 660 in 1981), and the fastest breeding (and dying) sheep in New Zealand, a reported 3 in 1976, 5087 in 1977, 3636 in 1979, 4219 in 1981 and 3048 in 1988. The 1988 figures also show 210 cattle and no domestic deer. It is almost the MOST SOUTHERLY OF THE INHABITED ISLANDS. In fact, there is damn all, besides 3000 miles of water, between Stewart Island and Antarctica. A great place to hike in the woods and, quite literally, get away from it all. (see: *mainland, North Island, South Island*)

sticking plaster: A BANDAID by another name. (see: *plaster, sticky tape, muslin*)

stickybeak: A stickybeak is someone who is always sticking their nose into other people's (usually your) business. A BUSYBODY. Some sources suggest that this term is derived from a (carefully unidentified) bird with honey-eating or moss feeding habits. Extensive research into the Australian (where the term appears to have originated) and New Zealand ornithological literature (by a distinguished ornithologist who kindly let himself be talked into the task) revealed no such bird name! I fear that these lexographers have been misled by the beak into assuming an origin without checking it. Never mind, I too would have liked to believe it was true. There is, however, a song from around the 60's (recorded on the *Kiwi* label, naturally) about 'Stickybeak the Kiwi' who invokes union demarkation rules and insists on pulling the sleigh in place of Santa's reindeer when they cross into the southern hemisphere. (see: *nosy parker, demarkation dispute*)

sticky tape: *Scotch Tape.* Evocative isn't it? Borrowed from Australia, this is the second most common term used for *Scotch Tape* (see: *Cellotape, drawing pins*)

sticky wicket: (A) A muddy or wet cricket playing field which leads to a bounced or batted ball showing much less life than on a (properly) dry playing field.

(B) A SITUATION in WHICH it IS DIFFICULT to do well. (see: *cricket, test, century, sticky wicket, wicket keeper*, etc., etc.)

stirrer: short for shit stirrer, a TROUBLEMAKER if you don't agree with him or her, a crusader if you do. If someone tells you that you've won the wooden spoon award, remember that is given for excellence in the stirring sport.

stockwhip: BULLWHIP; a more general term.

stockmarket quotes: In the U.S. the stockmarket is quoted in dollars and fractions of dollars. In N.Z. it is quoted in cents. Therefore a one point change in the U.S. is a one hundred point change in N.Z. Don't be fooled into overvaluing the N.Z. market or overestimating its volatility; both of which can happen if you forget to divide by 100.

stone: The weight of people (only) is calculated in stones. One stone equals FOURTEEN POUNDS. If someone says that he weighs 14 stone 9, he weighs 205 lbs. When it comes to human weights Kiwis think in stones and find the equivalent in lbs or kilos conceptually meaningless. (see: *pound, false friends*)

stones — stone fruit: stones are PITS and stone fruit are those cherries, apricots, plums, peaches, etc. that have a pit.

stonkered: (A) WORN-OUT — exhausted. 'I'm stonkered. Wasn't in condition to do the Milford Track as free walk, and I should have bloody well known it.' (see: *free walk, stuffed, buggered, knackered, beggared, clapped out*)

(B) INEBRIATED (see: *pissed, skinfull*)

straight away: You can't race your car on this one. 'Do it straight away.' Do it IMMEDIATELY. (see: *false friends*)

strap: a verb suggesting energetic contact between a length of leather and a child's hand or rear end. (see: *get the strap, cane*)

strawbs: STRAWBERRIES. (see: *veges, billberries, beaut*)

strides: Not what you do but what you wear when you are doing it. TROUSERS. (see: *false friends*)

strong-eyed bitch, strong-eyed dog: WORKING DOGS (female and male respectively) that exercise remarkable control over flocks of sheep or herds of cattle or deer or horses or geese seemingly just by crouching down and staring at them. The dogs are in turn instructed by the farmer's whistles. (see: *huntaway, dog trials, dogs, cocky*)

stroppy: RECALCITRANT. 'Young Trev is getting stroppy. I told him to clean up his room and he told me to do it myself.' (see: *Bazzer*)

'struth: a contraction of 'God's truth', meaning, SO HELP ME GOD. 'I saw a U.F.O. last night 'struth.'

*stuff: ENGAGE IN SEXUAL INTERCOURSE; although I must admit this one sounds a bit one sided. (see: (a) *naughty, shag, have it off, get one away, root, on with, false friends, bit of crumpet*)

stuffed: (A) BEAT — worn out. It most probably originally referred to 'post coitum' (see: *stuff*). However, it is now a reasonably polite term for tired, no matter how this state was achieved. 'After playing footie, (football) all day, I was too stuffed to go to the party in the evening.' (see: *football* or *footie, buggered, beggared, stonkered, clapped out*)

(B) It was probably used at first to refer to worn out machinery, as it does to tired people, but has come to refer to any BROKEN mechanism. 'This watch of mine is totally stuffed.'

sulky: No horses hitched to this one. It's a BABY BUGGY sometimes made of woven cane. (see: *pram, pushchair*)

sultana: An incompletely dried out RAISIN (usually from Australia). Sultanas, sometimes called 'golden raisins' are juicier and tastier than raisins.

sunbeams: When you are clearing the table after a meal and you find SILVERWARE THAT HASN'T BEEN USED and can be returned to the drawer without washing, these items are sunbeams.

sun shower — summer shower: Remember California sunshine, the liquid kind that falls from the sky? This is a short RAINFALL WITH the SUN still SHINING brightly.

Sunday papers: The daily papers in New Zealand do not have Sunday editions. Instead there are a series of independent weekly papers dealing with sports and/or scandal. Most of these are nationwide papers (unlike the dailies) and could be fairly described as the YELLOW PRESS. (see: *Saturday paper, false friends, local rag*)

super: (A) Superphosphate is the farmers' favorite FERTILIZER and one of the reasons for New Zealand's high pastoral productivity. It is usually spread by dropping it from light aircraft. Most of this super comes from aeons of layers of guano (bird droppings) deposited on the island of Nauru and which gives Nauru the highest per capita income in the South Pacific. Unfortunately, this very natural resource is likely to be exhausted in around 10 years. The Nauru government and some consortiums of individuals are taking foresighted steps, investing their surplus capital in real estate and other income producing enterprises in New Zealand and Australia against the evil day when bedrock replaces birddrop. Nauru is also importing topsoil to put into the cleared areas which would otherwise be incapable of growing anything. (see: *aerial topdressing, manure*)

(B) 96 octane PETROL. (see: *petrol*)

superannuation: SOCIAL SECURITY or retirement income.

supper: A snack before retiring, never refers to main evening meal. An evening party at home in New Zealand will almost always include a fairly substantial MEAL, called supper, SERVED 11:30–12:MIDNIGHT. (see: *dinner, tea*)

suspenders: aren't what holds up his pants, but rather what holds up her stockings. Suspenders are GARTERS and a suspender belt is a garter belt. (see: *braces, false friends*)

suss out: CHECK OUT or reconnoiter. You sussed out that situation really well.

sweets: A DESSERT of any kind. Would you care for sweets?' the waiter/waitress will ask you after the main course. (see: *entree*)

swedes: When the Vikings came to New Zealand. Well, no! but it makes a good story. Swedes are RUTABAGA a very large variety with firm white flesh. Driving through the countryside at harvest time, you will see roadside signs saying swedes $2.50 (or whatever) a sack. (see: (to) *come off the turnips, marrow, beetroot*)

swept up: FANCY, elegant, elaborate. 'That's a swept up new car you've got'. (see: *flash, tarted up, false friends*)

switches: Light switches, appliance switches, all kinds of switches, they are UPSIDE DOWN. Flipping up a switch turns it off; flipping it down turns it on. You may curse your own habits when trying to turn on a light in a dark room but take heart, there is a lot of U.S. gear, especially computer equipment, in New Zealand and the Kiwis find it just as hard to adapt as we do. (see: *hot points, backwards*)

swiz: A RIPOFF. 'It would take a major expedition to find any fruit in the fruit cake. What a swiz'.

swot: study-CRAM. 'I'm going to swot up on that subject.' During the period just before final exams, campuses are very thinly populated. Everyone is holed up, swotting.

swish: Ain't he sweet? How would you like to be called swish? Don't be upset. In New Zealand it is a compliment, meaning ELEGANT or SPIFFY. (see: *flash, false friends*)

T

T-bone: You know what a T-bone steak is, there's a big T shaped bone with a sirloin on one side and a fillet on the other. Well, in New Zealand, you get the bone and the sirloin but the fillet has been cut out for separate sale. (see: *fillet, butchery, false friends*)

ta: 'That was kind of you, ta.' That was kind of you, THANKS. (see: *thanks, you shouldn't have done that!*)

ta-ta: BYE-BYE. To go ta-tas is to go away. This is largely babytalk but as a cultural constant it is likely to be heard in almost any company.

T.A.B.: The Totalisator Agency Board; New Zealand's government owned BOOKIE PARLOR (betting shop for the Canucks). Takes bets as small as one dollar on all of the trots and gallops in New Zealand and some of the Aussie ones. (see: (have a) *flutter, trots, gallops, punt, punter, punting, divy*)

table a motion: Listening to Parliament you will often hear 'let it lie upon the table.' To a Kiwi (or a Pom) this means PUT IT ON THE AGENDA, while, to you and me it means to put it off for a future (perhaps indefinitely future) time. 'Sir Winston Churchill records that this confusion in meaning was the cause of a great deal of annoyance among the Allied leaders in World War II.' (see: *false friends*)

tablespoon: equivalent to a large U.S. SERVING SPOON. (see: *false friends*)

take: Where you might hold out a tray of chocolate and say, 'HAVE one' a Kiwi would hold out the same tray and say 'take one'. (see: *Kiwi, toilet*)

take a sickie: GOLDBRICKING. To take a day off ostensibly on account of sickness. 'Well I was sick of work'. (see: *9 o'clock flu, wag school*)

take-aways: Food TO GO. Whenever I refer to food 'to go' my Kiwi wife, who finds this phrase ridiculous for some unfathomable reason, says 'to go where?' Fast food places are called 'take away bars'.

(to) **take the mickey** (out of someone): is to RIDE them unmercifully. A friend recently described a scene in his local pub where someone was trying to take the mickey out of one of the local characters by imitating everything he did. After this had gone on for about thirty minutes the victim leapt upon the table and did a down trou. This was not imitated nor has any further attempt been made to take the mickey out of this particular character. (see: *sent up, down trou, drop your tweeds, brown eye*)

take to your scrapers: 'TAKE TO YOUR HEELS' or 'cheese it'. To depart at a run.

talk the hind leg off a horse: We all know somebody(ies) with this unfortunate talent. A LONGWINDED individual.

talking to the big white telephone: Leaning over the toilet to dispose of whatever over-indulgence you have been engaging in. (see: *Technicolor yawn, chunder, driving the porcelain bus, *spew, *puke, Wizard of Christchurch*)

talking with a plum in his mouth: You are in no danger of facing this accusation. It suggests that the individual is AFFECTING AN UPPER CLASS ENGLISH ACCENT, putting on airs. (see: *Pom — Pommie*)

tallboy: This prospective basketball player is made of wood, stands about 4 ft tall and has 4–5 drawers. It's the name for a TALL CHEST OF DRAWERS without a mirror mounted on top, sometimes called a highboy in the U.S. (see: *lowboy, duchesse*)

tamarilloes: A goose egg sized and shaped red FRUIT with a hard outer rind (not eaten) and a jelly-like inside with scattered seeds looking like red passion-fruit pulp. The name tamarillo was especially invented for the United States market as the New Zealand name, (see:) *tree tomatoes*, was not considered either descriptive or glamorous enough. (see: *Chinese gooseberries*)

tandem: A BICYCLE BUILT FOR TWO. There are tandems for rent at most resorts, and even tandem races.

tangi: A tangi is a Maori funeral.

taniwha: pronounced 'tanifa'. A SEA MONSTER in Maori legend. Of late they have been portrayed as benevolent monsters. (Puff the Magic Dragon?)

Tapanui Flu: Named after the town in which it was first identified in New Zealand, Tapanui Flu or M.E. (Myalgic Encephalomyelitis) is a disorder who's main symptom is pervasive lethargy on the part of the sufferer. There has been a controversy as to whether this was a convenient medical term for a psychological disorder, however, the balance of medical opinion now seems to be shifting toward a viral basis for this problem and outbreaks in other parts of the world that have been given other names are being recognized as the same disorder.

tapu: TABOO, e.g., burial grounds, tohunga, heads. Maori tapus still occasionally re-route roads or re-site buildings. (see: *tohunga, tangi*)

Taranaki: Taranaki was named for its most prominent feature, (Taranaki is the Maori name for Mt Egmont) a Fuji-like perfect cone shaped volcanic mountain that stands 8,264 feet high in isolated splendor. It consists of a large peninsular bulge of land three-quarters of the way down the west coast of the North Island, known as a dairying area (see: *Taranaki gate*). The volcanic land is lush and productive. This too is where the offshore Maui natural gas field's pipeline comes ashore and where part is reticulated around the North Island and part is run through a pioneering plant which makes gasoline out of natural gas. Population (1986 census) is 107,600 people, 1,672,000 sheep, 756,000 cattle and 9,000 farmed deer. The major metropolitan area surrounds and includes the city of New Plymouth having a population (1986 census) of 47,384. (see: *North Island, Motunui synthetic petrol plant*)

Taranaki Gate: An inexpensive and ingenious method of making a gate in your paddock fence. Named after one of New Zealand's richer dairying regions from which it has spread like gorse all over the countryside. This gate consists of two gateposts set deep in the earth. Firmly attached to one of the posts by loops of No. 8 fencing wire (the hinges) is a flexible, rectangular net of wire with a pole attached to the far end of the rectangle. This pole is in turn attached, top and bottom, to two loops of the same fencing wire that are firmly fastened to the farther gatepost. To open such a gate, you pull the top of the pole toward this gatepost and lift off the top loop. Then you let the pole sag in the other direction and lift it out of the bottom loop. To close the gate (and it is a gross misuse of hospitality not to), one reverses the process. The trick to closing the gate is to put the pole in that bottom loop first! (see: *cattle stop, Heath-Robinson apparatus, number 8 fencing wire, gorse, No.*)

tariff: The cost of your accommodation.

tarted up: something basically not beautiful or fancy has been GUSSIED UP. 'I tarted up my old bach by painting it yellow, then rented it to some American tourists for a month.' (see: *swept up, bach*)

(the) Tasman: That body of water (1200 miles across at its narrowest) that separates Australia and New Zealand. Named after a

Dutchman, Abel Tasman, who discovered it in 1642 (along with Tasmania) thereby earning himself a form of immortality but gaining his native land nothing at all in the first of his epic voyages. The TASMAN SEA. He named what is now Tasmania 'Van Dieman's Land' after the man who authorized the voyage and it kept that name for nearly 200 years. (see: *Trans-Tasman, Tasmania*)

tasty: Not long after a friend arrived in New Zealand she was at a luncheon and asked the person next to her, 'What kind of cheese is this?' 'It's tasty,' was the reply. 'Yes, it is,' she agreed. 'But what kind is it?!!' Tasty is a CATEGORY (or strength) OF CHEESE FLAVOR.

tats: There is an Australian LOTTERY called *Tattersalls* and one can purchase a 'Tatts' ticket in this relatively painless method of separating you from your money. OR, on the other hand if you are a criminal then your tats are the TATTOOS that you acquired from your fellow inmates during your last period in prison. (see: *boob, boobhead, gaol*)

tea: Refers to:
   (A) Mid-morning 'coffee' break
   (B) Mid-afternoon 'coffee' break
   (C) Evening meal
   (D) Occasionally any meal. As 'I'm going to get some tea.' 'Have you had your tea yet?'
   (E) The familiar tannic drink. If you want it black, say so, otherwise it is served with milk. If you want it iced you won't be considered any stranger than someone who wanted boiled *Coke* would be in the States. If someone decides to indulge this peculiar request of yours, you're likely to get a small glass of tepid tea with a single, small ice block in it. Be properly grateful! (see: *dinner, supper, ice block, smoko*)

tea chest: The favorite box used for moving purposes is a foil lined PLYWOOD CRATE roughly two feet high, 16 inches wide and 20 inches long, (there are also square ones that would be 20 inches wide and long) which originally entered the country carrying tea from Sri Lanka (Ceylon), India or Bangladesh (East Pakistan). The tea was in loose flakes in the box, so that if you go to your local tea importer (at least one in every main center) and pay them around $3 you can purchase one of these excellent containers with a few leaves still kicking around in the bottom. The other source of tea chests is from people who have moved here from other tea drinking nations (Great Britain, Canada, South Africa), who have usually sent some or all of their belongings in this fashion. In fact, shipping companies in those countries and in New Zealand use the tea chest as a unit of measure. If you say, 'I want to ship a tea chest', they don't ask how big or how heavy (except by air) but merely tell you how much. A warning to any Kiwis planning to send one back from overseas. Shipment to New Zealand may be slow but not too expensive. However, unless you are prepared to arrange Forestry (it's made of wood) Dept., Agriculture Department and Customs clearance yourself, it will probably cost slightly more than it did to send it to New Zealand to get the local moving company consignee to do these things for you, effectively doubling the cost of shipment. You can, however, pay the consignee company about $\frac{1}{3}$ of this amount for the privilege of allowing you to do these things yourself. Set aside two to four hours. Things will go faster if you hit the Government Departments at their 8 : 30 a.m. opening time, because they do not tend to be busy at this period.

tea towel: That household standby, the DISHTOWEL. It gets a bit more use in New Zealand than in North America, since dishwashers are less common in Godzone. (see: *tea, Godzone*)

Teachers' College: The former (and still the best recognized) name for what are now (as of Jan. 1, 1990) called Colleges of Education. This is a NORMAL SCHOOL in old U.S. parlance (a Normal School is something else here). It gives (teaching) 'Certificates', not degrees, after three years post high school study. (see: *College of Education, Uni, varsity, college, Normal School, School Cert., U.E.*)

tear off a tab — **tear off a scab: This is to OPEN a tear top CAN OF BEER. I must admit that the first time I heard the second description it made me too queasy to enjoy my beer. (see: *beer*)

technicolour yawn: To empty the contents of one's stomach through the oral orifice; often done as a response to an excess of alcohol in the system. (see: **spew, *puke, chunder, drive the porcelain bus*)

Telecom N.Z.: When the Post Office was restructured in 1987 Telecom N.Z. came into existence as a State Owned Enterprise on April Fool's day. Largely because of its mandate to act as a profit making corporation, it does not have the friendly efficient image of its Post Office predecessor. It also doesn't help that after its establishment it shed a very large percentage of its employees. In the U.S. I have heard the cry 'give us back our telephone company' after the major deregulation. That cry is being echoed by segments of the N.Z. population! The government (February 1990) has indicated that, for the right price, it would like to sell Telecom N.Z. Are you interested? Too late! Now (Aug. 1990), Telecom has been sold to a consortium of two U.S. phone companies. (see: *Post Office, New Zealand Post, Radio N.Z. Ltd., Railways Corp. N.Z., Television New Zealand, Rogernomics, restructuring, auroraed*)

telephone boxes: TELEPHONE BOOTHS. Telecom N.Z. appears to have just lost a battle with the Wizard of Christchurch. Telecom proposed painting all the traditionally red phone boxes yellow and blue. The Wizard (passively and noisily supported by many others) got out his paintpot and changed the Christchurch ones back to red as fast as they turned yellow. It appears that the power of Wizardry is not dead. All over the country telephone boxes are being refurbished in, you guessed it, red! (see: (the) *Wizard of Christchurch, Telecom N.Z., trad*)

telephone dials: As far as I can tell, New Zealand is the only place in the world where the numbers on telephone dials go from 9–0 rather than from 1–9 plus 0. Don't try to dial blind, you'll end up 180 degrees out of phase. Even some digital phones imported from overseas run their numbers backwards to make them correspond to the N.Z. phone computer system. (see: *tolls, backwards*)

television licence: In the U.S. one must have a license to broadcast. In N.Z., as in Britain, one must have an annual LICENSE TO OPERATE A TELEVISION RECEIVER. Technically known as the Public Broadcasting Fee this license fee ($74 per annum for black and white and $110 per annum for color) supports the two commercial-free radio networks (the National and Concert programmes), some of the programming on all three TV channels (both the two government owned ones and TV3), the New Zealand Symphony Orchestra, Maori radio, etc. All commercial sales of TV sets are reported to the Public Broadcasting Office and if licenses are not subsequently purchased by the TV purchasers the matter is followed up by letter or phone call. There is a mythology, probably borrowed from Great Britain where it does happen, that detector vans roam the streets pinpointing houses with TV's in operation and comparing their addresses with those of license holders. While the technology exists, I am assured that this has never happened in N.Z. and that the technology has only been used to detect sources of TV interference. Anyone who was misled by this entry in the previous edition of the *Kiwi-Yankee Dictionary*, please accept my apology. (see: *B.C.N.Z., Radio N.Z. Ltd., Television New Zealand., national programme, concert programme, wireless, Proms, TV3*)

Television New Zealand: This is the State Owned Enterprise that operates TV1 and TV2. (see: *B.C.N.Z., Radio N.Z. Ltd., State Owned Enterprise, national programme, concert programme, wireless, TV3*)

(a) tell-tale: This is your childhood TATTLETALE. After all, that's what a tattletale does; s/he tells-tales, unfortunately usually true ones, which the protagonist wishes kept confidential. (see: *tig*)

telly: Not Savalas although this is where you will see him; TELEVISION. (see: *goggle box, tranny*)

165

tena koe: pronounced 'tenaaque ay' means ALOHA or hello and good-bye. You may hear this one on television when the weather is presented.

ten bob each way: In July 1967 New Zealand went from pounds (£), shillings (s) and pence (d) to $ and ¢ but favorite sayings have a way of sticking to traditional language. A bob was another name for a shilling and to have ten bob each way is to have a 'dollar each way' or to 'COPPER YOUR BETS', covering yourself no matter what the result is. (see: *decimalisation, bob, as silly as a two bob watch, metrication, shilling, pound, quid, sixpence, penny*)

ten pin: The kind of BOWLING you do in your neighborhood bowling alley. (see: *bowler, bowling*)

terms of trade: BALANCE OF PAYMENTS. New Zealand sells luxury goods overseas. You may not think of them as luxurious but most of the world does. Beef, lamb, wool, etc. are what N.Z. lives on and the majority of the world's people can't afford; luxuries in all but a few countries. (see: *primary products, overseas funds, sheep*)

Territorials: The army RESERVES, weekend warriors, not to mention a fortnight in January. (see: *fortnight, January*)

test: a test match is a CHAMPIONSHIP game (of damn near anything, rugby most likely) between two terms representing different countries. One of these teams will be touring the other's country. Test matches have all the mystique of the world series, and Kiwis will stay up all night to see the satellite broadcast of such a game between New Zealand's touring All Black rugby team and that of Australia, England, Scotland or wherever the team happens to be. (see: *match, All Blacks, tour, touring, Springbok tour, side*)

Thames Valley: Pronounced 'Tems' like the river that flows through London, this is the 'local government region' comprising the Coromandel Peninsula and the regions around its base (Hauraki Plains, Ohinemuri and Piako). With 549,000 sheep, 579,000 cattle, 6,000 domestic deer and 58,665 people it is one of the rare areas where the cattle outnumber the sheep. The Coromandel was one of the richest areas in New Zealand during the late 1800's gold rush and with the increase in the price of gold is attracting the attention of mining companies once again. Those who prize the wild beauty and rural life of the area are resisting with protests and legal action and appear to be having considerable success with the partial 'greening' of the government. The town of Thames and its surrounding area boasted a total of 14,500 people at the 1986 census. (see: *North Island, Otago*)

thanks: I've noted elsewhere that one often says 'ta' rather than 'thanks'. Well, it is also common to say thanks rather than PLEASE. Rather like assuming your request will be complied with, and thanking in advance so you don't have to, afterward. 'Open the door, thanks.' Open the door, PLEASE. (see: *ta, the, false friends*)

that'll do me: THAT'S GOOD ENOUGH. 'How much do you want for that?' '$12.50' 'Here is $11.00' 'That'll do me.'

the: 'The' is often used instead of MY. 'The wife gave me a right bollicking when I came in last night.' (see: *right, bollicking, me*)

theatre: In usual parlance, this refers only to the live theater, other terms being used for the movies. Almost every hamlet in New Zealand has its own amateur theater company, the main centers having five or six of these plus a professional or semi-professional company. (see: *main centre, dress circle, Opera House, Town Hall, Concert Chamber, flicks, (the) Gods*)

'theft as a servant': Sounds much less grand (petty even) than EMBEZZLING. The old English value structure; if you work for somebody else, including large organizations, you are a servant. We retain the term for some purposes, e.g., public servant. (see: *Are you being served?*)

there's an old boot for every old sock: a phrase bearing reassurance for all those seeking spouse or paramour. (see: ***cock in a sock*)

there must have been a stray bull in the paddock: A comment purporting to explain such genetic and reproductive anomalies as two blue eyed parents having a dark eyed child or the birth of a child to a woman whose husband has been in Antarctica for 11 months.

thesis: The final piece of work which earns a graduate student his/her Masters or Ph.D. Usage in the U.S. and N.Z. are the same with regard to the Masters degree, but not the Ph.D. (see: *dissertation, football or footie, false friends*)

thick, thickhead: Used as an adjective describing an individual it implies that the person in question has a cognitive deficit. This is probably a shortened form of the phrase 'his head is as thick as a post' and made of the same material. STUPID. (see: *clot, no hoper, berk, jerk, clueless*)

thousand million: 1,000,000,000 is equal to a U.S. billion. A U.S. billion is less than a N.Z. billion by a factor of 1000. (see: *billion, false friends*)

throw a wobbly: Young children are often specialists at this, but most of their adult counterparts are capable of a spectacular TEMPER TANTRUM. (see: *do your bun, do a Hollywood*)

tickle the peter: To tickle the peter is to REMOVE MONEY FROM THE CASH REGISTER without recording the transaction. This could represent theft, or merely a reluctance to share with Inland Revenue. (see: *theft as a servant, on the fiddle, peter, Inland Revenue*)

tiddler: A tiddler is a LITTLE ONE. 'I saw the McKellar baby, she's just a tiddler.' 'I caught four fish yesterday, but they were all tiddlers so I threw them back.'

tig: You have played the game. You shut your eyes and count to 20, and then open them and say 'ready or not, here I come'. In N.Z. tig is TAG and when you catch someone you tig them rather than tag them. (see: *step on a crack and marry a rat, tell-tale*)

Tiki: Maori GOOD LUCK CHARM. I mentioned to a tourist guide in Auckland that I was a bit disturbed when the first thing his national airline did in Hawaii was hand me one of these good luck charms. He laughed and informed me that I had few worries on that score. The Tiki started out as a good luck charm all right — a fertility symbol worn only by women. (More recently, both pre- and post-European advent, men did take to wearing them.) Usually made of (see:) *greenstone*.

'time, gentlemen please': The signal that the PUB IS CLOSING, and you must drink up and go. (see: *hotel, six o'clock swill*)

tin: There are no CANS in New Zealand, only 'tins'. Don't be deceived by the fact that the two objects appear identical. There is no such thing as a can; and so it follows that you put your garbage out for collection in the rubbish tin. (see: *rubbish*)

(give a) tinkle: This has nothing to do with voiding one's bladder. 'Give me a tinkle.' 'Give me a PHONE CALL.'

tip: (A) The tip is the GARBAGE DUMP. (see: *skip, rubbish, false friends*)
(B) Under most circumstances it is not customary to offer honoraria. Don't tip please! (see: *no tipping*)

tip truck: This is one of those cases where Kiwi makes more sense than Yankee. A tip truck is a DUMP TRUCK. (see: *clothesgrips or clothespegs, hairgrips or hair clips, bottling, cement block*)

to do (Maths-English-Welding): Is to UNDERTAKE A COURSE OF STUDY in ...

to get your face smacked in (rearranged): BASHED. (see: *punch up, knuckle sandwich*)

toaster loaf: A loaf of sliced white bread whose slices are cut to the thickness you would expect in the U.S. or Canada. (see: *bread, sandwich, toasted sandwiches*)

toasted sandwiches: Imagine a sandwich, made with two half thickness slices of white bread, grilled on both sides with fillings such as cheese and tomatoes. Oh yes! In the South Island they butter the top of the sandwich after grilling it. (see: *sandwich, South Island*)

toby: (A) the MASTER WATER VALVE for a building, ordinarily located under a metal cover in the sidewalk outside. Who was Toby anyway? 'Turn off the toby so I can fix the tap.'

(B) a brand of fishing lure.

toffee apple: Shades of carnivals and fairs, cotton candy and CANDY APPLES. (see: *candy floss*)

togs: Not all kinds of clothing, but only one kind. Bathing togs, or a BATHING SUIT. (see: *false friends*)

toheroa: An ABALONE-LIKE SHELLFISH considered a great delicacy by most Kiwis. Open season on these is usually confined to five days per year on only two or three beaches across the country. Toheroa soup is canned in N.Z. and sold overseas, but the only place you can get it in New Zealand is in the larger tourist hotels. We once found some cans in a Melbourne supermarket, and brought them back to New Zealand.

Tohunga: Maori WITCHDOCTOR, priest, wise man, scholar, etc. (see: *Maori*)

toilet: A toilet is a room by itself with only this facility in it. The room is customarily unheated, even in modern dwellings. This makes the 'toilet as library' habit an unusual one in New Zealand, particularly in the winter. (see: *loo, bathroom, toilet paper, lav, bog, grot, dunny*)

toilet bowl: TOILET BASIN. A basin is only for washing. (see: *basin, bathroom, toilet, lav, toilet paper, lav, bog, grot, dunny*)

toilet paper: Unlike North America, where all toilet paper resembles facial tissue in texture, there are several grades in New Zealand. The most common is about the texture of old newspaper. If you are settling in for a long stay or merely traveling around the country, you may wish to purchase some *Fluffy, Rx* or (to my 'mind' not quite as soft) *Swansdown*. On the other hand, if you come from corncob country, the usual stuff (which I have carefully refrained from naming) may suit you just fine.

One more thing, the government purchases all its toilet paper in bulk and the wrapping on each and every sample reads: 'This Roll is the Property of the New Zealand Government'. I keep waiting to be asked to return after use. (see: *loo, bathroom, toilet bowl, toilet, lav, bog, grot, dunny, Snowtex*)

tolls: Tolls is the branch of Telecom N.Z. that handles LONG DISTANCE phone calls. When you dial for the long distance telephone operator, she (or he) will answer 'tolls'. If you want to make an 'operator assisted' overseas call dial 0170 and the international operator will be happy to help. Your local operator cannot handle these calls. Remember that it is the other half of the day and yesterday in North America. (see: *calls, telephone dials, Telecom N.Z.*)

tomato/potato: Tomato is pronounced 'tow mat oh', and potato is pronounced the way you learned it as a kid. Marvelous is the mind of man. (see: *tomato sauce*)

tomato sauce: If you were expecting ketchup, forget it! Ketchup can be purchased in small bottles sent out from England, but the standard tomato sauce in New Zealand is something else. It appears to be, in fact, just that. TOMATO SAUCE WITH NO PARTICULARLY NOTICEABLE ADDED SPICES. (see: *tomato/potato*)

Tongariro: This local government region surrounds Lake Taupo which is the largest fresh water lake in the North Island. In addition to superb trout fishing around Taupo it boasts a cluster of three semi-active volcanos, Mt Tongariro, Mt Ngauruhoe and Mt Ruapehu. It was quite an experience being on a volcano that is blowing its top, even if it was mostly steam and ash. However, in those days I was younger and more confident of my personal immortality. The largest gathering of folks is the town of Taupo, on the lakeside, with a population of 17,458 (1986 census). The whole region has 2,592,000 sheep, 236,000 cattle, 20,000 farmed deer and 40,793 people. (see: *North Island*)

toning: MATCHING. As a toning skirt and blouse. (see: *twin-set and pearls*)

too bad: Once when someone's mother had died, I said 'too bad' and I was thought to be insensitive. Too bad means HARD CHEESE or a form of crocodile tears. (see: *tough bickies, false friends*)

too right: 'That's too right mate.' That's a correct statement (opinion), and furthermore I AGREE WHOLEHEARTEDLY with my friend.

toot: One does not go on a toot in New Zealand. There are other ways to express this. One does, however, toot one's automobile horn as opposed to the rather vulgar American practice of HONKING it. (see: *on the piss, false friends*)

top dressing: The ACT of SPREADING FERTILIZER over a farmer's fields. This is often done from the air, and the fertilizer is most often superphosphate. (see: *aerial top dressing, super, manure*)

top of the milk: As the majority of Kiwis don't like their milk homogenized, a thick layer of CREAM accumulates at the top of your milk bottle (yes, we still have bottles). Many private recipes call not for cream, but top of the milk. The story has it that the first homogenized milk produced in N.Z. was made during WWII to accommodate the U.S. marines stationed here. They found it hard to adjust to shaking the bottle before opening it. (see: *milk, cream*)

topside: BUTTOCK STEAK OR ROAST. (see: *silverside, seasoned topside, butchery*)

torch: Put away your matches, a torch is a FLASHLIGHT. (see: *fire*)

tough bickies: HARD CHEESE. Isn't that just toooo bad. (see: *too bad*)

(the) tour: visit by a national representative team to N.Z. or from N.Z. to another country. (see: *touring, All Blacks, test, side, Gleneagles agreement, Springbok tour*)

touring: When a team of BALLPLAYERS (rugby, soccer, etc.) goes OVER-SEAS to play against teams in other countries, they are touring and are often referred to as 'the tourists', as are foreign teams when they travel to New Zealand. (see: *All Blacks, test, side, Gleneagles agreement, tour, Springbok tour*)

toy boy: A GIGOLO who is at least 15 years younger than the lady who keeps him. (see: *bit on the side, fancy boy*)

town bike: This is teenage slang for the most ridden members of their female compatriots. Why aren't there any names for promiscuous males? (see: *scrubber, lusty wench, Roman fingers*)

Town Hall: Not the seat of Government, but literally the TOWN MEETING HALL. Used for politics, entertainment, etc. it is most often the largest hall in town and is administered by the local government. (see: *dress circle, flicks, theatre, Opera House, Concert Chamber*)

trace wire: FISHING LEADER. (see: *bubble*)

trad: If it's trad, it's TRADITIONAL, and therefore sacrosanct. (see: *telephone boxes*)

tradesman: A tradesman is a SKILLED WORKER who is not a member of one of the 'professions'; hence a plumber, a panel beater or a painter would be a tradesman but a physician or a lawyer would be a professional. (see: *panel beaters, solicitor, M.B. Ch.B.*)

traditional markets: For primary produce means GREAT BRITAIN. (see: *primary products, freezing workers*)

tramping: HIKING, what's that? In New Zealand one, strike that, everyone goes tramping. Ask your Kiwi acquaintances if they own tramping boots and sleeping-bags. The answer of, conservatively, 98% will be 'of course'. (see: *freewalk*)

tranny: That Japanese or Hong Kong made device on which we listen to the morning news. A TRANSISTOR RADIO. This word appears to be another Aussie immigrant. (see: *Aussie, telly*)

trans-Tasman: The body of water separating New Zealand and Australia is called the Tasman Sea. Financially this is one of the widest bodies of water in the world, as it costs nearly as much to ship something across the Tasman as it does to ship it to or from the British Isles. Politically the gap is much smaller, but beware of thinking of Australia and New Zealand in one lump. In fact, at their nearest point, the two countries are 1,200 miles apart, have entirely separate governments and are always jockeying for position with each other. Like the Canadians say when talking about the U.S. 'going to bed with an elephant, even a friendly elephant, is risky business. He might roll over in the night and crush you.' Australia's 16,018,350 (1986 census) people looks elephantine compared to N.Z.'s 3,307,084 (1986 census). (see: *C.E.R., ANZUS*) (the) **Treaty of Waitangi:** A treaty between Her Majesty Queen Victoria's government and some of the tribal chiefs of the North of the North Island of New Zealand mostly signed on Feb. 5th and 6th, 1840 at Waitangi in the far north of the North Island. Maori versions of the treaty were then taken to most reachable parts of both islands over the succeeding eight months and were signed by approximately 500 chiefs. This treaty ceded sovereignty over the areas controlled by those chiefs to the Crown. Thus at least part of New Zealand was ceded (given) to the empire as opposed to being annexed (unilaterally claimed) by the Crown. In the case of the South Island the claim clearly came before the ceding. Wm Hobson, Esq., Lieutenant Governor of New Zealand, pointed this out in his proclamations of May 21, 1840 claiming the North and South Islands as he merely claimed the South Island and Stewart Island 'on the grounds of Discovery' (Colenso, 1890, *Signing of the Treaty of Waitangi*). I should mention that Colenso, who was a bilingual if not neutral, witness to the signing makes it clear that the paragraph which follows the treaty (the full text of which appears) below is nonsense and that the chiefs did not have a clear idea of what they were agreeing to and were well aware of this. Recent argument that they were misled by discrepancies between the Maori and English versions seem to ignore the fact that most, if not all (whether speaking in favour or opposed), made it clear that they didn't understand either version.

"THE TREATY OF WAITANGI
ARTICLE THE FIRST.

The chiefs of the Confederation of the United tribes of New Zealand, and the separate and independent chiefs who have not become members of the Confederation, cede to Her Majesty the Queen of England, absolutely, and without reservation, all the rights and powers of sovereignty which the said Confederation or individual chiefs respectively exercise or possess, or may be supposed to exercise or to possess, over their respective territories, as the sole Sovereigns thereof.

ARTICLE THE SECOND.

Her Majesty the Queen of England confirms and guarantees to the chiefs and tribes of New Zealand, and to the respective families and individuals thereof, the full, exclusive, and undisturbed possession of their lands and estates, forests, fisheries, and other properties which they may collectively or individually possess, so long as it is their wish and desire to retain the same in their possession. But the chiefs of the United tribes, and the individual chiefs, yield to Her Majesty the exclusive right of pre-emption over such lands as the proprietors thereof may be disposed to alienate, at such prices as may be agreed upon between the respective proprietors and persons appointed by Her Majesty to treat with them on that behalf.

ARTICLE THE THIRD.

In consideration thereof, Her Majesty the Queen of England extends to the natives of New Zealand her Royal protection, and imparts to them all the rights and privileges of British subjects.

W. HOBSON, Lieutenant-Governor.

Now, therefore, We, the Chiefs of the Confederation of the United Tribes of New Zealand, being assembled in Congress at Victoria, in Waitangi, and We, the Separate and Independent Chiefs of New Zealand, claiming authority over the Tribes and Territories which are specified after our respective names, having been made fully to understand the Provisions of the foregoing Treaty, accept and enter into the same in the full spirit and meaning thereof: in witness of which, we have attached our signatures or marks at the places and the dates respectively specified.

Done at Waitangi, this Sixth day of February, in the year of Our Lord one thousand eight hundred and forty."

Colenso, W., F.R.S., F.L.S. (1890). *The Authentic and Genuine History of the Signing of the Treaty of Waitangi*. Reprinted Christchurch, 1971: Capper Press, pp 38 – 39.

Some Maori tribes later revolted against the Crown (I don't know enough about the circumstances to judge whether the provocation justified the action) and had land confiscated. In the case of those tribes that hadn't signed the treaty I guess it was war and not rebellion, although Whitehall didn't see it that way.

Over the years, as it happened, more land was confiscated without mutual agreement. In the lifetimes of those alive today this happened during the World Wars and as recently as the 1950's. The land taken for military purposes, and sometimes actually used for those purposes, mostly did not find its way back into tribal hands. A recent effort to rectify what the government of today sees as excesses by its predecessors, called the Waitangi Tribunal, appears to be unrealistically raising Maori hopes and Pakeha fears. Race relations in N.Z. are certainly at a 20 year and probably at a 20th century low in 1990.

The present government sees itself as the direct descendent of that of Wm Hobson and consequently New Zealand celebrates Waitangi Day as the day it came into existence as an entity. (see: *Bastion Point, Waitangi Tribunal, Waitangi Day, sesquicentennial, Iwi Authority, Maori, Pakeha*)

Treasury benches: The PARTY IN POWER (with a parliamentary majority) traditionally occupies the SEATS in the parliamentary chamber to the RIGHT of the SPEAKER (chairperson). These are called the Treasury benches probably in recognition of the principle that 'he who pays the piper, calls the tune.' (see: *parliament*)

tree tomatoes: You may know these as (see: *tamarilloes*)

trick cyclist: PSYCHIATRIST (no comment).

trots: (A) MONTEZUMA'S REVENGE.

(B) That pursuit in which horses pull small carts containing single individuals around in circles in front of a large number of other people who have come to see them go round in circles and who place bets as to which horse, cart and driver will go round fastest. HARNESS RACING. (see: (have a) *flutter, GG's, gallops, T.A.B., punt, punter, punting*)

trundler: A two-wheeled shopping basket used by those who would rather roll their purchases home than carry them there.

try: RUGBY TOUCHDOWN (4 pts). A conversion is worth 2 points. (see: *football* or *footie, rugby, All Blacks*)

try it on: TO ATTEMPT SOMETHING, often used with regard to seduction or some new mode of employment for which you may not be qualified.

tuatara: The world's only surviving dinosaur. This appx. foot long lizard like creature (they can get up to 2 feet 4 inches and 2 lbs 3 oz) 'Sphenodon punctatum' is the only surviving species of the order Rhynchocephalia, having outlived the rest by something on the order of 100 million years. Individuals can live for 100 years or more. (see: *punga*)

tuck in: One tucks into tucker. It means BEGIN TO EAT. (see: *Kiwi grace, tucker, tuck shop, kai*)

tucker: FOOD by any other name would taste as good. (see: *tucker, tuck shop, kai*)

174

tuck shop: A shop located within a SCHOOL (STORE) selling mainly food. That is, things one can tuck into. (see: *tuck in, tucker, shop, bottle shop, chemist's shop, bottle shop, Op shop*)

tupping: What the ram does with the ewe. (see: *service*)

turf out: THROW OUT.

turps: Mineral TURPENTINE. In addition to using this for removing unwanted paint it is a great way to start your barbe if (!) you let it burn off completely before you start cooking. (see: *barbe*)

TV3: N.Z. has only three television networks and this is the only one which is not owned by the government. The Labour government has encouraged competition in this sphere and in most others. As a new enterprise, it is struggling for market share against its longer established competitors (Feb. 1990). (see: *Television New Zealand, Radio N.Z. Ltd., State Owned Enterprise, Labour government*)

twee: Just TOO PRECIOUS. The manners and home furnishings of the stereotype of a male homosexual might be described as twee. (see: *poncey, camp as a row of pink tents*)

21st: It is a New Zealand tradition that on a boy or girl's 21st BIRTHDAY, a large, coming of age PARTY is thrown. It used to be that this was the occasion for presenting, to the new adult, his or her first key to the parental house; symbolizing, and making possible the new freedom to come and go without supervision. 21sts still include the presentation of a key, but it tends to be three feet long, a foot wide, and made of foil covered cardboard these days. The symbol is all that is left as the real key (to house, car, etc.) has most likely been in the pocket or purse, of the party so honored for some years. (see: *age of consent, legal age for drinking*)

Twink: Yet another brandname that has become a generic one. This stuff is the N.Z. version of *Liquid Paper* or WHITEOUT. (see: *Biro, Snowtex, Clayton's, Kleensack, Witches-Britches, hoover, lux, Lilo, Fairydown*)

twin set and pearls: Toning (matching) jumper (pullover, sweater) and cardigan (jacket style sweater) worn together and topped off by a string of pearls around the neck is winter uniform for the well dressed matron who is off to the bridge club or a job in which she meets the public. (see: *toning, jumper, cardigan, jersey*)

two-toothed ewe: Most of the rams get slaughtered as lambs for export, as those N.Z. lamb chops your supermarket at home is hopefully trying to sell you. A few rams are kept for breeding and wool. Ewes, on the other hand, produce both lambs and wool so they are usually retained for these purposes. A two-toothed ewe is a TWO YEAR OLD FEMALE SHEEP. A prime age for breeding. (see: *hogget, sheep, lambing, primary products*)

U

undies: UNDERWEAR as worn by either sex. (see: *vest, singlet, spencer, Witches Britches*)

U.E. or **sit U.E.:** This was the UNIVERSITY ENTRANCE EXAMINATION. It has now been abolished and replaced by the 6th Form Certificate. (see: *6th Form Certificate, school, School Cert., Bursary*)

U.K.: A common way of referring to the United Kingdom of England, Scotland, Ireland and Wales, i.e., The BRITISH ISLES. (see: *G.B.*)

unco: An uncoordinated or CLUMSY school child, as described by peers.

Ug boots: Calf high BOOTS MADE by turning SHEEPSKINS INSIDE OUT (wool on the inside) and tacking on a shoe sole. I think the 'Ug' stands for ugly, which they are, but very warm.

Uni: UNIVERSITY. New Zealand has six of these: Auckland, Waikato (Hamilton), Massey (Palmerston North), Victoria (Wellington), Canterbury (Christchurch), and Otago (Dunedin); the last of these being the longest established. In addition there is Lincoln College, a tertiary level school of agriculture that grants a Bachelor's degree and intends to try to become a University in 1990. There are also hints of the establishment of a private school of business in Auckland that plans to call itself a university. The universities are divided into faculties or divisions (Arts, Science, etc.) unlike U.S. institutions that are divided into colleges. (see: *varsity, faculty, Teachers' College, school, college*)

union bashing: The definition of this term (like others, see: *mainland*) depends on one's point of view:

(A) 'Unwarranted and heavy handed interference in the normal process of collective bargaining between employers and unions.'

(B) 'The ridiculously pejorative description of the Government's mild attempts to control the worst excesses of unnecessarily militant unions whose actions are imperiling the economy of the entire nation.'

In most cases, it would appear that justice resides somewhere between the two. In any case the balance of power seems to have shifted (February 1990) to the employers and the Labour government is pursuing a 95% hands off policy toward labour relations, except insofar as their own employees are concerned. In the latter case they appear to have become one of the most overbearing employers. (see: *C.T.U., Labour government, P.S.A., restructuring*)

unit: (A) (Wellington only) suburban commuter train, SUPERFICIAL SUBWAY.

(B) A university course that runs all year round and is the equivalent in time required of 2–4 courses at a U. S. university.

Only the University of Otago retains this system in New Zealand although in 1970 every New Zealand university operated this way. (see: *Uni, Railways Corp. N.Z.*)

up himself: In practice this refers to someone who has a severely EXAGGERATED IDEA OF HIS OWN IMPORTANCE (and/or qualifications, intelligence, etc., etc.). It derives from the suggestions that someone with such strong narcissistic tendencies could find only himself worthy of his own concupiscent attentions.

up to muster: If something is up to muster then it's all there or it's UP TO SCRATCH. This originates from comparing the number of soldiers who turned up when a company was assembled with the list, or muster roll, of those who were supposed to be there. If they were all 'present or accounted for' the company was up to muster. (see: *muster*)

up the spout — up the duff: 'Milady, there's more in your belly than ever went in through your face.' (see: *bun in the oven, sprog*)

V

V8 gang: Teenage gang that specializes in using Yank tanks as transportation. An 8 cylinder engine being unusually large and powerful in N.Z. motoring. (see: *yank tank*)

vacuum tube: The inner, glass part of your thermos flask that keeps your hot drinks hot and your cold ones cool. It has nothing to do with electronics, pre or post transistors. (see: *valve, false friends*)

valve: (A) One of the vacuum tubes in your old radio or T.V. (see: *false friends*)

(B) A device for controlling the flow of (usually) liquids.

Varsity: This is not a letter you earn for athletic prowess, or the team representing your school, but another name for UNIVERSITY. 'Have you been to varsity?' is, Have you been to university? Only a limited proportion (20.5% full time and 5.6% part time in 1987) compared with other industrialized western countries (e.g., appx. 56% of U.S. students in 1984, including those who go to junior colleges and teacher trainees not included in the N.Z. sample) of the high school population goes on to university, although anyone over 21 is welcome to try, and all those who have done well enough in high school to be accepted by a university can enter at a younger age. It takes three years to earn an ordinary Bachelor's degree or four to earn a souped up Bachelor's called a Bachelor Honours degree. Despite the shorter period, I don't feel these students are any less qualified than their four year U.S. counterparts. (see: *Uni, faculty, Teachers' College, college, Honours, U.E., School Cert, false friends*)

varsity bunny: The other guy/girl. You know the one who always looks as if s/he just stepped out of a salon wearing the latest and most expensive gear. And s/he just has to sit next to you for contrast. (see: *BP, ski bunny*)

Vegemite: (see: *Marmite* and *Vegemite*)

(to) **veg out:** To act like a vegetable, or to DO SOMETHING MINDLESS (intellectually undemanding), e.g., watch TV. A university student phrase. (see: *veges*)

veges: Vegetables, another case where the Kiwi saves his breath. (see: *strawbs, speedo, beaut, chook, veg out, ciggies; runner beans, marrow, buttercup, butternut*)

venue: The LOCATION FOR ANY scheduled EVENT. We tend to use this only for the jurisdiction in which a court case is heard, i.e., 'change of venue.'

vermin: You don't need a hunting license to hunt vermin; rats and mice? Well, yes, but also deer, wallabies, opossum, rabbits, etc. In other words, almost anything (other than birds) you might wish to hunt. The N.Z. opossum is not the same as the American one, it has a beautiful winter fur coat and these vermin skins are purchased by the furriers for $1 – $12. Venison from wild shot animals can't be sold to the U.S. (regulations require inspection prior to slaughter) but can be sold to West Germany. The hunter can make over $400 for a big buck. Deer farming is now big business in N.Z. (see: *false friends*)

vest: (A) An UNDERSHIRT, usually one made of cotton, worn by a man or a child. (see: *singlet, spencer, undies, false friends*)
(B) (see: *WAISTCOAT*)

vicky verka: VICE VERSA.

villa: Many of the Kiwis you meet will live in villas. Does this conjure up visions of vine laden elegance clinging to the cliffs above the French Riviera? Forget it! This is a one storied house, usually made of wood, otherwise known as a BUNGALOW. (see: *gentleman's residence, property, false friends*)

viyella: A wool-cotton mix (55% – 45%) favored for men's shirts.

W

wag school: 'It's a beautiful day, too nice to be inside. I'm going to wag school today.' It's ... I'm going to PLAY HOOKEY today. (see: *9 o'clock flu, take a sickie*)

Waikato: The area and 'local government region' on the east coast of the North Island just to the south of the Auckland Region and just to the north of the peninsular bulge that represents Taranaki on your map. The most populous metropolitan area is that of the city of

Hamilton (and the 5th largest in the country as of the 1986 census) with 101,814 people. Waikato as a whole has 228,303 people, 46,000 farmed deer, 1,453,000 cattle (about half and half dairy and beef) and 4,375,000 sheep. This makes it one of the richest farming regions in the country. (see: *North Island, Auckland, Taranaki*)

Wairarapa: This local government region covers the southeastern portion of the bottom of the North Island. The largest town is Masterton (1986 census, 20,145). The regional population is 39,608 people, 3,437,000 sheep, 266,000 cattle and 6,000 farmed deer. The country race meeting on New Year's Day at Tauherenikau, where all the locals and a good number of Wellingtonians turn up with their picnic lunches to have a flutter on the GG's, is good fun. (see: (a) *flutter, GG's, North Island, Wellington*)

waistcoat: The third piece of a man's three piece suit; a VEST. (see: *vest*)

Waitangi Day: The Treaty of Waitangi ceding sovereignty over New Zealand to the British monarchy was first signed on the 6th of February 1840. This Treaty has never been ratified by either the British or New Zealand Governments, and it will never be, because under its provisions the Maoris would own entirely too much of New Zealand. The battle goes on in the courts and especially in a quasi-judicial body called the Waitangi Tribunal.

Despite the controversy and the fact that the Treaty will never be ratified, Waitangi Day is New Zealand's NATIONAL DAY as the 4th July is the U.S.'s. (see: *Treaty of Waitangi, Bastion Point, Waitangi Tribunal, Maori, Pakeha, Crown, sesquicentennial*)

Waitangi Tribunal: A quasi-judicial body (the courts have held that the government is not bound by its decisions) set up by the Labour government to hear and recommend resolution of claims made by Maori as a result of perceived violations of the Treaty of Waitangi since 1850. Most of these claims refer to land which was taken over by the Crown or to fishing rights. Property now in private hands was to be excluded from their brief, but it seems to be creeping in by the back door in those cases where what was once Crown land has been sold to private owners. Once a determination has been made by the Tribunal then the government must decide how (or whether) to implement it. (see: *Treaty of Waitangi, Bastion Point, Waitangi Day, Maori, Pakeha, Crown*)

walking: One quickly adapts to driving ON THE LEFT hand side of the road, or the exercise becomes academic because you are dead and so is some luckless Kiwi. However, the 'rules of the road' also apply to walking, and you've been walking a lot longer than you've been driving. You walk on the right, use the right hand door, etc. These habits have been reinforced and strengthened daily for every year of your life bar the first one or two. This means that you will find yourself performing an intricate dance when encountering a Kiwi on a narrow footpath, each of you reacting without conscious thought and neither understanding, at first, why behavior that has been successful all your life isn't working. Imagine, you come face to face with a Kiwi on the footpath, you courteously and immediately take a step to your right, with equal unthinking courtesy, he takes a step to his left. You are still face to face. Ah! the light dawns, you take a step to your left, however, he has now figured out that if you are an idiot, you are at least a consistent one, so he takes a step to his right. You are still face to face, etc., etc., etc.

In small towns, this problem is less noticeable, but in Auckland, for example, there is a yellow line drawn down the middle of major sidewalks to remind you to keep to the left and you quickly wonder why all the world is going the wrong way. Similarly, when a building has only one door there is no problem, but when it has two you will head for the door to your right, while the Kiwi going the other way will head for the door to his left, and on and on it goes. (see: *footpath, driving, backwards*)

Wanganui: This local government region extends from just below the Tongariro (Lake Taupo) region, southwest to the coast below Taranaki. Its major metropolitan area is the very pleasant city of Wanganui (pop. 40,758, 1986 census), near which is to be found 'Tough Old Woman Cove'. Sometimes it just doesn't pay to eat your enemies when they are past their prime! Remember that the only land mammal larger than a rat available to the pre-european Maori was man. The population of the whole region is 69,439 people (1986 census), 4,047,000 sheep, 297,000 cattle and 11,000 farmed deer. Do take a jet boat or paddle steamer ride up the Wanganui river. (see: *North Island, Tongariro, Taranaki, Maori*)

**wanker: There was a young lad who came across his parents engaged in exercising their marital prerogatives. He enquired as to the nature of this activity and was told that they were playing bridge. Later, his father found him in his bed and enquired as to the nature of his vigorous activity. The lad replied that he was playing bridge. His father then asked who was his partner in this enterprise. The lad said 'If you have a good hand, you don't need a partner.' This lad was a wanker.

This term is applied to any male you don't like, usually when he is out of earshot.

waratah: A steel fence post that is Y shaped with three equally spaced (apprx. 1 inch long) arms and usually about six feet in total length. These are easily installed with a sledgehammer and make great stakes for holding up trees and fences as well as serving as fenceposts. (see: *fencing, number 8 fencing wire, wire strainer*)

wardrobe: (A) a free-standing wooden CLOSET in which you hang your clothing. Older New Zealand homes assumed that you would have this piece of furniture and so these homes have no closets. For modern homes, the advertisements read 'built in wardrobes'.

      (B) Under specialized circumstances, wardrobe can refer to the clothing you put in the closet, e.g., 'The Wool Board has given Miss New Zealand a complete wardrobe entirely made of wool, so that she can represent New Zealand's products as well as its beauty at the Miss World competition . . .'

warrant of fitness: Every six months all motor vehicles, trailers, etc. in New Zealand, that use the public roads, must be safety checked for roadworthiness. Also, any vehicle offered for sale must have a warrant that has at least five months left on it. The window decal that indicates that your vehicle is roadworthy and also proclaims to the M.O.T. and anyone else interested the month when your next check is due, is your vehicle's warrant of fitness. Most garages and a few Ministry of Transport vehicle testing stations can and will check your vehicle and issue one of these for a reasonable price. (see: *M.O.T.*)

washhouse: A small outbuilding behind the main house where the LAUNDRY was traditionally done in a copper. These days, a modern or not so modern (wringer washers are not unknown) washer is likely to occupy this space. Dryers are considerably less common as sunlight and hot water cupboards seem to have some mystic virtue.

    Modern homes usually have a washhouse built in. Rental properties, even unfurnished ones, almost always come equipped with a clothes-washing machine, of uncertain vintage, as well as a stove and a fridge. It is a very unusual household indeed that sends clothing, bedclothes, etc. to the laundry. (see: *copper, air the washing*)

watching the dicky bird: What you do when you are having your PICTURE TAKEN.

water: If you want some of this stuff in a restaurant, you must ask for it. When it comes it is likely to be served in a thimble (well, a juice glass) and may perhaps contain a single ice cube as a sop to your accent.

    If, however, you ask for a jug of water they will think you are nuts but will cheerfully provide one and wait to see if you were really serious about drinking it. (see: *ice blocks, beer, jug*)

water biscuit: A large, saltless CRACKER. (see: *biscuit, scone*)

weather forecasts: I listened to these for years with mounting frustration since the official forecaster never utters a number, he only says: cold, cool, moderate, mild, warm, and hot. An anguished appeal to the forecasters produced the following information (which I must admit hasn't helped much, you will see why):

cold (during winter 6 degrees below normal)
cool
moderate (supposedly normal for place/time of year)
mild
warm
hot (during summer 15 degrees above normal)

What may you ask is normal? That depends on where you are along N.Z.'s 1,000 mile north-south axis and when you are in the year. Assuming you have such a table handy (I suppose someone must have), then the above information should help.

Fortunately, the unofficial forecasters now tell you what temperatures to expect in main centres and in your local smaller centres. Mind you, these are in degrees centigrade so you have to multiply by 5, divide by nine and add 32 to get Fahrenheit. Alternatively, you can get pretty close by multiplying by 2 and adding 30.

wedding breakfast: The first meal after a wedding, whether at 6 p.m. or 5 a.m. The closest equivalent would be a WEDDING RECEPTION.

wee: New Zealand has a Scots heritage and a wee anything is a SMALL one. (see: *wees and poohs*)

week: A week in casual conversation tends to be EIGHT DAYS LONG. There is some confusion about the first day of the week, Monday being the most popular candidate, but Sunday having its adherents. (see: *fortnight*)

wees and poohs: This is young children's argot for URINATION and DEFECATION. My favorite story in this regard concerns the Kindergarten teacher who answered her telephone to find herself engaging in the following conversation with a caller who had a suspiciously high pitched voice:

> Caller: Is that Miss Kennecot?
> Teacher: Yes.
> Caller: This is an obscene phone call. WEES and POOHS!

(see: *wee*)

Wellington: A small region at the bottom of the North Island including the capital city of the same name whose metropolitan area has a (1986 census) population of 325,697 people. This region extends a short distance north, taking in the coastal resort area and an even shorter distance east encompassing the Hutt valley. The region has 328,163 people most of whom live in and around the capital. There are also 226,000 non-voting sheep, 16,000 disenfranchised cattle and 1,000 underage for voting deer in this region. Making it the only region in the country where the people outnumber the sheep. The city of Wellington itself will remind you of a miniaturized San Francisco with Chicago's breezes. (see: *North Island*)

Wellingtons: This name has nothing to do with the city, despite what some spiteful Aucklanders might tell you. They are BOOTS. I'm sure the Duke's were leather, not rubber, but these are RAIN AND MUD PROTECTION, another name for (see: *gumboots, Southland slippers*).

West Coast: This refers to the west coast of the South Island. Kiwi's think of this narrow strip of rain forest, backed up against the N.Z. Alps and their glaciers, as the frontier, the wild west. Lots of sandflies, very few people and a frontier atmosphere. Climb on a glacier, visit the Pancake Rocks at Punakaiki and take your insect repellent. The West Coast has 34,942 people (1986 census), 462,000 sheep, 141,000 cattle and 9,000 farmed deer. (see: *South Island, sandfly*)

weta: A group of large cricket-like insects native to N.Z. The giant weta is the largest insect in the country and, while frightening in appearance, is not in the least dangerous. (see: *katipo spider*)

wetback: An illegal Australian immigrant who has waded 1200 miles across the Tasman Sea. Well no, but it makes a good story. A wetback is a set of pipes or a HOT WATER DRUM ATTACHED TO the back or bottom of a FIREPLACE or solid fuel stove. This way you can have your fire, or cook your dinner, and heat your water at the same time with the waste heat, thereby saving electricity. (see: *trans-Tasman, wetback destructor, destructor, false friends*)

wetback destructor: A vicious method of ... A SMALL CLOSED STOVE for disposing of any burnable rubbish, this one is EQUIPPED with an attached HOT WATER DRUM so that the waste heat is used to heat the water thereby killing two birds with one stone. (see: *wetback, destructor, false friends*)

wharfies: Wharfies are STEVEDORES. They are members of one of the best paid unions in New Zealand because in a very real way, matched only by the freezing workers, they hold the nation's economy in their hands. New Zealand is a trading nation. That means she sells her primary produce overseas and buys oil and manufactured articles. If she can't trade, everything grinds to a halt. In 1951 the troops were called out to break a wharfies' strike. The employers seem to have the upper hand now, however, a change in employers and working conditions, and a dispute between the wharfies and the harbour workers about who should do what work, led to a major shutdown of ports all over the country in 1989. The docks remain one of the two most vital, vulnerable spots in the economy. (see: *seagulls, freezing workers, primary products, terms of trade, overseas funds, C.T.U.*)

what the guts is: IT ALL BOILS DOWN TO. The two phrases seem to be related in sort of a cousinly way. Haggis anyone? (see: *guts*)

what's your line of country?: WHAT KIND OF WORK DO YOU DO?

wide comb: New Zealand sheep shearers use an electric shearing razor that is 1.04 inches wider than that used by Australian shearers. This makes Australian shearing gangs very unhappy when N.Z. shearers go over to compete with them. The wide combs (3.54 inches) making them just that much more efficient than the Australian (2.54 inches) competition. Australians are reluctant to adopt the wide comb because then they would have to reduce the size of their shearing gangs. Oh yes! The Australians also claim that their fine wools would suffer from the crude N.Z. instruments. (see: *shearing gang, rowsie, Golden Shears, sheep, blows, primary products*).

whilst: 'Whilst he took care of his business I took care of mine.' WHILE. (see: *amongst*)

whinge: whinge is a cross between whine and cringe. Some immigrants to N.Z. are more vocal about their COMPLAINts than others. One of these groups has become known as 'whinging Poms'. Unfortunately, when a group gets this label hung on them people cease to listen to the words. (see: *grizzle, bloody, Pom — Pommie*)

white goods: Kiwi's rely on primary produce for most of their vital overseas trade. However, there are a few areas of manufacturing in which New Zealand excels. One of these is MAJOR HOUSEHOLD APPLIANCES (e.g., stoves, refrigerators, washing machines, etc.) or white goods. In fact, at one point the Aussies were getting downright protectionistic about their inability to compete with these goods even with trans-Tasman (the Tasman Sea lies between New Zealand and Australia) freight rates (notoriously high) added. (see: *Aussie, C.E.R., trans-Tasman, primary products*)

white pointer: If you are out swimming and someone tells you that there is a white pointer about, don't look for a bird dog. Instead, swim quietly (don't thrash about) to shore and then look out to sea for a WHITE POINTER SHARK. (see: *false friends*)

whitebait: A SMALL, literally TRANSPARENT FISH. The adult is called a smelt, but the past tense is misleading. The juvenile or whitebait form is very tasty, baked into an omelet-based fritter called a 'whitebait fritter'. The whitebait are overfished and becoming scarce.

Whykickamoocow: An imaginary town located in the back of beyond; HICKSVILLE, NEW ZEALAND.

wicked: 'It's a bloody wicked day with a strong southerly blowing and the sky overcast.' It's a damn AWFUL day ... (see: *bloody, southerly, false friends*)

wicket keeper: The player in a CRICKET GAME who fills much the same role as the CATCHER in a baseball game. (see: *cricket, test, century, sticky wicket*, etc., etc.)

wigwam for a goose's bridle: An old, unusual and uncommon Southland term for something that is TOTALLY USELESS. 'That's about as much use as a wigwam for a goose's bridle'.

***Wilson's* Whiskey** and ***45 South*:** NEW ZEALAND'S own WHISKIES. Both are barley based, like scotch, but *Wilson's* is lighter and to my mind tastier than *45 South*. I suspect bourbon drinkers would like these better than scotch drinkers.

windscreen: That part of the car that screens you from the wind; your WINDSHIELD. (see: *accelerator, boot, bonnet*)

windy: (see: *get the wind up*)

wine biscuit: No alcoholic content and in North American terms it isn't a biscuit either. This is a cookie whose closest equivalent would be a GIRL SCOUT COOKIE. (see: *Girl Guides*)

wink wink, nudge nudge: This has gone from being a series of meaningful gestures to becoming part of the spoken language with the same meaning. It indicates that you should read between the lines for unspoken innuendo, risque; or less than the letter of the law. 'That sheila is really built, wink wink, nudge nudge.' 'What the Inland Revenue don't know won't hurt them, wink wink, nudge nudge.' (see: *sheila, Inland Revenue*)

winter woollies: This term is used to apply to all thick winter wear. However, it most often refers to underwear (LONGJOHNS). (see: *central heating, undies, vest*)

wireless: That device developed by Marconi that carries voices between two points without intervening bits of copper. Despite T.V., RADIO is alive and well in N.Z. (see: *Radio N.Z. Ltd., national programme, concert programme, Television New Zealand, State Owned Enterprise, TV3*)

wire strainer: Now why would anyone want to strain wire? This is a clamp and leverage DEVICE which is USED to put tension on fencing WIRES so they can be PULLed TAUT before being fastened to fence posts. (see: *fencing, number 8 fencing wire, waratah, primary products*)

Witches Britches: Believe it or not, this was a brand name for a fancy version of winter BLOOMERS for younger women. Like other brand names, this one has become a generic term (for ladies' long undies). (see: *spencer, undies*)

within cooe: I think this one is on loan from Aussie. Originally it meant within calling distance, but now it usually just means HANDY or around. 'Is your mate Bazzer within cooe?' (see: *Aussie, Bazzer, mate*)

(the) **Wizard of Christchurch:** An ex-sociology Lecturer from Australia has managed to convince the Christchurch City Council to appoint him the town Wizard. He holds forth in the town square, wearing a loincloth (Alley Oop style) and occasionally whipping out a little white telephone on which he purports to talk to God. His off-duty costume includes top-hat, tails and a silver headed cane (although he will on occasion wear this with open sandals). He has founded a political party, the Imperial British Conservative Party, dedicated to re-establishing the Empire with (I suspect) Victoria as its head. Unfortunately, despite my approval of its other policies, I can't support this party because it is violently anti-Jewish and anti-Catholic which leaves a bad taste all round. The Wizard could safely be described as a hard shot. He has some subordinate Wizards (which makes him the Archwizard) such as the 'Duke of Wellington', the 'Wizard of Dunedin', 'Mergatroid — Wizard Itinerant' (the itinerary includes Australia) and the 'Wizard of Australia' (who lives in Melbourne). (see: *lecturer, hard shot, telephone boxes, Queen's Birthday*)

Works Corp.: Works and Development Services Corporation (NZ) Ltd. Formerly the Ministry of Works and Development or the GOVERNMENT CONSTRUCTION DEPARTMENT, now a State Owned Enterprise which has to compete with private firms for government contracts. On the other hand it can now compete with private firms for private contracts. Neither side has, as yet (February 1990), comfortably adjusted to this new state of affairs. It still builds dams, roads, buildings, etc. and the 'works' are mostly public works. It still has an army of engineers, draftsmen and laborers who move around the country in an endless round of build and repair. (see: *State Owned Enterprise, Ministry of Works lure, Railways Corp. N.Z., Rogernomics, restructuring, auroraed*)

*wog or **W.O.G.:** WORTHY ORIENTAL GENTLEMEN. When the British were in Egypt (the first time), the powers that were felt that it would improve relationships with the local populace if their troops ceased to refer to their Egyptian counterparts as 'dirty black buggers' and similar endearing terms. Therefore, it was decreed that: 'Henceforth, you will speak of the Egyptians as Worthy Oriental Gentlemen.' Wog is now a epithet applied to any non-European and just about as nasty as 'dirty black buggers'. We've a few of our own: wop, mick, kike, etc. (see: *boong, coconut*)

wonky: If something is a bit wonky its AWRY or ASKEW. 'There is something a bit wonky about that business deal.'

wooden aspro: Prison argot for a clout on the head with a truncheon. (see: *guest of Her Majesty, gaol, been inside*)

Woolworths: In N.Z. this organization has given up the 5 and dime business and is a chain of SUPERMARKETs. (see: *false friends*)

wops or wop-wops: Nothing to do with Italy. The wop-wops are the BOONDOCKS or BACKBLOCKS. (see: *booze, false friends*)

'Words': Spelled differently but pronounced and meaning the same as their U.S. counterparts. The N.Z. (British) spellings below are, with three exceptions (rumour, savoury, marvellous) to be found as less preferred, but acceptable, variants in a standard U.S. dictionary. The British do not extend the same courtesy to the U.S. spellings. These lists are by no means exhaustive.

N.Z.	U.S. (preferred)
appal	appall
behaviour	behavior
centimetre	centimeter
centre	center
cheque	check
colour	color
favourite	favorite
flavour	flavor
gaol	jail
gramme	gram
harbour	harbor
honour	honor
kerb	curb
kilometre	kilometer
labour	labor
licence	license
litre	liter
marvellous	marvelous
minimised	minimized
neighbour	neighbor
parlour	parlor
personalised	personalized
practise	practice
programme	program
pyjamas	pajamas
rumour	rumor
savoury	savory
splendour	splendor

subsidised	subsidized
technicolour	technicolor
theatre	theater
travelled	traveled
visualise	visualize

worked a treat: WORKED VERY WELL. 'That method of minimizing my income tax worked a treat!' (see: *goes like a bomb, 'Words'*)

(the) **Works:** This is the meatworks or SLAUGHTERHOUSE for export lamb and beef. (see: *freezer, abattoir, freezing works, gemel*)

wouldn't have a clue: Somewhere between 'I don't know', and 'I don't bloody care'. (see: *bloody, oh yeah*)

wowser: A wowser started off to be a teetotaller, but has expanded in meaning to cover any sort of PURITAN attitudes.

X

X-rated: Only the journalist who is describing the book or movie has rated the entertainments so described. The government censors use a different system (see: *flicks*). This description is, however, widely used and understood to imply a high SALACIOUS content. (With thanks to Mrs Bear who provided a desperately needed X. Whoever heard of a dictionary that included only 25 letters?) (see: *Patricia Bartlett, flicks*)

Y

yachtie: A yachtie is a YACHTSMAN OR WOMAN. A representative of that substantial percentage of Kiwis who spend their free time sailing in one of New Zealand's magnificent harbors or for those with larger craft, round the coast or even round the world. (see: *concrete yacht*)

yahoo: This one is courtesy of Jonathan Swift and *Gulliver's Travels.* Remember the brutish manlike creatures in the land of the intelligent horses? Well, a yahoo is a LOUT, and to 'yahoo around' is to do nothing constructive noisily. (see: *larrikin, yob-yobbo*)

Yank Tank: This device does not bear General Sherman's name or that of any other general. It's your everyday V8 family CAR. In New Zealand, where the average car is a *Toyota* size and 4-cylinders, these rare dinosaurs look gigantic. Top this off with the 42.5% import duty plus 12.5% GST (on the total of the following: the initial cost, plus the import duty, plus the cost of transportation, plus the cost of transportation insurance) and U.S. cars become fiscally impractical as well as oversize. Mind you, the Japanese have to pay the same duties. (see: *V8 gang, mini, GST*)

Yankee shout: DUTCH TREAT. And you thought the Scots were renowned for their parsimony! (see: *shout*)

yob-yobbo: A yob is someone who is between a slob and a lout. This term gets applied, almost exclusively, to young males.(see: *yahoo, larrikin*)

you shouldn't have done that!: A very sincere THANK YOU. (see: *ta, false friends*)

Your Worship: This is how MAYORs are formally addressed. In other circumstances, vilification is more probable than worship.

you're the dizzy limit: a description that hovers somewhere between exasperation and admiration.

Z

Zambuck: The nickname of the personnel of the St John's Ambulance Service. This name is friendly but slightly derogatory as Zambuck Ointment was once considered the sovereign remedy for bruises and the St John's men (in those days all male) who attended (and still attend) all sporting events were purported to rush out onto the field every time someone was bruised and anoint him with Zambuck Ointment. (see: *St John's Ambulance Service* or just *St John's*)

zed: The pronunciation of the 26th letter of the alphabet, the one we call ZEE. Any time you see the name of something which has N.Z. as part of it you should say N. Zed. *Sesame Street* is changing what kids call the letter but not what it is called in acronyms. (see: *Radio N.Z. Ltd.*)

zippers: Another case in which the men's reflexes will betray them; you ladies are O.K. All N.Z. made, jacket zippers for both sexes have the slide attached to the left hand side (as in ladies' clothing in the U.S.). If you've been zipping up your jackets for years without looking at what you are doing, you are in for a culture shock. You can't do it, until you've totally retrained yourself. (see: *backwards*)